W9-CEI-365

IN A ROCKET
MADE OF ICE

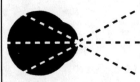

This Large Print Book carries the
Seal of Approval of N.A.V.H.

In a Rocket Made of Ice

AMONG THE CHILDREN OF WAT OPOT

Gail Gutradt

THORNDIKE PRESS
A part of Gale, Cengage Learning

GALE
CENGAGE Learning·

Farmington Hills, Mich • San Francisco • New York • Waterville, Maine
Meriden, Conn • Mason, Ohio • Chicago

GALE
CENGAGE Learning®

LIBRARY OF CONGRESS CATALOGING-IN-PUBLICATION DATA

Gutradt, Gail.
  In a rocket made of ice : among the children of Wat Opot / by Gail Gutradt.
    pages cm-(Thorndike press large print biography)
    ISBN 978-1-4104-7333-2 (hardcover) — ISBN 1-4104-7333-3 (hardcover)
    1. Orphanages—Cambodia. 2. Orphans—Cambodia—Social conditions. 3. Orphans—Services for—Cambodia. 4. HIV-positive children—Cambodia—Social conditions. 5. Children of AIDS patients—Cambodia—Social conditions. 6. Large type books. I. Title.
    HV1300.3.G87 2014b
    362.73'2—dc23
    [B]   2014028920

Published in 2014 by arrangement with Alfred A. Knopf, Inc., a division of Random House LLC, a Penguin Random House Company

Printed in Mexico
1 2 3 4 5 6 7 18 17 16 15 14

Dedicated to Wayne Dale Matthysse
and the children of Wat Opot

CONTENTS

PART FIVE: DEPARTURES

FOREWORD:
DR. PAUL FARMER

Wat Opot Children's Community, pencil drawing by Pesei

With humility and discernment, Gail Gutradt introduces us to Wat Opot, a thriving community of over fifty children and young adults, many of them members of the first generation of Cambodians to grow up living with HIV. This community is the life's work of Wayne Dale Matthysse, a U.S. Marine Corps medic who, having failed to prevent the deaths of two Vietnamese children on one gruesome day during his wartime service, has since served the orphaned, poor and ill in Central America and Southeast Asia. He and cofounder Vandin San opened Wat Opot as a hospice for people with AIDS in the years before antiretroviral medications were available in Cambodia. With the advent of effective therapy, Wat Opot has been transformed from a place in which the abandoned and castoff received end-of-life care into a source of hope and opportunity for its young residents, whose aspirations have grown apace. Gutradt's admiration for Matthysse's inexhaustible dedication to Wat Opot — as well as for his capacity for drawing on the resources, cultural and personal, that he sees all around him — is leavened by a frank account of what it's like to lack other resources, money usually, needed to prevent suffering and early death.

Gutradt's deep comprehension emerges from her own narrative, woven together with the individual stories of children at Wat Opot as they receive their initial AIDS diagnosis and then begin a lifetime of treatment. She charts their reflections as they assimilate the loss and abandonment they've experienced within their families, and as they come to understand the raucous, dynamic community at Wat Opot as home. Gutradt doesn't shy away from examining the power imbalance between volunteer caregivers and those to whom they minister, the limitations of a visitor's ability to care for the chronically ill, the unintended consequences of well-meaning projects and the often-agonizing moral dilemmas involved in caring for the sick and dying when certain resources are scarce.

In a Rocket Made of Ice offers readers rare access to the extraordinary people of Wat Opot, as well as substantive insight into the complexities of caring for the poor and sick in the developing world. Much more than a story of hope in the face of grim news and chronic disappointment, Gutradt makes a compelling case for the efficacy of ingenuity, imagination and a commitment to human dignity when we accompany each other through adversity.

Paul Farmer, MD, PhD, is Kolokotrones University Professor and Chair of the Department of Global Health and Social

Medicine at Harvard Medical School, Chief of the Division of Global Health Equity at Brigham and Women's Hospital in Boston and cofounder of Partners In Health. He also serves as UN Special Adviser to the Secretary-General on Community-Based Medicine and Lessons from Haiti. Dr. Farmer and his colleagues have pioneered novel, community-based treatment strategies for the delivery of high-quality health care in resource-poor settings. He is the author of *Infections and Inequalities: The Modern Plagues,* among many other titles, and has written extensively on health, human rights and the consequences of social inequality.

AUTHOR'S NOTE:
INDECISIONS AND DECISIONS

In 2001, when Wayne Dale Matthysse and Vandin San founded Partners in Compassion, a tiny nondenominational nongovernmental organization (NGO), there were no AIDS drugs in Cambodia, and no means of testing for HIV either. The very idea of children "growing up with AIDS" would have seemed impossible.

Today, some treatments are available, and Wat Opot, a self-supporting program of Partners in Compassion, has evolved into a visionary community where HIV-positive and HIV-negative children live together as family. And because they are growing up side by side, the fact of AIDS deeply affects all the children. Whether they have been orphaned or watched their friends and siblings die, live with HIV or AIDS themselves, or are nurturing younger siblings who are infected — or if their family or community has been touched in some other way by the disease — these children are growing up with AIDS.

During my first five-month visit to Cambodia I had no thought of writing a book. I was not a writer, but I became one, because I found a story so worth telling. I am not a journalist, nor is this a book about AIDS in Cambodia. All the statistics you need are available online in the many publications of the United Nations and the Cambodian National AIDS Authority. But behind the spreadsheets are real people whose lives are acutely affected by abstract policy decisions, trade agreements and political dramas. As the African saying goes, "When elephants fight, it is the grass that gets trampled."

When you first meet the children you would be hard-pressed to guess who is HIV positive and who isn't. I first wrote *In a Rocket Made of Ice* using the children's real names, but then realized that this breach of privacy might cause a child to be stigmatized in school or in the village. Neighbors know that some of the children at Wat Opot are HIV positive, but not which ones, and even after children leave Wat Opot this information could jeopardize their careers and social prospects. It is still a child's own personal decision whom to tell, and whether to tell, and when.

For this reason I have chosen to change the names of most of the children and adults, both HIV positive and negative, and to not name the children in the photos or put their pictures with their stories without their permission. Thus the inclusion of any child's picture says nothing at all about his or her HIV status. The names of some volunteers have been changed as well.

Renaming people is no small matter. Cambodian names are meticulously chosen with due consideration given to meanings and portents, and I found the struggle to change the names of my friends profoundly unsettling. I consulted many Khmer baby-name lists and names of friends of friends on Facebook, looking for more than forty new but common names that were easy to pronounce for a non-Khmer reader. Although I tried to find a name suitable for each child in sound, poetry and meaning, and in some instances asked a child to choose his or her own name, I apologize for any choice that might make a child unhappy.

Khmer is difficult for an English speaker, and I am ashamed to admit that in four long stays at Wat Opot I learned very little. Complex vowel sounds, implosions, unfamiliar gymnastics of mouth and tongue and my own aging brain made it hard for me to learn more than a smattering of words. Moreover, at Wat Opot there is a conscious effort to help the children grow up speaking and understanding both Khmer and English. Volunteers sometimes lapse into a hodgepodge of the two languages, but Wayne is careful to speak in complete, well-articulated English sentences, as a model for the children. During my time with them their English grew by leaps and bounds, while my Khmer remained risible.

Khmer words in this book are transcribed as this foreigner heard them, with no claim to accuracy. As Khmer has its own unique alphabet, descended from the ancient scripts of India, a child may spell his name in English one way today, another way tomorrow. A visit to any Khmer Facebook page will confirm the variations of spelling. Nicknames abound, often formed of the final syllable of a given name. Thus, Sothy becomes simply Ty. There are also affectionate pet names, such as Srey Mom (Precious Girl), or descriptive nicknames such as Srey Map (Chubby). Sometimes a child may decide they want to be called by another name entirely.

Throughout the book I have tried to make the Khmer words available to an English-speaking reader, and any inaccuracies are not a mark of disrespect for Khmer culture but simply my attempt to make foreign words accessible to people who may never have heard the language spoken and are unfamiliar with complex phonetic notation. Some of my transliterations come from pronunciation guides in Khmer-English dictionaries and guidebooks, but even these disagree. "Thank you" might be written *o-ku!n.* Or then again, it might be *or-gOOn.* What to do? In the end I have tried to write words and names in such a way that the reader will not trip over them or feel stuck. Although Khmer differs from Thai or Vietnamese in that it is not a tonal language, in a few places I have included stress indicators. Thus, Malis, a girl's name meaning "Fragrant Jasmine," is not pronounced like the English "malice," but the more graceful *mah-LEE.*

Over the years, Wayne has worked on a document he calls his *Statement of Passions and Beliefs.* Many of the quotes in Chapter 19 and throughout the book are from these writings; others are from a series of taped interviews by Andy Gray, mostly on matters of spirituality; and some are excerpts from Wayne's letters to me, or from my own journals, notes from conversations with Wayne during many a long evening.

Choosing just a few images from more than six thousand photographs taken over seven years felt like a treasure hunt. Over time, images and words have intertwined into a tumble of beloved faces and memories, and together they form a journal, the images complementing volumes of late-night notes written by candlelight. Now and then, as I worked on this book, a photo triggered a metaphor that became in turn the seed of a story. Thus, a simple image of a kite flying in the smoke of a cremation inspired the tale of the singing kites. (There are, of course, many others, but I leave them to the reader's imagination.)

Sometimes I was concerned that the camera might come between me and the kids. I needn't have worried. When they had enough of my prowling about, someone would sneak up behind and goose me just as I was about to snap a photo. I soon learned when it was time to put the camera away.

From 2005 to 2012, I spent a total of almost fifteen months at Wat Opot. I made four trips: October 2005 to April 2006, January to May 2007, December 2009 to January 2010, and December 2011 to March 2012. Most of my stays were during the dry season, when there is often no rain at all for four or five months, so when I picture Cambodia it is rarely the radiant washed colors of the rainy season I recall, but more often sun-faded surfaces covered with a patina of dust. December and January are cool months. The children wear sweaters in the morning and we all sleep under thin blankets at night. Toward the end of January temperatures begin to rise, and daytime heat may climb to the triple digits. Everybody naps.

After my second visit I thought to take a year off from volunteering to write a book, but one year stretched to nearly three. I spent one of those years being treated for cancer, but stayed in close touch with the people of Wat Opot. During the long summer and fall of chemotherapy and radiation I often longed to return one more time to see the children. Their experiences and mine were becoming intertwined as I found myself dealing with serious illness, and memories of their courage and joy often sustained me. Sometimes it seemed I might never see them again. I poured my longing and love into telling their stories.

Though slow and measured in some respects, life at Wat Opot can also be disorienting. There are dozens of children and an ever-changing stream of volunteers. Travelers you meet for a day may later return and stay for months — or not at all. People arrive on short notice: NGO groups, college students, government officials, donors. The children too come and go, sometimes returning to their families, leaving for university or taking a job. Sometimes — rarely, these days — they die. The structure of this book reflects my own leaving and returning, learning a little more each time, becoming closer to Wayne and the children as we have all grown older. What we learn about each other in life is not revealed all at once, but slowly, in increments, through a variety of interactions and events. Wayne calls these, simply, "the things we go through together." So I ask the reader to relax into the chaos, knowing that life is not linear, but can perhaps better be viewed as a spiral, as we revisit certain events and people, explore expanding dimensions, recognize contradictions and deepen our love for each other.

In the end it all comes back to the children. Despite the name changes and other complexities, I invite you to do as I did: Stay a while with the children of Wat Opot and meet them as who they are, whole and vibrant, with their powerful personalities and enormous souls.

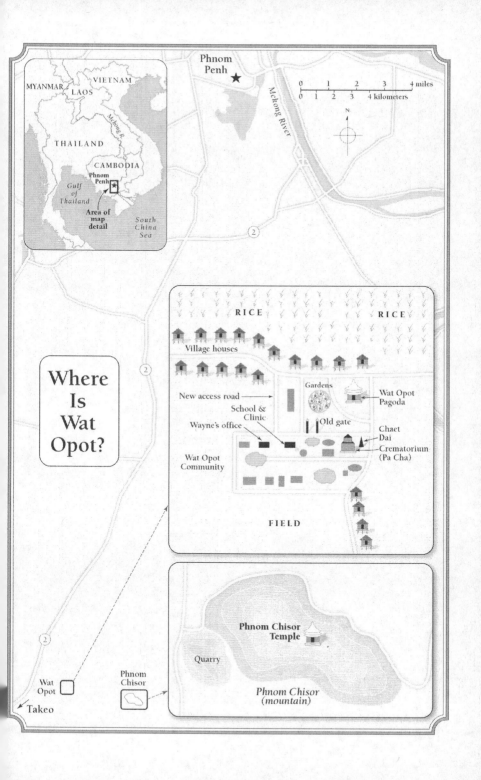

■ ■ ■ ■ ■

PART ONE:
SANCTUARY

■ ■ ■ ■ ■

1
SITA

Shhhhhh. Listen. Sita is waking the day.

Sita turns on her portable radio the moment she wakes up. She raises the volume as high as it will go, way past the point of distortion, then twists the dial back and forth searching for something that pleases her: the trailing melodies of Buddhist mantras, a marching band playing the national anthem of the Kingdom of Cambodia, karaoke tunes, monks chanting, more mantras, marching, karaoke, monks and on and on and back again.

I open my eyes. It is still dark outside, and only the dim differentiation of wall from ceiling, sky from wall, barely perceptible through the pink mosquito net, shows where my single window looks out onto the world. In the distance a rooster crows weakly, sounding cross. Is it too early for him as well?

29

A wandering many-voiced chant arises from the Buddhist temple next door, the morning prayers of young and aged monks. One dog barks. From across the way another answers.

Sita is playing a Western song now with lyrics in Khmer. Her cheap speakers crackle under the strain.

A gecko begins chirping on the stucco wall.

On the porch outside my room Wayne is still a snoring mountain. His mosquito net is tucked into the black fleece blanket on his bed. Wayne says he sleeps outdoors so he can hear the children when they cry, and manages to sleep, often uneasily, through noises less urgent.

Somewhere in the children's quarters a baby cries out from a dream and is comforted. Wayne rolls over and draws his body upright, dangling his feet over the side of the bed. He wears yesterday's black trousers, dried mud still on the cuffs from working in the garden. The crying has stopped now so he sits quietly, wrapped in his blanket, collecting his thoughts for the day, breathing himself awake, perhaps praying. A pair of small feet drop over the other side of the bed and stumble off toward the bathrooms behind our house. Mister Phirun, at nine years old the oldest boy with AIDS, sometimes wets the bed. None of the boys wants to sleep with Phirun, so Wayne lets him crawl in with him sometimes when he is worried or lonely. Wayne wakes up often during the night and he will carry Phirun out to the yard, hold him at arm's length to drain and return him to bed without waking him.

Wayne calls all the kids Mister or Miss, especially the very little ones who run around with no pants. It is a matter of respect for the children but also on occasion affords much-needed comic relief, as in "Mister Vantha! Where *are* your shorts?"

The children begin to wander in from their various sleeping quarters, gathering near the bathrooms outside my window. They are still half asleep, most of them, and sit in dazed solitary silence on the bamboo slat bed next to the wall in the manner of small children softly awoken, holding their toothbrushes and soap and waiting their turn in the bathroom. Their towels are draped about their shoulders or dangling unconsciously from their hands. Now and then a little one nods off to sleep as he waits, and his towel drops to the ground and he draws his bare shoulders in and up against the morning dampness and hugs himself and looks even smaller than before.

Now Sita squats by the faucet outside her woven mat house and draws a little water to wash herself. She wears a worn flowered sarong hastily tucked in above her breasts, and her hair tumbles uncombed about her neck and shoulders. In spite of the radio, in spite of the insects and the chirping gecko and the whispers of children, in spite of dogs and roosters and monks chanting, the air has until this moment still possessed the integrity of night. But when Sita opens the tap her simple gesture signals the onset of the day's activities, because somewhere else Mr. Sary has opened the valve that allows water to flow down from the holding tanks on the roof and the water hits Sita's plastic bucket with a noise like a string of small firecrackers. In the bathroom next door I hear the cistern beginning to fill and the children splashing about, giggling and whispering, washing themselves modestly under their clothes.

Sita has lived here, on and off, for six years, her residency interrupted by a series of transgressions, petty thefts and infractions that have made her at times unpopular with her fellow residents and unwelcome in the community. Each time she has left and failed to make a life for herself in the outside world Sita has returned, tentatively at first, testing the boundaries, subtly insinuating herself, promising that she has mended her ways, until finally Wayne's resolution fails and he persuades the other women to allow Sita to move her few belongings back into her small house.

As with nearly everyone here, her life has been a series of the setbacks and rejections, catastrophes and abandonments, that beset people infected with HIV/AIDS the world over. Such stories abound, every imaginable permutation of sorrow and many that are unimaginable. Sita's own story includes elements not uncommon: an abusive father, a lover who impregnated her and infected her with the HIV virus, then the death of her baby and beatings from her family and, when her illness became public knowledge, a village that tormented her and made of her a pariah. Perhaps like many poor women she has sometimes been forced into prostitution, at least informally, to feed herself. Wayne considers these things when he advocates for her in the community, and the others relent because, after all, Sita's life has not been so different from their own.

The daylight has begun to come up now

and Sita emerges from her house, dressed for the day, and begins sweeping the pounded dirt courtyard, bent over her short broom. Her dusty sarong has been properly tied, falling in a modest pleat from her waist. She wears a black blouse with panels of openwork lace, a garment that hints of the dressier ensemble it may have been part of before being sold as surplus from the sweatshops of Phnom Penh. Her high cheekbones, full mouth and high forehead give her a face that might be called sculpted rather than pretty, with a trace of knowing irony in her eyebrows. Yet I have seen her transform, and once, when she was clearly smitten by a young volunteer, she became girlish: radiant and unguarded and wonderfully soft. I could see then the beauty Sita had been and the wife and mother she might have been and the passionate woman she can be.

She moves aside a grass mat barrier to reveal a small space adjoining her house. It is no more than eight feet on a side and forms a tiny walled garden on one side of which Sita has planted pink, orange and red zinnias. Once the garden was open, but the bony cows that are allowed to graze freely in the dry season, topping Wayne's young mango trees and eating whatever else they can find, made a meal of Sita's flowers. So she has enclosed it, a hidden jewel, radiant in a dusty world. It is her refuge, her pride and her testament, like her radio that blares forth its witness every morning to the world and declares before Heaven, "Yes. I am still here. Listen! I am alive!"

2
A WORKSHOP FOR SOULS

My favorite way to arrive at Wat Opot is by tuk-tuk, an open-air surrey made of welded rebar and decorated with a bright fringed canopy. The tuk-tuk is the poor man's chariot and can accommodate several generations of a large Cambodian family, or one Western visitor with luggage for a lengthy stay. It is towed behind a motorbike, attached by a ball hitch. On the back of the tuk-tuk is a sign welcoming "Responsible Tourists" to Cambodia and announcing that the driver is "Absolutely Against Child Sex Tourism."

You hail a driver outside the Golden Gate Hotel on Street 278 in Phnom Penh. He knows you by now, knows all the volunteers and knows which of the ornamental gates off Highway Number Two South to turn through to access the rough dirt road through the village of Sramouch He and on to the Wat Opot Children's Community.

The trip takes about an hour and a half, as the tuk-tuk is slower than most other forms of public transport, but more enjoyable than being crammed with your parcels into a crowded bus or shared minivan and even nicer than riding in the back of a private taxi, whose air conditioner and windows may not work and whose driver's taste in music — always loud — may not agree with your own. In this surrey you can see and be seen, make funny faces at children along the road, enjoy the view of life and, if the rains come, you can let down the plastic shades and breathe the moist ozone-scented breeze that will settle the dust at last.

Wat Opot (a wat is a Buddhist temple, also called a pagoda) is a small village sanctuary, which in 2000 donated five acres of unused land for a small project to provide palliative care to some of Cambodia's poorest people who were dying of AIDS. The temple itself had been desecrated in the late 1970s by Khmer Rouge forces who had used it to store corpses. The land in question was known to be haunted.

Wayne Dale Matthysse, an American who

had been a medic in the Vietnam War, began the Wat Opot Project with a young Cambodian Buddhist, Vandin San. Over the years it has grown from a hospice into a vibrant community for children whose lives have been impacted by HIV/AIDS. About a third of the children are HIV positive, and all have lost at least one parent to AIDS. At any given time between fifty and eighty-five children, HIV positive and HIV negative alike, live together at Wat Opot as family, along with a number of adult patients.

On the last day of October in 2005, three months after my sixtieth birthday, I arrived in Cambodia and took the first of many tuk-tuk rides to Wat Opot. I had imagined Cambodia to be somewhere between Conrad's *Heart of Darkness* and Coppola's *Apocalypse Now.* The night I arrived I wrote in my journal,

First impression of Cambodia is that it is like the other poor places — same materials — bam-bam [corrugated tin] roofs, concrete or wooden houses — and except for the temples no decoration — along the roads very few places that are new, none that are fancy. Some neighborhoods in Phnom Penh with little row houses. But overall the dust, people making small market, nothing extra. Still, a lovely sweetness and quick response to a smile. I am met by the director and cofounder of the program, Vandin San.

Then south to Wat Opot. Arrival, meetings, many children and helpers. The kids are wonderful, beautiful — one boy runs out and hugs me. Lunch is fish from the little pond and string beans, rice, fruit, fried potatoes. Wayne gives me the tour — suggests some projects — I am still numb, exhausted — going through the motions of civility. I crash in late afternoon and wake for dinner saved for me — crash again till 4 a.m.

Wayne tells a litany of stories, of children here who have been abandoned or exploited — sold to prostitution, stripsearched when they visit family for any penny or anything worth selling. Adoptive parents who bought a boy, dropping him off at Wat Opot when they suspected AIDS. They wanted a child to raise who would care for them in their old age, not one for themselves to love and care for. Men getting drunk, raping their wives. Now the woman is pregnant, has AIDS or has a sick baby. Stories on top of stories. Women here who have lost children, now caring for the children of other women who have died. Wayne seeing God even in the least of these.

Where does the social contract break down? Where is the heart lost? Is it poverty, or some flaw in human nature? Is this the natural state, and the rest only stories that make us play out care and kindness? Or are these perversions caused by the collapse of culture, trauma of history, poverty and fear? For my part I will need to focus on the children, in the present, on being kind and giving them whatever I am able, and not whether one or another is HIV positive. Just be with them as they are and love them as well as I can.

When my friends heard that I would be going to Cambodia to volunteer for five months they questioned whether I might instead stay for a shorter time, "to see whether you like it." I had never spoken with Wayne, the director, but had received a few enthusiastic emails, welcoming me in spite of my inexperience and lack of professional qualifications. Rebecca, a pediatric nurse who had been volunteering at Wat Opot for some years, had phoned me when she was in the United States. She had first met Wayne when she visited Cambodia with a Christian mission group. She could see that he needed help and had begun praying that he might find someone who could make a commitment to the project. After a while she came to realize *she* was that person. Rebecca left her job and grandchildren and moved to Cambodia. She had now been living at Wat Opot for about five years and told me stories of the children, how they would love me, teach me Khmer and guard me from all harm.

Although I grew up in a Jewish family in New York City, as a child of the 1960s I had also dabbled in Eastern philosophies. I had little experience of Evangelical Christianity, and the sort of fundamentalism that was gaining political clout in the United States seemed more foreign to me than Cambodian Buddhism. I wondered how Rebecca and I would get along. Wayne, in contrast, although he came from a devout background, seemed dedicated to making Wat Opot a nonsectarian refuge, free of proselytizing. In the end I told myself that there would surely be things I wouldn't like, and if I knew I'd be leaving soon I would never try to come to peace with them. I figured I'd better plan to stay awhile.

Before many weeks had passed at Wat Opot, I would find that the problems were different and the joys more profound than I could have imagined. I will tell you about both in this book, and to that extent I could not help but write a book within a book, one about *une femme d'un certain âge* who goes off to find her soul by volunteering in the so-called Third World. It's a familiar theme in this isolating age, and although some of my own story inevitably crept in, the book I hoped to write is not about that. It is the lives of the children I want you to know about.

I arrived at Wat Opot at a time when anti-retroviral medicines (ARVs) had only recently become available to treat the first generation of children with HIV/AIDS. In those days, Cambodia had one of the highest infection rates in Asia and many children were being born HIV positive. But things had begun to change. Médecins Sans Frontières — Doctors Without Borders — had arrived in Takeo Province in 2003, bringing the first ARV program to a simple clinic in the provincial capital, also called Takeo. It's a small city, about an hour south of Wat Opot, with a current population of approximately 39,000 people. Very sick children who formerly would have perished in the AIDS epidemic were for the first time on medication, and they were clearly beginning to grow stronger. The problem now was how to nurture these traumatized children who had watched their parents and friends sicken and die, who might themselves have been close to death. How to convince them that with care they might grow up, go to school, live near-normal lives? This was a time when widespread attention turned to the epidemic in the developing world, before the economic downturn and relentless military spending spilled the seed of the largest donor nations, a time before people with AIDS would once again begin leaving the hospitals to die at home because there were no services or medicines for them. This was a hopeful time.

And I would like you to see how a good man with fifty dollars in his pocket and very little backing walks into the chaos of a post-apocalyptic country and wrests from the devastation a small island of compassion and comity. Those of us who yearn to "do something" in the world need such models, need to study real people who are not stopped cold by a lack of funds or support from international institutions or by the sheer enormity of the problem, people who are far from perfect but who can live in the reality of the moment and perceive what is needed and how to meet those needs with the materials at hand.

Wayne does not regard the Wat Opot community as existing only for the benefit of the children, although that is assuredly its primary purpose. Rather, he opens the gates to anyone on a journey who stumbles upon this place and feels called to linger with the children. Asked one afternoon whether there is any thread that unites the volunteers who have passed through Wat Opot, Wayne replied simply, "Loneliness and the need for touch." Even if people show up not realizing what is lacking in their lives, when the first child comes to hug them something changes, opening them in a way they likely could not have named before, answering a hunger that many of us in the West do not even know we have. Still, for all our hungers and traumas and our need to love and be loved, our compulsion to see ourselves as kind and useful in the world, maybe in the end we are only another passing caravan, a footnote in a long history. For us it is a brief visit, and then we leave and again we are alone. We come and go. But the children, in a sense, are eternal.

What Wayne did not mention on that occasion was the opening of the heart to compassion, which happens to many people who visit. After I had finished writing the first chapter of this book, I sent it to Andrew, a young Australian volunteer on whom Sita had developed a crush. Sita used to come to Andrew's room late at night and he would have to ask her to leave — very politely and kindly, because he was a sweet man — but it was difficult for him. And he would complain to me that she was putting him in the painful position of having to reject her night after night. But after he read the story he told me it helped him to appreciate and love Sita. This made me realize the power stories can have to transform the way people feel and love. I began to understand that Wat Opot was — is — a workshop for souls.

3
FAMILY PICTURES

Mister Sampeah [*sam-PEE-ah*], the first child to greet me when I arrived at Wat Opot, was all elbows and knees, mischievous eyes and a wide toothless grin. There I stood, apprehensive and exhausted after a thirty-hour flight, and it was Sampeah who ran out from a huddle of momentarily shy children to throw his arms around my knees. I felt my heart burst open, and from then on nothing was ever the same.

Sampeah's story is a mystery. Wayne guesses he was about four years old when he came to live at Wat Opot. Late one night an ambulance pulled into the clinic to drop off a woman patient. She had been beaten unconscious and her wrists showed rope marks where they had been bound together. The ambulance attendants were riding in the front seat, and when they opened the back door out jumped a skinny little boy with no front teeth. No one had seen him climb in and hide behind his mother's stretcher. Before Wayne could ask any questions the ambulance and its attendants disappeared into the darkness. Wayne wondered whether Sampeah had lost his teeth defending his mother from her attackers, but like many questions about Sampeah this one will never be answered. His mother died that night without ever having regained consciousness.

No one knew where Sampeah came from or whether he had family who might have been looking for him, but one day, when he was playing with the other children, one of the Khmer staff overheard him say the name of a village. Wayne asked him whether this was his home, and would he perhaps like to visit to see whether they could find his family. Sampeah's reply was a stifled "No!" and a face so fraught with anxiety that Wayne would never ask him again.

After dinner my first night I walked with Wayne to the crematorium for the brief memorial service that is held there each evening. The children chant a prayer invoking the name of the Buddha and sing a Christian hymn of thanks for the lives of their loved ones.

An unruly group of kids fell in behind us on the dirt path, calling out, "Meestah Wayne go *pa cha*!" They shouted and sang and jostled each other, hanging in clusters from our arms and hands. I wished I had more fingers.

The crematorium — *pa cha* in Khmer — stands on the far eastern edge of Wat Opot's slender strip of land. It is an austere white structure, square, with seven levels tapering toward a pointed top. Chimneys in the upper levels allow the smoke of burning bodies to rise and blossom, pure white against a blue blue sky.

On the western face of the *pa cha* are three doors. The door on the left opens to a small chapel with a simple white sarcophagus where the dead can rest until family and monks arrive for the funeral. A painting on the wall shows a beam of light ascending from the ocean to the clouds. In the center, behind steel doors, is the furnace itself. As a body is consumed by flames, bones and ashes sift down through a grate onto a ragged sheet of corrugated tin and are collected through a low door on the rear of the building.

To the right of the furnace is a tiny chapel called the family room. Inside, we crowded onto floor mats across from a wall of pictures of parents and friends who had perished of AIDS. On that first night, Wayne explained that after each cremation the children help to wash and select the bones for the little brass urns that sit in a glass case underneath the photographs. Each urn is carefully tied with a web of string and bears a tag with a name and a tiny portrait.

Behind the *pa cha* is a small memorial stupa called the *chaet dai.* It is painted the saffron of monks' robes, brilliantly brushed over with gold paint. Any ashes that are not put into urns are added to the remains of hundreds of other souls in this communal crypt.

The children love to climb on the *chaet dai,* and even mourners at a funeral do not mind their noisy play. People say that it comforts the spirits of the dead to hear the children's laughter.

During the service my new friend Mister Sampeah snuggled close to me. Several other children climbed in and out of my lap, their hair smelling of the incense we had just offered to the souls of the dead. Afterward, Sampeah took his mother's urn from the glass case. With both hands he held it out so I could see her picture and said simply, "Mama." He knew just where to find her. He could visit her and hold her and introduce her to his new friend, and it comforted him.

A year later, when I returned to Wat Opot, I watched as Sampeah introduced his mother to another new volunteer. I had my camera with me that night and asked him whether I might take his picture. The memory of that first evening had remained vivid in my mind, but there had never been a moment when it seemed anything but greedy to ask him to pose with the urn. He was delighted, and I was able to give him a large print of himself holding his mother's ashes. You can see her face on the tag tied with string to the lid. Sampeah is smiling his vast, guileless smile. His second teeth are starting to grow in.

Mister Veha and his little sister Miss

Kolab, whose mother had died earlier that week, were there that day and asked me to take a photo for them as well. So Veha fetched their mother's photograph down from the wall and they sat together on the cool tiles outside the crematorium. Veha put his hand under Kolab's chin and lifted her head to pose her just so.

For Sampeah and Veha, and for Kolab, who is too young to remember, these photographs of themselves with their mothers are the only ones they will ever have.

Two years later, in an elementary school in Northeast Harbor, Maine, I was talking with a group of fifth graders about the children of Wat Opot. Unlike most adult audiences, who want to know whether I had a bathroom or bottled water, or what kind of camera I use, or where the funding comes from, these kids identified powerfully with the children in the photographs, and their questions were different: "You say these kids are poor. How come they don't look poor?" and "If they know they are going to die, how come they look so happy?"

I was touched — awestruck really — at how their questions seemed to find the heart of the matter.

4
Exit, with Cookie

Miss Chan Tevy [*chan teh-VEE*] stands in the open doorway, her head held a little to one side. She walks toward me smiling, part eight-year-old, part diva, and altogether winning. She thrusts out an open palm and demands, *"Saboo!"* It is the eighth time tonight. "I *gave* you shampoo," I tell her. "I gave you shampoo for tonight and shampoo for tomorrow and shampoo for next week. What do you *do* with it all?" She considers this question seriously for a moment. She is wearing a white T-shirt with the word "ANGEL" in rhinestone studs. Then she tips her head to the other side, once again puts out her hand, smiles her most appealing smile, and says, "Cookie!"

I bring the biscuit tin from my room and give her one of the big ones with the chalky strawberry filling. She scowls. *"Bpee!"* she insists. "Two!"

It's a warm evening and the air feels perfect after a hot day. There's still a soft glow in the sky and we are waiting for Mr. Sary to fire up the generator. This is my favorite time of day, when everybody gathers after

dinner just to play and touch and be together.

Wayne and I sit on the bench in the yard,
and the kids pile on. Everybody wants to
cuddle. Miss Srey Mao, who is four years
old, climbs up on Wayne's knee and busies
herself plucking hairs from his arm. Little
Socheat leans back and relaxes into Wayne's
lap. Wayne tickles him and he doubles over,
laughing. Mister Poi runs up and blows on
the whistle he has made, a blade of grass
held between his thumbs. The sound is
wispy and Poi looks disappointed, so Wayne
shows him how to adjust the grass until it
makes a satisfying squeak. Mister Vantha
plucks a fresh blade of grass and the two
boys run off together, chirping happily in
the darkness. Mister Kosal muscles Socheat
out of the way, scrambles up Wayne's outstretched legs and slides giddily down again.
Socheat runs off to play with Miss Malis,
who grabs his hands and swings him round
and round in the air.

Pesei [*pe-SIGH*] snuggles up to me. He
has just tucked a sprig of bright orange
bougainvillea behind each of Baby Mai's
ears. Baby Mai is beaming, basking in the
attention. A few inches away, not quite
touching anyone, sits Pesei's sister, Miss Jorani. Needy but aloof, she is very much the

55

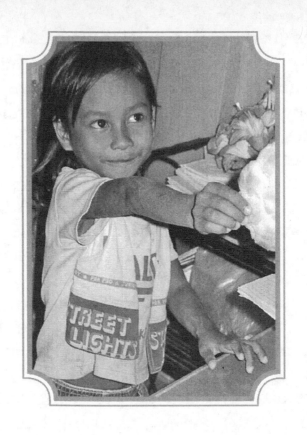

young teenager. Other kids jump rope and play volleyball. Mister Ratha, somewhere between twelve and sixteen, strikes a cool pose on a big red motorcycle. Little kids play and squabble and cry and come for comfort and run back out to play again. Older boys turn cartwheels. Bicycles careen by in the dark. It is on evenings like this, all of us together at the end of the day, that Wat Opot feels most like a family.

The generator coughs and the lights splutter on. Wayne peels the children from his lap and walks slowly toward the office to prepare for the evening clinic. Miss Srey Mom and Miss Ve Not have strung a piece of green twine across the path between the bougainvillea tree and the fence. Ve Not is five years old, tiny, and the string is just high enough that she must stand on tiptoe to reach it. The little girls are having fun pinching blossoms from the flowering trees and balancing them over the green string to make a flower garland. A simple and charming game. They hold the flowers daintily between thumbs and index fingers. The blooms tip back and forth in the breeze like bells, or miniature Chinese lanterns. Lavender, scarlet, white.

I wander over to admire their work.

Miss Chan Tevy drops her jump rope and runs over to play with Miss Srey Mom. They laugh together. Yet out of the corner of my eye I detect an odd movement, something not quite natural. It is only for a moment, a tiny jerking of Chan Tevy's body; she goes on chattering as if nothing has happened. Then it happens again. A little spasm. She does not seem to notice, but I watch carefully as she adds a hot pink flower to Srey Mom's garland. Over the next few minutes the spasm repeats several times.

Thoughts race through my mind: seizures? I have heard that over time AIDS can attack the brain — but . . .

"Chan Tevy?"

I hear alarm in my voice. I hadn't meant it to be there. She looks straight at me, but her eyes don't seem to focus, and this time her spasm is stronger, more dramatic. I gather her up and carry her into the clinic. She is light like a baby bird and she feels so vulnerable, shuddering in my arms.

"Wayne! Something's happening with Chan Tevy."

I set her down and she drops to the floor and begins to convulse, arms and legs jerking wildly, eyes rolled back.

Wayne glances up from his computer and goes on typing.

"Wayne!"

"She's faking it," he says, trying hard not to grin. "That one gets a reaction every time. Run along, Sarah Bernhardt."

Miss Chan Tevy allows herself a quick, satisfied glance at me and disappears out the door. I sink onto a stool, exhausted.

It's time for their meds. The children gather outside the clinic doorway. Serain urges them into something resembling a line, little ones in front. She monitors the doorway, directing the children with a bamboo rod, but her ferocity is all show. Along with Wayne and Rebecca, Serain is the backbone of Wat Opot. Every morning she arrives on her moto — gold jewelry and platform shoes, her hair just so, sometimes dyed black, sometimes red. Washerwoman, night nurse, tender of the dying, cleaner of god-awful messes, she is cheerful, industrious and, in my mind, superhuman. When there is nothing more pressing she collects old candle ends, softens them on a hot stone bench in the sun, and kneads and rerolls the wax to make new candles. Or she manicures the edges of the lawn with tiny scissors. She takes care of me like a mother and I love her. She is also fiercely protective of Wayne and brings him enormous bedtime bowls of sesame noodles. He groans loudly that she is trying to kill him, but he never refuses.

Every day Serain studies English from a tattered phrase book. "Madame, speak English?" she asks me. We each call the other "Madame." She points to an arcane circumlocution in this antique primer and together we pronounce a phrase, something on the order of "When does the parade of the matadors commence?" Then she will try to teach me something in Khmer, which always ends with the children laughing uncontrollably as Serain struggles to keep a straight face. I am convinced she keeps changing the pronunciation. The sessions end when she pats me on the cheek affectionately and says, "Madame speak Khmer very good!" Her English never seems to improve — but then neither does my Khmer.

One by one the children come into the office to take their medicines, the youngest first, Little Run, with his astonished eyes and enormous, translucent ears. As usual his nose is running. He is carrying a liter water bottle that seems much too big for him and he is wearing only a faded T-shirt that covers him to his knees. He is four, but already he can find his pills in the basket marked with his name. Mr. Sary checks the pillbox to make sure Run is taking the right dose, and then Run swallows his medicine, drinking deeply from his bottle. Mr. Sary gives him a cookie, and he runs off to play. I watch Run go through this procedure, morning and night every day, and each time I have the same thought: "He is so small."

Large and small they come, first the children infected with HIV, who must take their medicines punctually, twice every day, lest the virus develop resistance. All of them take pills except Mister Vibol, who is nine years old. Before he came to Wat Opot he was living with his grandparents in the village. To these elderly farmers, as to many villagers, HIV was a death sentence, so they didn't send the boy to school or give him his medicines regularly. Vibol developed resistance to the first-line antiretroviral drugs, and now he must take the second-line medication, a foul-tasting liquid that must be stored on ice.

He takes a deep breath. Mr. Sary reaches across the desk with a fat plastic syringe and squirts a measure of medicine into his mouth. Vibol takes a big gulp of water. He is trying not to gag. Wayne is still unsure how he is responding to these new drugs — so many skin infections, such frequent fevers too. We just can't know how much organ damage he has sustained, and Wayne worries about him, worries whether he will even survive. Sometimes Vibol seems withdrawn and frail and comes by for a moment just to rest with my arm around him, or he sits alone, out by the crematorium, softly playing his harmonica. But when he is well he is all boy, joyous and gangly, running with the others like a yearling colt. So for

He painted his mother bathing him
"because she loves me very much."
The young artist passed away not
long after painting this picture.

now all we can do is hope, and send him to school, and love him.

After the clinic, after the generator has stopped grinding and the children have settled down and the world is quiet again, Wayne and I sit in the darkened office, talking into the night with only a small candle for light. He begins to reflect on Miss Chan Tevy, and how he and Rebecca first discovered her at her aunt and uncle's house in a nearby village. Chan Tevy was the first child to live at Wat Opot.

"She was stitched into a hammock on the front porch. She was ill, only skin and bones. The aunt had put her there so that *she* could go out into the field to plant rice."

Seeing my expression change, he adds, "I know it sounds like abuse, but really it isn't. It's a necessity here. Chan Tevy lived with her uncle and aunt until she was two years old, and though we had no ARVs in those days she responded well to the vitamins and antibiotics we brought for her. Then testing became available and we had them bring her into the clinic, and when she turned up positive for HIV the uncle said he didn't want her in his house anymore. They had an argument right here in the office, but her aunt took her home anyway. About three weeks later the aunt brought her back. She said her husband had not come home and would not give her money for food until Chan Tevy was out of the house. Now and then she'll visit the aunt and uncle, but she's been living here ever since.

"Rebecca spent more time with her than with the other kids, and I believe much of Chan Tevy's acting ability comes as a result of her learning to manipulate Rebecca. I recall one time when Rebecca was going to give her a cookie but pulled it away just as Chan Tevy reached for it. This continued a couple of times. Finally, Rebecca gave her the cookie. Chan Tevy took it and then, looking straight at Rebecca, she threw it down on the ground. I don't think their relationship ever really developed beyond that point."

Miss Chan Tevy stands in the doorway to my room, her head a little to one side.

"Cookie!" she says.

"Bpee?" I reply. "Two?"

For a split second she looks surprised. Then she grins and holds out both hands. *"Bai!"* "Three!"

Now I'm grinning too. "Chan Tevy, you know I'm really happy to see you. Did you come to give me a hug?"

She climbs into my lap and throws her arms around my neck. We sit together for a little while, both of us, I imagine, wanting nothing in the world so much as this moment.

Then she runs off, a cookie in each hand.

5
MISS SREY MOM: THOSE WE ARE GIVEN TO LOVE

Miss Srey Mom was new to Wat Opot, and she stood in the twilight of her first evening with the children playing games all around her, knowing no one, seeing no one. She was only six years old, and alone. Behind her on the white stucco wall was a giant red AIDS ribbon and the words

WELCOME
WAT OPOT PROJECT

I approached her, put my hand gently on her shoulder, but she had turned deep inside. Blinded and deafened by grief she did not respond, though I thought I felt her body shudder when I touched her.

"I need to wait," I thought.

The car brought her and the car left without her. Two older sisters were in the car. Srey Mom's parents had both died of AIDS, and

65

her sisters were supposed to take care of her. But they were pretty and young, and anxious to marry. In Cambodia the quality of a woman's life is still largely determined by the man she marries, and it was not long before these young women realized that a promising young man, a good prospect, would have no interest in marrying a woman with a sickly young sister infected with AIDS. So they brought Srey Mom to Wat Opot.

Her sisters gave Wayne a plastic hamper with hair ribbons and bright new clothes. Srey Mom refused to look at them or say goodbye when they left. She just stood there, very still and very small. But after the car drove through the gate and down the road past the Buddhist temple, after it disappeared down the village road toward the highway, Srey Mom began to cry. She cried for hours, cried for her mother, her father and for everything that had been lost and taken from her. She was perhaps too young to know the words for what she was feeling. She just cried.

I had only been at Wat Opot a few weeks myself when Srey Mom arrived. She was the first new child to come while I was there. I was still adjusting to the loud all-

66

night music from the wat that lacerated my sleep, and to the constant demands of so many children with unfamiliar Khmer names. It would take me months to learn their stories, who was related to whom, which adult was responsible for which child. And that was just the beginning, the bare facts, the illusion of knowing. To begin to know these children, to meet them as people, would take much longer. In the dance of personalities there are some I will never know.

Perhaps because I was new myself I understood a little of how overwhelming it can be for a child to arrive at Wat Opot, this trauma heaped on top of all the other abandonment, the death of their parents and loss upon loss of anything familiar or loving in their lives. So I made a special effort to befriend the new ones, to sit with them on their first evenings, to check in with them until they made friends and began to fit in. Like them, I felt far from home. I too needed to be close to someone. And as my heart began to open, I started to contemplate what it is to love a child who might die.

A few evenings later, I was sitting with the women and children in the dormitory watching Korean soap operas on television. It's a quiet time of settling in for bed before the generator goes off. The villain made his entrance, greeted by a chorus from the children.

"Ot la-or!"

"Baaaad!"

Over in the far end of the room Miss Srey Mom was getting ready for bed. Like all the kids, she took out her own pajamas, showered by herself, combed her own hair. She went about this quietly, competently. In a normal life a mother would be doing all these things for her, and she would not be going to bed surrounded by strangers, but held warm and safe in the arms of a loving family.

She stood on tiptoes on her sleeping mat and pulled down the mosquito net and lay down, but after a while she slipped out of bed and walked over to where I was sitting. She looked up at me for a moment, and I smiled and said, "Hi, Srey Mom." Then she found her way into my lap, wrapped her arms tightly round my neck and clung to me just like that, slipping in and out of sleep. Her hair was still damp from her shower and she smelled sweet and clean in her new pajamas.

■ ■ ■ ■

Over the next few days, Srey Mom was my shadow. She needed to play or be held endlessly. When another child tried to climb into my lap she fought them off. "I have two knees," I would laugh, "and lots of love." But she needed all I had, both arms, both knees, all my love.

Miss Kalliyan walked by. She made a show of snubbing me. Although she was thirteen years old, she could not tolerate my giving so much attention to a new girl. Miss Kalliyan acted the same way when I made ginger tea for Miss Malis when she had a cold.

All of these children have had love, and what they most need snatched away from them through death or desertion or betrayal. Some have better strategies than others for filling their needs, but as with all of us they struggle, and they often do things that bring just the opposite result from what they have hoped for. The hitting, sulking, aggression and demands are just clumsy ways of asking, flailing around for something they cannot name. They don't know any other way to express their pain and need and their anger at being abandoned. There are so many children. It is hard for them to always have to share everything, never to be first, never to get enough.

The second year I returned to Wat Opot I brought a large suitcase full of Legos that were donated by the children of a friend in Maine. There were thousands of pieces. Finally, I thought, we will have enough so that all the children can play. They will build amazing things.

I unzipped the suitcase in the middle of my porch. The kids stood round, astonished. They had never imagined such a toy. Day by day the pile grew smaller. I became the Lego Police, frisking the kids as they left the porch so that they would not smuggle away pieces in their pockets. But one day on my way to dinner I watched Mister Kosal bopping across campus, flying three strips of Legos arranged like an airplane, and making sputtering put-put noises. He was overjoyed, absorbed in his wonderful toy, and it struck me that while the pedant in me was fixated on the idea of the children being able to build complex structures and learn principles of mechanics, the kids as always were using their imaginations to transform sticks and leaves and rocks into toys.

Within a month or two, very few Legos were left in the toy box. Several times a day Socheat would present me with some pieces he said he'd found. I began to suspect he was sneaking them away just so he could make a show of returning them, so I always thanked him profusely. But maybe — no, probably — the other children were happy just to reach into their pockets and touch something special from another world that was theirs, and theirs alone.

I wake up suddenly from a nap. Someone is banging on my door.

"Chee-um!" Blood.

Rebecca, the nurse, is in Phnom Penh, and Wayne has sent for me.

Srey Mom is in the dormitory, coughing up blood. By the time I arrive the children have gathered around her, a circle of protection, while Wayne tries to listen to her heart sounds above their chatter.

Madame Ketmoni [*ket-mo-NEE*], an adult patient who looks after Srey Mom, tells Wayne that the bleeding started in the pickup truck as they were riding back from Takeo, where they'd seen the doctor. Wayne questions Ketmoni persistently, in English and Khmer. Maybe it is just the drug Srey Mom is taking for tuberculosis. That can

71

turn sputum red and might be mistaken for blood. Maybe that's all it is, just a carsick child and some red-stained vomit. But Ketmoni is adamant, and a little offended that Wayne should doubt her report.

Wayne asks everyone to be quiet while he listens intently through his stethoscope. He knows that if Srey Mom's heartbeat is fast and weak, she is bleeding internally, and he can only put her to bed and wait for death to take her. But her heartbeat is strong, so he suspects it is only a little old blood that she is coughing up. And it is the weekend and the doctors at the hospital have all gone home until Monday. There is nothing to do but watch and wait.

Wayne tells me that sick children can go downhill very fast and that in America a child with HIV and TB would be put on the critical list. Srey Mom cannot be given antiretroviral medicines until her tuberculosis has been treated, and there is not enough medical technology in Cambodia to treat what may be happening inside her tonight.

Years later, when I asked Wayne to explain how a child like Srey Mom, who might have been confined to a ward in the West, was allowed to run and play with the other children at Wat Opot, he spoke of the need to accept things as they are. "Death was just around the corner for many of these kids, and neither I nor she thought she would be a survivor. So it was important to treat it casually so she didn't get scared and give up."

Later, in bed in the hospice, Srey Mom is hungry, and I ask Madame Ketmoni to bring her some food. Pesei is there, next to me. His father and mother died of AIDS; he shares this moment's anxieties. He nursed his own parents, and his presence is a quiet offering. He will do what is needed. Ketmoni returns with Srey Mom's dinner. I feed her and remain close by. Then Ketmoni hugs me. It is the first time she has shown any affection toward me — and, for that matter, my first toward her. On this night we are both mothers.

It is later still, nearly lights out. Srey Mom has climbed out of bed and is sitting on the ground throwing up blood. The children stand in a ring around her, but not too close. They understand about AIDS and blood and everyone knows which children here are HIV positive. Wayne says the bleeding might be coming from her stomach or her lungs, or perhaps it's just a blood vessel in her throat, opened by her persistent coughing.

We lay her in bed again, and I sit with her. She moves my hand to her chest, right over her heart, to ease the pain or perhaps to ease her loneliness, and I leave my hand there, patting her gently until she falls asleep.

It is almost midnight when Ketmoni comes for me. Srey Mom is coughing up a lot of blood. By the time I get there, Wayne has put a large block of ice on her chest, as much to keep her still as to try to stanch the bleeding. The blood is bright red, so it is probably not from her stomach. It could be from her lungs, but she has been coughing heavily and Wayne is still hoping it is only from her throat. Srey Mom looks small and scared. Wayne tries to insert an IV by candlelight. He is blind in one eye from when he was wounded in battle as a medic in Vietnam, and his "good" eye has a cataract, so he strains in the dark to find a tiny vein. We bring the candles closer, as in some arcane ritual. But in spite of Wayne's training and his years of experience, tonight he cannot find a vein. For now it's impossible.

Wayne is exhausted. He was up all the previous night nursing a dying man, so he asks me to stay here in the hospice with Srey Mom. All through the darkness and into the morning I wake up every hour or so to replace the ice on her chest, or to give her medicine to keep her from coughing. Wayne figures that if the blood is only coming from her throat, and if we can keep her still, the lesion may heal. So many ifs.

Her coughing wakes me once more. She is restless and feverish. Her shirt is soaked through and in her sleep she has thrown off the ice. Nearby, Serain, in mask and gloves, moves quietly among the patients, speaking softly in the darkness to comfort and calm a frightened woman.

I am reminded of something Rebecca had told me when I first arrived, about how patients come into the world rocked by their mothers, but how there is no one to rock them as they leave. So I hold Srey Mom in my arms and rock her and stroke her flushed, frightened face.

At dawn I place my palm on Srey Mom's forehead; at last her fever has broken. Once more I notice the crickets and chuckling geckos, the howling dogs and hurdy-gurdy sounds of the wat. From two rooms away I hear Wayne snoring. Serain studies English by candlelight under her pink mosquito net. Patients moan and shift, their thin bodies rustling on the plastic mattress covers.

It's daylight when we carry Srey Mom back to her own bed. I sit by her side, rubbing her back as she drifts into a deep sleep, and suddenly I have a vision of myself as part of an eternal lineage of mothers and fathers who have sat up for countless sleepless nights with sick children. I am hot and exhausted and still worried, and I close my eyes and feel the touch of my father's hands as he used to give me alcohol rubs when I was small and had a fever, and my vision dissolves into tears.

Pesei's sister Miss Jorani has been doing her school lessons on her bamboo bed nearby. She walks over quietly and fans me with her notebook. She kneels down and looks up into my face and asks, "You cry?"

I nod. "Yes, I cry." She reaches out her hand and touches my arm for a moment. Her touch is gentle and cool. Then she goes back to her lessons.

Over the next few days, Srey Mom's throat heals and there is no more blood. I bring her a little doll to comfort her and keep her still, and children come to sit with her on her bed, or play nearby.

Only when it is over, when she can play

and run with the other children again, can I bring myself to ask Wayne the questions I dared not articulate when we did not know whether Srey Mom would live. How can you open your heart completely and love the child who needs it most, the one who might die? And how can you go on loving the next one and the next, after they do?

Wayne's calling has been to work with the dying. In this new world, where children can grow up HIV positive, there are different challenges. How can we help them to live with AIDS? What sort of lives will they have? What work can they do? As the first generation of HIV-infected children entering young adulthood, will they be able to marry or have children of their own?

But for me in this moment it was a question of how to love, whatever the outcome. Not without attachment — how could that be possible? But to accept that love and grief, caring and mourning, are manifestations of the same fierce instinct. For when we close our hearts, out of fear of pain, we do unspeakable violence to the children and to ourselves. We distance ourselves from life, and from all opportunities to share with them the joy of living. In the end, to shut our hearts would bring us to an untimely and tragic death-in-life. And worst of all, for the children this would be the final, the cruelest abandonment.

6
BOYS WITH BARBIES

Wayne and I tried to keep Srey Mom in bed until her throat healed, but that proved to be a difficult task. As soon as she began to feel better she wanted to run around and play. But before we could stop her the exertion would reopen the wound in her throat, she'd start coughing up blood, and we would have to begin all over again, keeping her motionless for hours with a block of ice on her chest. I brought her toys and books and sat with her, but it was hard for her to keep still. She was only six. Between tuberculosis and AIDS she had been sick most of her life, and, as Wayne put it, "Srey Mom doesn't do sick well."

A donor from the United States had sent a box of Barbie dolls, but Rebecca had forbidden me to let the girls play with them. Rebecca was trying to teach them not to be concerned with appearances and to concentrate on developing their minds and spirituality and self-confidence. She felt that the dolls, with their ample busts, constricted waists and impossibly long legs, would undermine the self-image of growing young women and nullify everything she hoped to accomplish. I saw her point, yet it seemed such a waste to withhold them. But although I could foresee the fun they would have, and that it would likely overshadow any enduring harm, I respected Rebecca's wishes, and the dolls remained hidden away.

But today was Sunday, and Rebecca had taken the girls and the smallest boys into the village to attend church. Only some of the older boys stayed behind. A wicked impulse formed in my head: I just had to see what those boys would do with the Barbies. After all, Rebecca had not said the *boys* couldn't play with them!

I dumped the plastic anorexics and their accessories onto the bed next to Srey Mom — a dozen Barbies and scads of outfits: from spangled gowns to minute bikinis, silver sandals, cat's-eye sunglasses, patent leather boots and spiked heels with polka-dotted bows on them. Srey Mom and I were having a wonderful time, and before long the word went out and every boy on campus (and a few more I'd never seen before) came running from all directions toward the dorm's open door. With a whoop they fell to. They did what boys do: they investigated, dressed, undressed, peeked, giggled,

prodded, tossed, guffawed and beheaded, and then put them all back together and returned them to me, miraculously whole and virginal.

I loved the rollicking way these boys played with the dolls. Like girls, they too enjoyed assembling miniature outfits, meticulously doing up the tiny buttons and snaps, and delicately, almost reverently, combing the dolls' long blond hair. These boys had no preconceptions, no sense that this was girl stuff. They were totally open.

About that time Rebecca came back with the girls, who joined the party at Srey Mom's bedside. Not that I could have hidden the fact of the dolls from them anyway.

Nope, the Barbies were out of the bag, and there was no getting around that. Rebecca saw how excited the kids were, and all in all she proved to be a good sport about the whole thing.

The lovely Miss Kalliyan held the doll she had just dressed close to her heart. Her eyes were shining and she uttered to me perhaps the only English sentence I had ever heard her speak: "Gail. I want."

Maybe Rebecca was onto something after all.

Eventually the boys wandered off, but the girls stayed. I had some chores to do, but when I returned something caught my eye. Among the Barbies was one single dark-skinned doll, and she lay on the table, abandoned.

Just about any cosmetic product I saw in Cambodia, from face cream to underarm deodorant, contained skin whiteners. Cambodians know dark skin will peg them as a peasant who works in the rice fields. A few days before, I had talked with one of the girls about the perils of some of the home-brewed skin bleaches for sale in the local markets — I had heard that some even contain mercury. She was a natural beauty, and I explained to her how worried I was that she should feel it necessary to bleach her lovely face into what would look like an ashen gray mask. She listened politely but uncomfortably, not wanting to disagree with an elder, but I could see how socially compelling it was for her to have lighter skin. Years later, when we knew each other better, this young woman would tell me that her father's mother had not wanted him to wed her mother because she had dark skin and came from a poor family.

Today I noticed she was sharing a doll with another girl, so I offered her the orphaned Barbie. Her reaction was immediate, phobic and physical. "No!" she exclaimed, withdrawing her hands and jumping back. She actually seemed frightened, or so it seemed to me, that some of that darkness might rub off on her.

A while later I wandered back, curious to see how they'd worked it out — or hadn't. As there were many more girls than dolls, I was certain someone would be tempted to break the taboo.

I was not prepared for how they actually solved their problem. Someone switched the heads on two dolls, so there was a brown face on a white body, and a white face on a brown one. I supposed their logic went that now each of the two children could have a doll that was at least partly white.

7
OPENING THE GATES

A wrought iron gate, left casually open, marks the boundary between the Wat Opot Children's Community and the grounds of the Buddhist temple next door. On each side of the gate a yard or so of fence, no longer plumb, struggles to assert itself from amid the weeds. This is the formal entrance to the campus.

When I first came to Wat Opot, drivers would turn off the main highway and travel a mile or so down the dirt road that runs through the villages, and then turn onto the temple grounds. Your taxi or moto would drive right through the Buddhist wat itself, and in through the northern gate. But by the time I returned the next year a new access road had been built along the outer wall of the wat. The need for a second road puzzled me, but Wayne would explain that the monks had been disturbed by the attitude of some of the moto drivers. The wat grounds are sacred, and when you come inside it is proper to remove your hat. Some of the moto drivers who were new Christians had begun to flout this custom.

The new road meant that Wayne had to build another entrance, on the western end of the compound: a wooden fence with a latched corral-type gate, broad enough for trucks and cars. This gate, one might reason, would keep hungry neighborhood cows from raiding our crops. But opening and closing the gate meant getting out of your vehicle twice; this was too much of a nuisance for most people, so usually the gate stood open. Cows wandered in and out at will, grazing on flowers and feasting on the struggling vegetable garden. In truth, the gate was irrelevant: even when it was latched, the cows simply leapt over the fence.

Then too, all those cows could just walk around to the other side of the volunteers' housing and amble onto campus unimpeded. They spared neither the thorny pink bougainvillea bush nor the succulent philodendron vines that shaded our porch in the dry season. So Wayne installed yet another fence with a sort of turnstile, but the kids ducked under it, and even though it was no moon gate the cows jumped over it all the same.

Back on the north side, a little ways down from the old main entrance, behind a small

silted pond where the monks collect water for their gardens and almost hidden among the weeds, is a set of crumbling concrete steps that allow access between the temple grounds and the Wat Opot campus. From the gazebo where we gather for breakfast every morning, we have a lovely view of white cows descending the staircase for a breakfast of their own — the tender crowns of young mango trees that Vandin planted across the field from the crematorium. Once, Wayne spent a slow afternoon building a teetering construction on the topmost step. He balanced cinder blocks and wood scraps and a couple of fat rusty springs from a truck suspension. He hoped the cows would knock pieces off as they tried to brush by and be spooked by the noise, but they just stepped placidly over the debris and ambled onward. Wayne might have installed a more serious barrier, a set of cables or a gate with a spring, but in that moment he just enjoyed playing with blocks.

There is no gate on the south side of the campus, which backs onto the open field that stretches all the way to Phnom Chisor. (*Phnom* means mountain or hill in Khmer.) A barbed wire fence strung between cement posts seems to do the job. It also makes a dandy clothesline; the barbs take the place of clothespins and keep the laundry from blowing away. This explains the odd pattern of tiny holes in certain garments at Wat Opot.

Finally, behind the crematorium on the east end of the campus and secured by a rusty lock and chain stands yet another wrought iron gate. But next to that a little stile, wide open, allows unhindered passage for children and cows alike. Along this side of the campus runs the road that defines the village, where we took our early-morning walks.

When Wayne and Vandin were first searching for land, the plot of scrub that would become the Wat Opot Children's Community was not what they had in mind. They had visited a number of villages, hoping one of them would donate land for the project, but local people feared this terrible new plague whose cause they did not understand.

Finally, the head monk of Wat Opot offered Wayne and Vandin a plot of unimproved land that local people believed was haunted by ghosts. The temple grounds formed a natural barrier between the project and the village. On the far side lay only open fields. This desolate setting offered a quiet, discreet place for people with AIDS to live and die, out of sight of the neighbors.

In the early days, while the clinic was being built, Wayne came down from Phnom Penh every week to take care of patients. The village and wat were in sad condition after the war years. The temple itself stood open to the weather and to wandering animals; worse, its statues and murals had been desecrated. Wayne hoped that the improvements he and Vandin were making to the land might inspire and encourage the monks and villagers and that the new clinic and hospice might benefit this poor rural community. After the partners filled the land, after they built a clinic, planted orchards and constructed a crematorium, the government improved the local road and people began fixing up their houses. Over time the monks installed a new tile roof on the temple. They hired a local artist to restore the murals that show the life of the Buddha. The artist also regilded the statues and repainted the Buddha's compassionate smile. Today there are gardens and reflecting pools, and the temple is once again an important part of the community.

In the beginning, the people of this tiny village told Vandin they had never heard of AIDS. That sad knowledge would come soon enough, when their neighbors began to sicken and die. By the time I arrived in 2005, fear of AIDS had begun to create barriers between the villagers and Wat Opot in spite of educational outreach by the monks and Home Care staff. Sometimes when I took the children to the local market, I would see their faces suddenly darken, their eyes drop. I could not persuade them to tell me what shadow had passed over them. Then I would become aware of a knot of people nearby and overhear them whisper the word "Opot." It would take time to change their attitudes, to open the many gates between the village and Wat Opot, and it would happen in unexpected ways.

Papa Steve the Giant Tasmanian was an expansive, florid man with a contagious smile, wild white hair and startlingly black eyebrows that danced like a pair of unruly toupees over his bright blue eyes. To the children he was a human jungle gym. *"Tomaaaaah!"* they'd say. Huge! "Same-same Meestah Wayne." They giggled and poked, fascinated by his considerable belly. Steve hugged and teased and windmilled the big boys over his shoulder. Having few healthy men in their lives, the children thrived on his exuberance. And the little ones delighted in the shiver of fear they felt

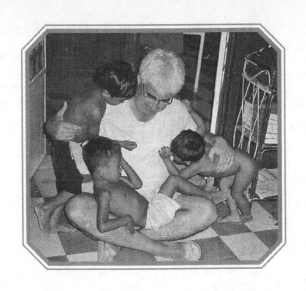

when the giant hurled them high into the air and then feigned barely catching them in his huge safe hands. But for all his buoyance, Papa Steve would also dive into intense private conversations with troubled children, dialogues that struck me as mystically empathic and reassuring, in spite of their lack of a shared language.

I had barely settled in for my first winter at Wat Opot when Steve showed up. A teacher, businessman and computer consultant, this fifty-year-old Australian had also worked in community development. He had briefly volunteered at Wat Opot the year before, and now he was back for a longer stay. We became friends at once and went walking together most mornings. He would scratch at my door before cockcrow and we would set out by starlight, feeling our way along the rutted road. Steve would call out his hearty "G'day!" and the villagers would respond drowsily — and, truth be told, a little grumpily — their voices hoarse from sleep and the smoke of early-morning fires.

Steve had a cell phone camera, and once daylight had come he would snap pictures of people we met along the way, especially the children. The camera was small enough not to be intimidating, and it had a screen so the children could look at themselves. They were enchanted. Steve took hundreds of pictures.

On our next trip to Phnom Penh Steve had lots of the best photos printed and he passed them out to the village children. By watching the flow of pictures we began to discern who was related to whom in this seemingly random mass of children and grown-ups.

After a few weeks, we found that the villagers were dressing their children up in the dark and waiting with them by the side of the road at dawn so Steve could stop and take more formal pictures. Children who would normally swarm the camera for a chance to be photographed stood awkwardly in their best clothes, clutching some prop appropriate to a studio portrait — a parasol, or a fancy hat — and their parents would slick their hair down and poke at them and pull their shoulders back and plaster their hands to their sides, creating that most unfortunate of images, the static, posed, little soldier-child. In a spirit of conspiracy with each kid, Steve obliged by taking the portraits the parents wanted, and then snapped happily away as the tiny victim escaped captivity and began behaving like a child again.

More trips to Phnom Penh. More little prints given away.

Several venerable *yei,* village grand-mothers, approached Steve to make por-traits of them. They asked for larger prints so their families would have something to remember them by after they died.

People began inviting us into their court-yards, offering us a cup of water or a ripe mango. After a while they brought out sick children and older relatives whose faces were new to us, and began asking us for medical advice. Since we were foreigners from Wat Opot they assumed we were doc-tors, but of course we had no medical advice to give, encouraging them instead to come to the clinic with their questions. One little baby looked so puny we urged his mother to bring him to Wat Opot right away. Another woman seemed too ill to move, and we arranged for the Home Care nurse to visit her in the village. Steve sent one girl with scoliosis to a clinic in Phnom Penh, giving the child's grandmother from his own pocket the five dollars she needed for travel and clinic fees — for a rural worker almost a week's wages. The next time we saw the girl with the curved spine she was wearing a brace.

People began inviting us to weddings and memorial celebrations. Steve took more photographs and gave away more prints.

More people began to bring their injuries, illnesses and health care questions to Wat Opot. There were no crowds or lines to stand in, it was nothing dramatic, but these were people who until then had not thought to come to Wat Opot for help or, if they had, would have been too frightened of catching AIDS to have passed through any of our many gates. Their newfound trust marked a beginning, and I marveled at how naturally the shift in attitudes had progressed, from a few roadside snapshots to the opening of the gates, and a little less fear.

Wayne and Vandin envisioned Wat Opot as an outpatient clinic for people infected with HIV/AIDS and, before antiretroviral drugs became available in Cambodia, a hospice with a dozen beds for the dying. In the first few years more than three hundred patients — adults and children and little babies — had died of AIDS there and were cremated with dignity in the *pa cha.* This included the parents of some of the children who now live at Wat Opot, children who are growing up taking profoundly powerful medicines that came too late for their parents, but that may offer them near-normal lives. To all appearances they are healthy, save for the fact that they must endure side effects from the medication, suffer recurring opportunistic infections and grow up wondering in every new social situation how being HIV positive will impact their lives.

Wayne and Vandin began to be concerned for the future prospects of this first generation of children to grow up HIV positive. As more of the kids survived, the focus of the project began to change — from tending to the dying to preparing the children to live in the rest of the world, outside Wat Opot. For much of their education the Wat Opot children would be going to the local schools, sitting next to kids from the village whose parents might worry about their own children catching AIDS.

Wayne hired local teachers to work with

the smallest school-age children and also to offer classes especially for older kids who had not attended school before. These kids would otherwise have had to start in the village school at a first-grade level, and Wayne recognized that having to sit on tiny chairs among the littlest kids would be mortifying.

Education in rural Cambodia is just beginning to recover from the dystopian fantasies of the Khmer Rouge years in the late 1970s, when intellectuals were routinely murdered, and being able to read, or simply wearing eyeglasses, could cost you your life. An expatriate librarian in Phnom Penh told me that when she arrived in Cambodia some years before, not a single book remained in the university library. The Khmer Rouge had burned everything. So village children are being taught by a first generation of mostly young, mostly rural teachers, some of whom are educationally only a few years ahead of the children they are teaching. These teachers are underpaid, and sometimes their paychecks are late or do not come at all, so they have to find outside work, often during school hours. Wat Opot children will go off to school in the morning only to return a few minutes later, complaining, "Teacher not come today."

Our own Wat Opot teachers hold classes

every day after lunch to supplement the government education, but some days this is all the schooling the children receive. When the village teachers do come to school, classes are large and noisy and the children mostly learn by recitation and rote. And because their wages are low, teachers all over Cambodia, at every level of education, expect bribes from their students for grades and permission to graduate — a disaster for the many impoverished students. As Wayne observed, "The only thing worse than ignoring children with physical and mental disabilities is to give them a second chance at living but no opportunity to make a life for themselves."

In 2007, Mary Dunbar, a good friend of Wayne's and of Wat Opot who has worked in Cambodia for many years, approached Wayne with the notion of starting an art program for the children. She knew a talented young Khmer artist named Rith Houeth, who had illustrated a number of pamphlets and posters for NGOs. If they could raise money for supplies and a small stipend, he would be willing to come down from Phnom Penh once a week and hold art classes for our kids. The Schmitz-Hille Foundation in Germany agreed to fund the program for an initial two years. Because this generously sponsored art program has been so fruitful, the foundation has continued to support the project to this day. Recently they donated money for full scholarships for three promising students to study art and architecture at the Royal University of Fine Arts in Phnom Penh.

During my first season at Wat Opot I brought paper and supplies for the children and they spent many happy hours drawing, so I knew they had lots of creative energy. But under Mr. Houeth's instruction their work was transformed. He taught them discipline and perseverance and close observation. They learned how to use colored pencils and oils and watercolors. Now, instead of whipping through one sheet of paper after another, they would work for hours on a single painting, and over time their art became much more developed and refined, beautiful and personal.

As Mary Dunbar and Wayne originally intended, the art program is another way for the children of Wat Opot and the village children to become comfortable with each other. Working together, Mr. Houeth's students have painted murals on the walls of the new schoolhouse at Wat Opot. One panel shows a family of elephants, frolicking and playing and trumpeting with joy.

Wayne is surprised by how successfully the mural project has helped open up the relationship between the Wat Opot community and the villagers. Monks bring visitors to see the mural, and the village children proudly escort their parents through the gates to see their work.

I was particularly moved by comments of children from the village who came to Wat Opot to help paint the mural. One little girl named Poilin, age thirteen, when asked whether she had any fear of working alongside children infected with HIV/AIDS, replied simply, "There was no problem. We achieved everything together."

8

ANTS-IN-A-LINE VILLAGE

Sramouch He is one of several small villages on either side of the dirt road that runs between National Highway Number Two and Wat Opot. Its name translates as "Ants' Parade," or "Ants-in-a-Line Village," due to the abundance of huge clay ant hills that people found when they came to settle here.

Like the ants, the children of Wat Opot have put the finely digested clay of the ant hills to good use. (The insect workers at their feet do literally ingest, digest and excrete the soil, transforming the yellowish-white earth to a sticky clay.) The children have recently begun harvesting the ants' clay to make sculptures. They started with masks and figures and portraits of the other children, but more often they are moved to sculpt the figure of a child held in its mother's arms.

On either side of Wat Opot, villages line the road, but all of them look more or less the same and I could never quite tell where one village ended and another began. Houses along the road are mostly traditional wooden structures. A few are brick or cinder block with ornamental iron window grates. The downstairs is wide open, without walls, and the single upper story, which rests on stilts and is accessed by a simple wooden ladder, forms both an enclosed living quarters and a ceiling and sunshade for the lower story. A floor made of widely spaced boards allows air from below to circulate and cool the upstairs room, but it is on the ground floor where the family spends most of its time, at least in the dry season.

Most houses are simply built, with little ornamentation. Now and then the whole structure, or perhaps merely a window

frame or banister, is painted with a color where plain wood might do. On a rough wooden door, a painting of the sun rising over a shining sea, two beams of light ascending to heaven to become a cross, marks the home of a lay pastor.

Exterior walls may be of wood, tin or woven mats; wooden house posts two feet off the ground rest on concrete piers to keep them out of the rainy season floods. The roofs are corrugated metal, or new or old thatch. Birds, finding there a comfortable home with all the nesting material they could wish for, flutter in and out all day long, chattering and carrying food to their young.

A few prosperous families have houses

with shingled or tiled roofs, shutters of a faded blue against weathered wooden walls, concrete stairs and perhaps carved and painted bargeboards. Sometimes there are cast concrete roof ornaments of the Wheel of Dharma, or even auspicious trumpeting elephant finials such as one finds on the roofs of temples.

By contrast, a poor family's home might be a casual arrangement of lean-tos and roof lines — angles and materials scrounged from everywhere: woven palm fronds, corrugated tin, plastic tarps patched into place with random battens and, when there is nothing else, cardboard from flattened paper boxes.

Until recently, electrical power lines stopped at the main highway and villagers made do with car batteries to power a single lightbulb or, now and then, a small television. Every morning a man would come by with a cart, pick up spent batteries, recharge them with a generator and drop them off at the front door, much like an old-fashioned milkman.

Tall trees shade the road and produce edible fruit in season. Loaded carts with upward-sweeping prows groan by, pulled by white bullocks with massive humps and thick, curving horns. Their heavy heads sway back and forth to the hollow tunk of cow-bone bells. A young girl steps daintily down a flight of stairs, holding up her flowered sarong. Her mother appears from behind the house, upon her head a bundle of firewood silhouetted against the rising sun. Its branches glow like antlers in velvet.

In the outdoor living area beneath the raised house, all of a family's material life is on display: rusty biscuit tins, cooking pots, calendars saved for their glimpse of the exotic (a fast car, a snowy landscape), hens, beds of slatted bamboo, hammocks, sandals, a sneaker missing its mate, buckets crowded with live catfish, plastic sleeping mats, bags of rice, plates of food. Stretched between beams are various overhead lines of thick or thin rope from which are suspended laundry, tarps, patched quilts hung as curtains against the sun. Tacked to one of the posts, a curling picture of a fat baby smiles at an unseen parent. Photographs and political broadsides: the king and his father, the prime minister and his wife, a yellow Corvette parked in front of a European palazzo, Easter bunnies.

A boy stands on tiptoe to scoop water from a burnished concrete jar. With one cupped hand he parts a froth of buoyant green algae. Rainwater, channeled from the roof during the downpours, is saved in a row of lidded jars. In the long dry season, when rivers and ponds turn to dust, this may be the family's sole source of drinking water.

Animals are everywhere. Next to a fence of lashed bamboo and brambles, a squirming litter of piglets lies nursing. As I pass by, a man waves to me excitedly. His cow has just given birth. She is held steady by wide bands to the overhead beams of the upper story of the house. Proudly he shows me the neat stitching of the episiotomy he performed on the mother. The calf is already nursing. In the front yard the man's son scrubs the flanks of an enormous white bull, like a proud American kid from the 1950s polishing his prize Chevy.

Except when it rains, the family lives, cooks and naps in the shade under the house. Girls meticulously prepare tie-dyed wefts on wooden frames, which women weave into the legendary iridescent Khmer silk. Chickens bustle about their feet. A full-faced old *yei* sits on her woven mat warming her bones in the sun just like Hotei, the fat joyous Buddha. Red betel nut juice drips from the corner of her mouth. *"Hoap papaya?"* she calls out, inviting me to share a ripe fruit from a tree next to the house.

Children run about, with or without clothes. Older kids dressed for school in white shirts with book bags and fresh-faced girls with dark skirts pedal by on heavy bicycles. Village women wear nearly anything they can afford: sarongs and tops of contrasting patterns, mismatched and incongruous by our lights, but after a while making a strange new sense. Pink flowers with leopard skin prints, metallic blue Lurex, an argyle sweater. But if you attend a local wedding you will see these same ladies, transformed by makeup and radiant as temple dancers, costumed in the jewel-like silks woven by their own hands in the village.

Some families set up neighborhood shops under their homes and make small market to earn what money they can. For making drinks they may have an ornate cast-iron ice shaver with bottles of sweet syrup in poisonous reds and greens the shades of antifreeze. Slabs of brown coffee jelly are diced up into the flavored shaved ice, and this concoction is served not in a cup but a plastic bag. You sip it through a thin straw. It is cold and invigorating on a sweltering afternoon.

Other shops display Angkor beer in bottles, Fanta in cans, packets of shampoo

in long strips. A small girl sells cigarettes from a rusty tin showcase. There is cooking oil, fish sauce, raw palm sugar and fried snacks, all hanging in plastic bags from hooks in the rafters, safe from the predation of animals and small children.

The egg vendor rides by. He drives carefully, skirting the ruts and ridges. Ten layers of egg crates are balanced on a board cantilevered across the back of his moto, the whole miraculous construction secured by a web of bungee cords. Quick mental math

gives me the sum: 1,080 eggs. The egg man lifts his cap politely in greeting. Live catfish swim in a bucket of green water clutched between his knees.

In the village someone is celebrating, and the music clangs through the sultry late-afternoon air. I follow a narrow footpath through the mango grove and far out into the rice fields. Now the rice is green, but soon it will ripen to gold, divided by wind-breaks of green hedges and trees, and the people of the village will harvest it and then dry and winnow it on mats in their door-yards. Finally, in the vast lands surrounding the village, nothing will remain but a brown stubble. Out here, the sounds of human existence, of weddings and funerals, memorials and festivals are distant, blown away by the wind. Now the light is soft and luminous, like a painting by Corot, but soon there will be only silence and dust, and the hungry cows foraging.

9

WALLS

Another evening comes, and Wayne and I have gathered with a small group of children at the crematorium to remember our dead friends and family. On the wall are photographs of some of the three hundred family members who have died, many of whom were cremated at Wat Opot. One photo shows Srey Mum, who died when she was twenty-two days old, a puffy-eyed infant with mittens, propped up on a pillow. Someone has tucked a sprig of yellow flowers behind her picture, where it remains, the leaves dried to a muted olive, the flowers still bravely bright against the gray wall. Another shows both Im Kong, four years old, and his mother, Bun Tevy, who was thirty-six. They died within a month of each other. There are many children and many more adults. The portraits hang side by side in regular rows.

When I first saw the wall I thought of Dust Bowl quilts from the 1930s. Wayne has toned the photographs with the same pastel colors a poor woman might have chosen when she shivered in a sod house in Oklahoma or East Texas, stitching butterflies onto a patchwork quilt made of feed bags and praying for an end to the raging wind. In a sense, the same gales howl outside Wat Opot, and its crematorium wall is a patchwork of lives cut off by AIDS.

One simple act doomed each person on that wall. A rural husband or boyfriend, a farmer from the village, went to the city or the karaoke parlor, a little extra money in his pocket, and had sex with a prostitute or lover, male or female. He brought home a disease that killed him, doomed his wife and infected his unborn child. More than a few young men told Wayne that they had had sex only once in their lives. They were innocent, fourteen or fifteen years old, and went with their friends to a brothel on a dare. They had never heard of AIDS. Maybe it was their birthday.

Wayne has placed the memorial booklet he designed for his own father's funeral in the lower corner of the glass case that doubles as an altar. His father's photograph looks out at us, every inch the stalwart churchman Wayne has described.

More children arrive and jostle into the tiny chapel, tumbling and laughing. A quick snake escapes out the door and slips through a drain into the bushes, tasting the air.

Wayne lights a fragment of white candle on top of the vitrine that contains the urns with the ashes of the dead. Each vessel is bound with a string that attaches a small faded photo. Wayne lights a bundle of incense from the candle and flicks it up and down to extinguish the flame. He sits in his battered wicker chair, sits heavily tonight because he is tired from working in the sun all day. He has been building an arched stone bridge across the canal where the ducks swim. He stretches his bare swollen feet out in front of him. Mister Kosal and Miss Kiri scramble onto his lap, soon defending their territory against all invaders.

Miss Punlok perches herself on Wayne's outstretched legs so she can see her mother's picture on the wall. Vanny died only a little while ago. She was once a pretty woman. In her photo she wears a flowered dress with a scalloped neckline, and looks worried.

Wayne passes me the lighted incense sticks to give to the children.

Miss Punthea settles herself daintily under the window, accepts the incense and holds it precisely upright between her palms. Mister Vantha lies flat on his tummy on the cool concrete floor. Mister Veha lifts his little sister onto his lap and together they hold a stick of incense. Sampeah tries to set Vantha's hair on fire with the lighted tip of his incense Pesei, seated against the wall, leans forward and brushes the glowing ash from Vantha's hair and glares at Sampeah. Vantha is oblivious. Sampeah giggles. Miss Punthea says, "Shhhhhhh."

Once, when Wayne went to Phnom Penh and I did not have the key to the crematorium, I suggested to the children that we just gather on the tiles outside and have the service there. We could see the photographs through the window. But someone objected that there would be no incense. "It will be okay. We can pray outside," I said. And they answered, "But if we don't burn incense, the dead will not hear us."

So I am surprised when Pesei does not accept his stick of incense. There is a picture of his parents on the wall, standing together on a happy occasion. They were an attractive couple, his mother striking in a red embroidered dress, his father handsome and young in a suit and striped necktie. Pesei does not exactly refuse the incense, but he looks away when I offer it. I say his name softly — "Pesei?" — and offer it again, thinking he did not hear me. But he is clearly troubled, and too polite to argue about something that disturbs him.

We begin the service to remember our loved ones, the one simple daily practice, which is voluntary for the children yet forms the spiritual core of our days.

"*Namo Tassa . . . ,*" "Hail the Fortunate One," we intone in Pali, invoking the Buddha, "*sama sam poot . . . ,*" "freed from suffering, fully enlightened through his own diligent efforts." In Cambodia this invocation begins all rituals. "Now," Wayne says in English, "in loving thanks for the lives of our family and friends, we sing . . ." and the children sing enthusiastically, "Thank you, thank you, Jesus in my heart." They punch each syllable equally, opening and closing their mouths like hand puppets, so it comes out, "Tank yooo tank yooo Jeeesaa een my haaaaaat!" There follows a moment of passably silent prayer, and the offering of incense. "Ahhh-men!" they finish, bobbing the incense up and down three times —

111

"Satout, satout, saaa-tout!" — before they escape and begin turning somersaults in the warm evening air.

I notice that Pesei does not chant the Buddhist invocation.

Later, Wayne tells me that one of the local Christian ministers has warned the children that burning incense is a heathen Buddhist practice; anyone who offers their deceased parents the blessings of the fragrant, sacred smoke will be sent to Hell.

10
PESEI

Before I went to Cambodia I enrolled for a month in an English teaching course at a nearby college in Maine. As things turned out I never taught English formally at Wat Opot, but one of the delights of that month was living in a dormitory with foreign students one-third my age who had come to study English. They were from Japan, Korea, Taiwan, Russia, Mexico and Mali. I soon lost interest in the textbook and concentrated on being a conversation partner for any of the students who wanted to practice English. I looked for real-life situations where they could use their new skills. None of the students had a car, so I organized outings to the local supermarket. This was also a dorm-life survival strategy, as summer meals at the university, which were catered by fast-food franchises, could not support sentient life-forms. The foreign students were dismayed and politely scandalized by the burgers and pizza and fried messes passed off as nourishment by an American institution of higher learning.

We decided to avoid the dining room and fend for ourselves. Down in the basement was a kitchen, and there we gathered every evening to cook a banquet of dishes from our native countries. As we ate together we talked and laughed into the night. I felt like den mother to the Peaceable Kingdom, envoy to the United Nations on a good day. This was one of the happiest months of my life.

The foreign students were hardworking and earnest, and they were the guinea pigs for our teaching. One day our professor wrote the words from Norah Jones's song "Come Away with Me" on the board, and spent an hour parsing the meaning and developing a vocabulary list from the lyrics. Then he asked the teaching students to build another lesson on his.

The song is about two young people who run away together in the night, away from the world's hypocrisy, to a mountaintop where love never ends. As an exercise, we asked our students to picture themselves as one of the lovers, to think ahead one year, to imagine what might have happened in the meantime and to write the first letter home to their parents. It seemed like a simple task of imagination, but I was surprised to find that for many of my students, what we were asking was impossible.

"Oh no, I could never wait a year, I would have to leave a note when I left, asking them to forgive me. And I would call them the next day so they would not worry."

"My parents have worked so hard for me, I could not do that, even if I were in love."

"I could not run away with someone my parents did not approve of. They know what is best for me."

One young Korean girl summed it up when she burst into tears and said, "I could never do that. I cannot even pretend. It would hurt my parents too much."

Americans come from a culture of leaving. How else could we have come up with this idea and considered it nothing more than an innocuous exercise? This was my introduction to Asian family values.

Time and again in Cambodia I saw or read about people putting their duty toward family before their self-interest. Were family and self, I wondered, inseparable? Older siblings at Wat Opot accept without question that they will take care of their younger brothers and sisters. I observed no sense of struggle against this, only a question of how best to accomplish what is needed. So when Pesei — who did not, after all, burn incense for his parents that night — began preparing to take on responsibility for his sister, it seemed to him natural, his duty. He would find a way to do it.

The day Pesei turned sixteen he began seriously questioning how he would take care of his younger sister, Miss Jorani, when they leave Wat Opot. Both are HIV negative, come from a middle-class family and have lost both their parents to AIDS.

After their mother's funeral, their grandmother wanted them to return and live with her in the village, but these two bright youngsters insisted on staying at Wat Opot, where they could obtain an education rather then face a lifetime of labor in the rice fields. Each wanted to reclaim a life lost when their parents died.

There was also a danger that if they returned to the village Miss Jorani might be sold. As a lovely young girl without parents, Jorani is vulnerable. I don't know whether the children thought about this, nor whether this particular grandmother would have done such a thing — people do all sorts of things when they are desperate — but Jorani would fetch a good price from an Asian businessman or a sex tourist or, more terrifying, from someone with AIDS who believed he could be cured by having sex with a virgin. Despite laws against it, and a highly visible campaign to warn pedophiles that they will be prosecuted, child prostitution thrives in Cambodia as in other poor countries.

Sometimes it is the sense of family obligation that drives young women into the sex trade. I heard one story about a young girl whose family had run up seemingly insurmountable debt. She was the oldest child, and to her fell the duty of helping her parents. Her parents took her to Phnom Penh to earn money as a prostitute. After some time she scraped together the cash needed and called for her parents to take her back to the village. They came to Phnom Penh and collected the money, but they would not take back a daughter who, they said, had "ruined herself."

Many rural Cambodians do not know their actual birthdays, so everyone gets to be a year older on Khmer New Year. This leads to some anomalies, as a child born the month before the New Year will be officially a year old after one month. In our local school, children are not admitted until they reach a certain minimum height. It gets confusing. So when Pesei turned sixteen, there was no way of knowing how old he was chronologically. Maybe he was only fifteen and a little bit. But just after his sixteenth birthday he began pondering what his life might be after he leaves Wat Opot.

It's a hot afternoon in April, right after Khmer New Year, and I'm walking across the Wat Opot compound. There's been no rain since January — not a drop — and it is well over a hundred degrees every after-noon. I am sneaking away to the cremato-rium for a nap, the only place I know with a midday breeze. I like to rest in the shadows there, on the cool tiles. I figure I will have five minutes of solitude before the kids find me, maybe ten if they don't notice my sandals out on the front steps.

Before I know it, Pesei falls into step with

me, looking serious.

When I first met him, Pesei told me he wanted to go to medical school so he could help his people. Now he says, "I don't really want to be a doctor."

"Is that true?" I ask, disappointed. Many of the kids have no realistic plan for their lives, or they continually fantasize about being film stars or karaoke singers. I had been impressed by this thoughtful boy as I watched him one day, sitting cross-legged in front of another boy who had hurt his neck, gently putting his friend's head through range-of-motion exercises. I could already picture the stethoscope dangling from Pesei's back pocket as he sat there, holding the boy's face between his hands, skillfully guiding his head from side to side. He had a healer's way about him.

"Yes, it's true," he said. "You tell foreigners you want to be a doctor and help your people so maybe they will help you go to school."

Slowing the pace of our walk, I laugh and throw my arm around Pesei's shoulder, enjoying his candor.

"So tell me, what *would* you like to do?"

"I want to make movies. But I have to take care of Jorani. She has to go to school. *She* wants to be a doctor. I want to leave here when I am eighteen and go to Phnom Penh. Where will I get money? Who will help me?"

His questions tumble out. He has obviously been worrying, and I wonder how, starting from this dirt road in Cambodia, surrounded by rice fields, this boy will find a way to make all this happen.

"Have you talked with Mr. Wayne about this?"

He shakes his head, looking intimidated. "Maybe you talk to him for me?"

"How about I set up a time with him when you won't be interrupted by the other children?"

He looks at his foot, moving the sand around in patterns. I realize how alone he feels, how much he needs a parent.

"If you want, I can come with you and help you tell Wayne what you have told me."

A pretty day. We find Wayne sitting in the gazebo, watching the children as they play under trees heavy with green mangoes. Some of the little kids are giving each other rides in a wheelbarrow. Older boys are collecting trash. Others are playing tag.

The ice-cream vendor from the village arrives on cue, ringing his bell. Wayne has just given the children their snack money, and the vendors know it. With infallible instinct they race their wagons and pushcarts to be first through the gate to relieve the children of their allowances.

"They must have spies," Wayne complains. But he looks content and relaxed. Wayne loves to sit back and survey the scene and watch what everyone is doing, like a happy god enjoying his still-unsullied Eden, or an inventor who has crafted an impossibly complex Rube Goldberg apparatus that for a few minutes operates smoothly, miraculously, on its own.

He turns to Pesei.

"First of all, Pesei, you need to believe that the universe wants you to have a good life. So don't worry about money."

Pesei looks dubious.

"When I opened Wat Opot I had exactly fifty dollars in my pocket, and there was nothing here. Nothing. No buildings, no clinic, no fishponds. Just some rice fields that everybody thought were haunted. Now, seven years later, look around you. All these children, the hospice, the dormitories, the school and all the programs we've had, and the food we've eaten for seven years, and these mango trees. And you know what? I still only have fifty dollars in my pocket. You already speak English better than many of the people working for NGOs in Phnom

Penh. You are smart and good-looking. You will have no problem finding work. You could walk in and get a job right now, and with a few years more English you'll be even better. You have the tools to do this now. You don't have to worry about who will help you. Just study hard, and trust, and don't worry about the money. It's not about money, I promise you. Work hard, and you will be given what you need."

In less than a week, events are to prove Wayne right.

The story begins with the arrival of a delightful German artist named Alfred Banze. Alfred has been touring the world with a multimedia art program called the Banyan Project, demonstrating the sacred interconnectedness of people, community and nature in lands where banyan trees grow. He spends a few days with children in each country in a free-form mix of creative activities, leading them in painting, drawing, dance and performance. The children's paintings are cut into abstract shapes and spliced into strings of paintings by children in other countries, mimicking the aerial roots of the banyan tree. Alfred carries these strings, some of them twenty or thirty feet long, wadded into a little backpack, and he extracts them with a flourish, as in some wonderful magic trick performed with vivid scarves floating in air. We watch, mesmerized.

Traveling with Alfred is a young Norwegian filmmaker. He has come along to document Alfred's playful explorations with the children. I tell him about Pesei, and ask whether he could use an assistant, someone to help carry his gear in exchange for a few tips on filmmaking. He can do better than that, he tells me. He has an extra video camera, and he will gladly teach Pesei to use it. They will film the workshop together.

I corral Pesei and tell him about the plan. He is excited but scared. He has been playing tag with the little kids and is covered with dust. I suggest he wash his face and put on a clean shirt.

"You are going to your first job," I tell him.

That afternoon the children gather with Alfred in the dining room for the first day's workshop. The filmmaker is getting his gear together, but Pesei is playing with the little kids again.

I fetch him aside and tell him, "This is not a time for play. This is the time to learn." He looks at his feet.

"I don't know what to do," he says. I realize how intimidated even the most confident of our children become when faced with strangers from the world outside Wat Opot.

"Come on," I say. "I'll introduce you."

By afternoon, Pesei is operating the camera without supervision. And by the end of the third day he has directed and shot his first film, a story about a boy growing up in a village in Cambodia whose parents are dying of AIDS. Children in the village tease this boy; he is very lonely. The children of Wat Opot are the actors. For many of them it is their story, too.

As the workshop ends and the visitors are packing their car to leave, Pesei hangs back.

"Maybe you should thank your teacher before he goes," I suggest.

He looks confused. I explain to him that when someone does something special for you, it makes them feel good if you thank them. It's a gift you can give them. And perhaps they will remember you in a nice way.

"I don't know what to say."

I suggest some phrases, and he asks me to write them down so he can practice them. We role-play for a few minutes, and then he walks to the car to say goodbye. I watch him chatting comfortably with the young film-maker.

All at once I notice I am smiling. I feel very much like a parent.

We who grow up with attentive and sensible parents take the most basic skills of living for granted. If you walk down the road in any village in Cambodia, a mother carrying her infant will place the baby's palms together to greet you properly as you pass. When Miss Punlok's mother, Vanny, finally died in the hospice, Thida, one of our mothers at Wat Opot, looked after Punlok at the cremation. I watched as she held the little girl on her lap and, reaching around her from behind, gently held Punlok's palms together and showed her how to offer incense to honor her mother. Thida's eyes were soft and sad. She has four children. Perhaps she was wondering who will show her youngest son what to do at her own funeral.

11
Chaos Theory Dominoes

We are all on the porch outside the office. I have brought several large sets of dominoes from the United States, and this afternoon I've shown the kids a simple version of the game. They play with panache, snapping the tiles down on the tin tabletop. *Pop! Pop! Pop!*

Dominoes turns out to be the great equalizer. Girls compete with boys and little ones trounce their elders. After a few games, a couple of the older boys get tired of Miss Srey Aun beating them. She is perched on a stool, surveying her prey, undulating like a cobra.

Wayne's secretary has gone to lunch and the coast is clear. Mister Ouen and Mister Vuth slip inside the office to explore and, moments later, emerge with their prize — two large yellow plastic bananas. For reasons I have not yet understood, the children find these plastic fruits hysterically funny. With a flourish, Ouen and Vuth whip off the banana scabbards revealing two robust pink plastic penises used for condom demonstrations, and begin a swashbuckling fencing match.

The boys quickly tire of that game, and there is a scrimmage of kids trying to gain possession. Miss Jorani, who at thirteen is usually reserved and modest, makes a dive, manages to beat out the little kids, grabs both penises, holds them up to her head like horns and starts running around the yard bellowing like a bull. Then it is a free-for-all, kids running after her, dominoes flying everywhere, until we all collapse in laughter.

Later that afternoon, Miss Jorani informs me that she will never marry a Khmer man. After all, it was her father who had affairs and brought home the virus that killed both him and her mother.

12
MISTER OUEN

Chewing. Loud and persistent and closer to my head than one might wish such a sound to be. I turn toward the source and open my eyes. A white cow, all hunger and bones, is stripping philodendron leaves from the grille that runs around the porch. Every day Serain threads the vines back and forth and through the bars to weave a translucent green arbor to shade the bamboo couch where I come to nap, or try to nap, on hot afternoons.

One placid brown eye stares back at me. I close my eyes again. "Wayne will have a cow," I think foolishly, still dull with sleep and heat.

Someone has left the front gate open again, and the neighborhood cows wander in and out, scavenging anything green. It is the dry season, late April, and there has been no rain since New Year's Eve. No, there was one day when a few drops fell. The sky darkened and a wind came up; I ran outside and stood with my face to the sky, but it was over in a minute, leaving only a few pockmarks in the earth here and there to release the faint, yearning scent of damp clay. And then it passed. Most days it is like a photograph from the 1930s, and Wayne and I are tenant farmers, shading our eyes with our hands and peering into the sky, discussing that one tiny cloud near the mountain, way over there, willing it to come our way and bring rain or a patch of shade or a little variety to the endless blue sky. But it never does.

Local custom and simple kindness dictate that at times like this your neighbor's cattle may forage freely. But already they have topped all the young mango trees and decimated the squash, and now this one is eating my shade.

Ouen is walking by. "Mister Ouen!" I call. *"Goa!"* Cow! Ouen grabs a switch and gives the cow a whack across her skinny flank. She is blasé, goes right on chomping, and Ouen flails at her until finally she turns to face him. Ouen puts his face right up to the cow's face, his one weak, nearsighted eye close to her brown eye. He curls his lip and mutters something in Khmer, and then whacks her smartly across the shoulder. I fear for a moment that she is going to charge him — she is strong and she has large horns. He hits her again, and then he keeps hitting her. But the white cow is inured to such treatment at the hands of rice farmers and small boys. Finally she trots off toward the gate, disdainful of Ouen's shouts of *"Hoi!"* Once outside, she will jog around the perimeter until she finds another vulnerable spot, or she will simply leap the fence and make a meal of the bougainvillea. Wat Opot is a merry-go-round, encircled by cows, jumping up and down and over the fence and back again. And I'm still half dreaming.

Wayne never met Ouen's father, who infected Ouen's mother with HIV and then grew sick himself. After he died, Ouen's mother turned to prostitution to feed her child. Ouen is HIV negative, but he has a congenital deformity. The external tissues of his right eye are slightly misshapen, and the eyeball itself is pure white with neither iris nor pupil. His left eye, though normal to look at, is exceedingly weak. Deformities of this sort are common in Cambodia and Vietnam; it is possible that Ouen's mother, who was Vietnamese, was exposed to Agent

Orange during the war. If so, Ouen's deformity is relatively minor compared with the many horrendous images I have seen: children born without eye openings or features, their faces as flat and unmarked as tortillas.

Ouen and his mother lived in a small house in Takeo, the provincial capital, about an hour away from Wat Opot. Ouen did not go to school. When his mother was first sick a man in town took them in, but when she became too ill for Ouen to take care of her they were brought to the hospice at Wat Opot.

Late one night, sitting in the office, Wayne told me the story of Ouen's first year at Wat Opot.

"Ouen was only nine or ten at the time, and he did a good job of caring for his mother. But he did not get along well with the other children because they often teased him about his eye. His mother improved after coming here, but in time she began slipping again and her joints became very painful. She wouldn't let anyone massage her except Ouen, but she would often scream out in pain when he did. One night the children came running to get me because Ouen, helpless, frustrated and in tears, was hitting his mother with a stick. I

131

took it away from him and he went running out of the room and started pounding the wall with his fist. He refused to go back into the room and sleep with her like he usually did. I checked on her in the morning. I could see that she was failing fast. I told Ouen to go in to see her, but he refused. I then said, 'Ouen, your mother is dying.'

"Ouen stared at me to see if I was telling the truth and then walked in to where his mother was lying. Because he does not see well he got close to her face and looked his mother straight in the eye and with tears flowing he kissed her on the forehead as she took her final breath."

That was in 2003, before I came to Wat Opot. After his mother died, Ouen began to go to school, but the children still teased him and called him One Eye. When I first came to Wat Opot two years later I noticed that whenever there was a fracas it seemed like Ouen was right there in the middle of it. He had a bad temper and was always getting into trouble, and I admit I found his demeanor menacing. But mostly he ignored me, and I avoided him. One night, as I watched him walk across the compound with his usual scowl, carrying a large butcher's cleaver, I had the fleeting thought that this was a kid I would not want to meet in a dark alley. The words "apprentice ax murderer" came to mind. But I also realized that my anxiety was in part simply a reaction to his appearance, that it came from a down-deep fear, a primal instinct to cull the herd of the weak or deformed. It was the sort of aversion that forms reflexively before you even think about it and then has to be noticed, defined and consciously unraveled. "He's just a little boy," I told myself, and I became determined to change how I responded to Ouen.

I began talking with him whenever we met, asking about his day, smiling, making him feel welcome rather than steeling myself against whatever mischief he might get into. The change in his behavior was immediate. Within days he was smiling back at me, and once, when I greeted him by taking his face in my hands and saying, "And how is my beautiful Ouen?" I saw for the first time his sweet, vulnerable smile.

Wayne's own eye trouble began when he was a medic in Vietnam. One day, on a battlefield near Da Nang, he was helping a wounded soldier when an explosion sent shrapnel into his eye. He was airlifted in a helicopter that then crashed en route, and the next thing he knew he was in a hospital. A cornea transplant failed, and when a doctor explained that they had run out of options, Wayne settled into life with one eye. But over the years a cataract had formed in his one good eye, and when I met him he had been almost blind for a long time. He had tried to arrange for cataract surgery through the Veterans Administration, but he was never in the States long enough to get through all the appointments and paperwork and bureaucracy. And he never had enough money to get it done privately.

It was a problem that needed handling, but Wayne thinks about everyone but himself. After all, this is a man who once told me that if he accidentally became infected with HIV he might decide not to take antiretroviral medicines because they are not available to many other people who are poor and ill.

As his eyesight dimmed, Wayne turned inward; depressed and remote, he seemed resigned to blindness.

One afternoon, as I watched Wayne once again struggling to find a tiny vein to insert an IV in a sick baby's arm, I saw that something needed to be done soon, not only for Wayne's sake but for the well-being of the children. I spoke with him about it and encouraged him to investigate local options, but I could feel him resisting. Finally, Wayne admitted he was afraid that yet another doctor would tell him there was nothing to be done, that it would just continue to get worse and that he would soon be totally blind.

As Ouen approached adolescence and the children continued to tease him, he grew angrier and ever more alienated. One day Wayne decided to take Ouen to the eye hospital in Takeo to see whether anything could be done. The clinic is run by the Catholic organization Caritas, and makes eye care available at little or no cost to all who need it.

The doctors told Wayne that with a little cosmetic surgery Ouen's eyelid could be corrected, and they could fit him with a prosthesis that would give him the appearance of a normal eye. It was all very simple. Almost as an afterthought, Wayne asked the doctor whether they ever performed cataract surgery, and the doctor answered, "What are you doing this afternoon?"

Two days later Wayne and Ouen returned from Takeo. The children swarmed about and welcomed them home like heroes.

Wayne was wearing his black cowboy hat, and they both had snazzy black sunglasses. They lazed under a welcoming tamarind tree in the center of the compound, telling tales of their adventure and copping an attitude of bluesy cool. They were happy and amazed. After a few days Wayne began to see better and, with a few ups and downs and adjustments over the next year, his vision in one eye is approaching 20/20. He marvels at leaves on trees, chain-link fences, the colors of flowers, the faces of children.

Even though Ouen's vision could not be helped, his sightless eye now appeared normal. He was thirteen years old and quite handsome, and the other children, excited by his transformation, no longer teased him.

About a month after his surgery, Ouen was due back at the eye hospital for his follow-up appointment. Wayne was in Phnom Penh for a few days and Ouen asked me to go down to Takeo with him. Ouen could have managed on his own; he had already traveled alone on the bus when he visited relatives in the provinces on Khmer New Year. But I could see he wanted company and moral support, and he seemed relieved when I offered to go with him. So the next morning we walked to the main road and flagged down a bus.

We reached the hospital at about 8:30 a.m. Under a thatched canopy a crowd of patients sat close together on wooden benches, avoiding the glaring sun. They were a mixture of old and young, sightless and seeing, some with obvious injuries or cataracts, others with deformities that in the West might have been corrected when they were children. I was the only Westerner, and everyone looked up curiously when we entered. They had been waiting for hours with nothing to do, and here we were — the floor show.

Ouen needed to stand in a long line with his identity card to retrieve his medical records, but when I tried to join him he put his arm around me and led me back to the bench. Although it was early, the day was already hot. He searched out a place for me to sit, negotiated with the neighbors to slide over and make a space, made a great show of dusting it off first and then, holding me by my upper arms, backed me up to the bench and gently settled me into my seat.

The people watched us, clearly amused, and pleased to see him treating me with the respect due to a *yei* of my advanced age and graying hair. It was the proper Khmer thing to do, but so different from his casual behavior at Wat Opot that I had to struggle to keep a straight face and mop my neck with my *kramah* — the traditional Cambodian checkered scarf — and act appropriately decrepit. Knowing himself to be the center of attention, Ouen played his role to the hilt, and in that moment I loved him as I have rarely loved anyone in this world.

At about this time I became friends with Rinin, a young girl who lives with her mother in a tailor's shop in the public market a few kilometers down the road from Wat Opot. By day, Rinin's family living space is open to the busy fish and vegetable market outside their door. Her mother's sewing machine sits at the threshold to advertise her trade. There is a clouded glass case with buttons and lace trim, fancy bras and spools of thread, and inside the room in a larger showcase hang the dresses that Mama sews for her customers, shimmering confections of Khmer silk that turn even the humblest rice farmer into a stunning lady of fashion. The family's belongings sit on high shelves, carefully wrapped in plastic to protect them from the grit of the marketplace.

Rinin is bright and motivated and her mother pays for her to study with an English tutor every day after school. The first time I met Rinin she parroted a list of questions from an antiquated English primer.

"How many chambermaids do you have?" she asked, proudly enunciating each word. I was from *Amérique,* so I must be rich and have many chambers in my home, and certainly a maid to tidy each one.

"I have no chambermaids," I said. "Not even one. How many chambermaids do *you* have?"

"Oh, I do not have any chambermaids," she replied, glancing at their all-in-one-room home. "I am very poor. And very small," she added emphatically. She was in fact quite tiny, but with prominent ears that bore tiny gold earrings.

"No," I said. "You are rich and *very* fat."

"And you are very thin and very *young,*" she answered, catching on to the game right away.

This became our usual greeting, whenever I would visit her family. "And how are all your chambermaids?" I would ask. And if I brought along a guest to meet her I always told Rinin that they were fabulously wealthy and had dozens of chambermaids.

Each time I came, Rinin and I would sit for an hour with her schoolbooks. I brought her some storybooks in English and she made a habit of underlining any word she didn't know. Then she would look it up and write the definition in the margin in her minuscule, precise hand. She was hungry to learn. Her mother worked hard to pay for her tutoring, and she hoped to send Rinin to college.

I usually visited Rinin and Mama on Sunday mornings. Once, I took some of the kids with me, thinking they might like to meet my new friends, but they were silent and sullen, resentful that I had a connection outside with another child, someone who had a mother and spoke English better than they did. After that I tried to keep my two worlds separate. I felt bad about not inviting Rinin and Mama to Wat Opot, and it would have been hard to explain to them why. They were very kind, and whenever I went to the market Mama would send me home with bags full of fruit for the children.

One afternoon I woke from my nap to find Rinin at my door. She had come by moto to say hello, carrying several large pineapples and a bag of papayas from Mama. Rinin prattled on in her best English, unaware of the effect her visit was having on the children, who watched us with jealous curiosity. I introduced her to some of the kids and was aware that a few of the older boys were eyeing her with some interest.

Before she left, Rinin pulled me aside. She looked quite concerned, and announced in a voice easily audible to anyone nearby, "Mommy Gail, I think the children here are not respectful to you in Khmer."

I cringed. "What do you mean?" I imagined untranslatable epithets uttered behind all those friendly smiles.

"When they speak to you they do not call you Madame Gail. Only Gail. That is not polite."

Knowing that the children overheard every word, I wanted to spare them any embarrassment. "Well, Rinin," I began, "thank you, but these children do not have a nice mama like you do to teach them. Anyway, here at Wat Opot we are less formal. We are friends, and we all love each other very much."

After Rinin left, Ouen came and shyly put his arms around my waist. He peered up into my eyes and, looking quite grave, asked, "Maybe we should call you Madame Gail?"

"No, I would rather you just call me Gail," I said. "And I will call you *Mister* Ouen."

13
YEI

The moto is a primary means of transport in Cambodia. This small motorbike is the people's taxi in the city or countryside. All manner of baggage is carried: twenty brace of live chickens tied by their feet, straining sacks of rice, buckets of water with fish swimming in them and great placid hogs, their enormity crammed into openwork lattice baskets. Small plastic bags — red, green, pink and black — carry palm sugar paste, cooking oil, fish sauce and pulses. The bags dangle from the handlebars like translucent Christmas ornaments.

But this is child's play. Your clever driver introduces cantilevering: a board engineered across the back of the bike can support a double-wide construction of several dozen Styrofoam coolers, a carved wooden wardrobe with mirrored doors, a maze of rattan chairs, a squawking, teetering poultry market in cages lashed ten feet high. Thus the moto becomes the poor man's moving van. It is also his ambulance, and I have seen patients bouncing along on stretchers attached crosswise to the back of a moto, complete with an IV drip.

And whole families. Three or four slender Cambodians plus children of assorted sizes often ride on one bike. The father drives, and a child or two are sandwiched between him and his wife, who rides sidesaddle. Finally there is Grandmother, her grandchild in her arms, riding backward, appended to her seat by Grace itself. Between the father's legs rides the youngest son, holding the handlebars, proudly pretending to steer. And when there is an accident — and there are many such misfortunes — it is the little one in front who often suffers the worst.

This morning I glance out my front door as such a family arrives on foot at Wat Opot. The stunned father clutches his child's body; the mother is limping behind. They have all been injured, but Wayne is concerned for the boy, who flew over the handlebars, slid along the ground and struck his head on a rock. One side of his face is brilliant red where the skin has been scoured away by gravel, and the bruise on his forehead is dark and swelling fast. Wayne hands the boy a hundred-riel note — enough for an ice cream — to distract him, and sets about debriding and disinfecting the wound. The boy squirms, frightened, and tries to burrow into his father's arms. His father holds him on his lap and comforts him, his face soft and burdened. He moves his hands here and there over his son's body, stroking and patting him, perhaps to reassure himself that the boy has no hidden injuries. The boy grimaces and recoils again from the sting of the antiseptic. His mother stares straight ahead, stunned, never once looking at her husband or son.

Wayne speaks in a low voice; his movements are deft and precise — a relaxed economy of motion he learned caring for the wounded on the battlefield in Vietnam, and in years of emergencies here and earlier in Honduras. He works without gloves, holding the gauze pad by one end and cleansing the wound with the other, never allowing blood to touch his fingers. Wayne once told me he has had three needlesticks with HIV-contaminated needles — all while working with gloves. He prefers to know exactly where his fingers are.

The Wat Opot children sit on the window ledges, watching. Even the youngest children understand that *chee-um,* blood, is serious business.

Wayne examines the father, but his injuries are slight, and turns to the mother, who has been sitting a little apart. She has hurt her knee, but again, it is nothing much. He gives them some pills for pain, and they rise to leave. They do not offer payment, and he asks for none.

Soon an old *yei* arrives asking for medicine for her broken wrist. Occasionally people from the village come by for first aid. It has taken some time for them to understand that they are welcome here, and it has taken years for many of them to overcome their fear of catching AIDS if they step through the gates of Wat Opot. Sometimes when we are at breakfast they come to the office, shyly waiting, as peasants do, fearful of being seen as a bother. Yet in their poverty and their history and their patient humanity reside the enormous weight of their entitlement.

The old woman's face is wrinkled but, since Cambodians smile a lot, her wrinkles go in nice places. Her hair is the merest stubble of white. She walks with a staff, but she is upright and strong and her eyes are clear. She is wearing a neat sarong and a long-sleeved jacket over a white blouse. The fabrics are thin and faded, but they are carefully mended. Her *kramah* is folded precisely over her shoulder like a tartan. Perhaps she has been at the temple, or maybe she has dressed for this occasion. She has been back several times with the same complaint; her wrist mends too slowly, and it pains her. It is her left hand; she can still wield a small scythe to harvest rice with her right hand, but then her left hand cannot grasp the walking stick to steady herself as she stoops in the slippery rice paddies. She is perhaps eighty years old.

Because she sees me as an elder, or maybe because I am a woman, she approaches me first. I find the camaraderie with the old women here in Southeast Asia delightful. In Vietnam I was invited in for tea by two

sisters on a dirt path behind the main streets of Hoi An. They had high cheekbones and pearl necklaces and the supple elegance of retired courtesans.

Now the *yei* greets me formally, palms pressed together, and then we hug. She gives me a Khmer-style kiss — a nuzzling with the nose, a little snuffling-sniffling sound, and then we just hang out, holding hands and smiling. Some of the kids gather around her. They sit at her feet in a sort of dreamy calm, totally at ease, while she lays her hand on each one in blessing. I give her some watermelon and Mister Ouen asks her a question that triggers a burst of laughter. Someone translates for me. He has asked her, "*Yei*, how can you eat watermelon when you have no teeth?" The ancient woman joins the laughter and her whole face crinkles up. Ouen's face is shining.

How deeply relaxed the children have become with her, affectionate and light in a way I have never seen before. The change is palpable. It is the presence of something you did not realize was missing until you saw it, the sense of relief you feel when, after a long and terrible journey, you are home. And I think, what must it be like to be raised by well-meaning strangers who may love you but who do not speak your language, or know who you are, or have anything but an outsider's intellectualized and generalized understanding of your culture and people, and of your life for that matter. And then to have someone deeply rooted in being Khmer, as this old woman is, appear in your life and remind you of who you are.

I massage some moisturizer into her wrist. I want her for *my yei*.

I suggest to Wayne that we should hire this venerable lady to visit once a week for a few hours and sit with the children. She is old and her wrist will be a handicap in her work and home life, and a little money would help her. She would be good for the kids; they could experience that gentle, grounded part of themselves. Everyone else in their lives is either preoccupied with their own illness or working with foreigners. But she is their history, and the earth they walk on. She has survived it all: Pol Pot, the war, the American bombings. But more important, she remembers the way it was before, remembers all that has been lost from these children's lives. She could tell them the stories they otherwise would never hear. We won't know what she says, but it's none of our business. It's Khmer stuff, and that's what they need.

Wayne likes the idea, but days pass and it never happens. I feel sad. It was a good idea.

14
"She Died Like This . . ."

Wayne tells the story of a village family with four daughters. The eldest, twelve years old, was caring for her mother, who had AIDS. After the mother died, the father could not take care of so many children. So he kept one middle daughter at home to cook and keep house for him and brought the other three to Wat Opot. He wanted the twelve-year-old and the seven-year-old to go to school. The youngest, a baby of nine months who had been born HIV positive, arrived with her sisters. She was receiving antiretroviral drugs, but Wayne saw that she was very ill and probably would not survive.

The three daughters slept in the same bed every night. As the youngest grew weaker Wayne moved them all into the clinic. The baby would cry if her sisters were not with her, so Wayne let them all sleep together to comfort her, even on the night he thought she might die.

Wayne slept right outside the room so he could monitor her labored breathing, and around 5 a.m., when he heard the rattle in her throat fall silent, he knew the baby had died, lying between her two sisters.

Death is not pretty, and Wayne does not like to make the family see the worst of it, so he washed the baby's body and laid her out prettily with her hands across her chest, in a new dress, along with a few flowers. Wayne sent word to the father, and when he arrived Wayne told him that his baby daughter had died peacefully during the night.

At which point the younger sister, the seven-year-old, piped up. "No, she did not! She died like this . . . ," and she twisted her face into the awful grimace of death.

But it was the twelve-year-old sister whose grief was most complex. She had been caretaker of both her mother and her baby sister and both had died. Bitterly, she blamed herself.

15
UP THE MOUNTAIN

Many mornings I wake up early, my sleep succumbing to the blare of chanting from the wat, or I may be drawn to move about and get what exercise I can, because by breakfast we are already sweating and for the rest of the day, until early evening, movements must be slow and measured, interspersed with naps taken alone or in the company of assorted children.

But now, before dawn, an immaculate stillness. With the moon as my flashlight I find my way out through the eastern gate and onto the dirt road through the village. Sometimes I set out alone but always, if we have overnight guests, I offer to guide them on a walk through the sleeping village and up the mountain to the ancient temple.

Phnom Chisor is one of two small mountains that rise from the fertile belly of the rice fields surrounding Wat Opot. So flat is this area that one is able, with a little searching, to pinpoint the region of Wat Opot on a Google map by scanning due south from Phnom Penh, pausing halfway to the town of Takeo, tipping the map toward the horizontal plane and watching two small green mountains rise from the otherwise unrelieved monotony of the topography. It is easy to recognize Phnom Chisor. The semicircular bite of a granite quarry is visible on the southwest flank of the mountain, where workers mine veins of stone the color of rain clouds. For some, this enterprise is a badly needed source of income. For others, it is a desecration of the sacred; this mountain is twice holy, having, in addition to the ruins of the Hindu temple, a living Buddhist wat.

Today I set out at about 4:30 a.m., hoping to watch the sunrise from the mountain and to walk there and back in the coolness of early morning. I suppose I could use a flashlight, but the beam destroys my night vision and lessens the delicious mystery of walking in the dark. I prefer to Braille the ruts and puddles with my toes and proceed slowly, relishing the scents and sounds of the somnolent landscape.

Now and then a ghostly bicyclist weaves along through the mist, rusted chain rasping his progress through the stubborn darkness. A few people have emerged from their homes, crouching around tiny fires in their front yards, burning trash, warming themselves, too sleepy to say hello.

I reach Phnom Chisor and begin climbing the hundreds of steps to the mountain temple. A festival day is coming, and there are prayer flags everywhere. Thousands of triangular pennants flutter from lines stretched diagonally across the courtyard. The flags are made of unlikely fabrics: polka dots, tartan plaids, purple zebra stripes. These are the leavings, the tiniest snippets, gleaned from garment factories in Phnom Penh, from the unrelenting labor of the sweatshops, salvaged and sublimated into prayers in the morning breeze.

I cross the courtyard of the contemporary Buddhist pagoda that shares the mountaintop, rousing the sleepy white temple dog, who feigns aggression and then retreats into indifference. At the edge of the mountain I stand for a few giddy moments catching my breath, gazing out to the east, down the steep ceremonial staircase to the rice plains below. The rainy season is just ending and the fields are still bright green. In a few months, after the rains stop and the rice is harvested, all will be dun-colored stubble, with a few exhausted trees defining the edges of the rice paddies. Winds will raise the dust into a cloud of grit that will obscure the horizon. Then the puddles will dry, the ruts will bake white in the sun and the hard-pounded clay will crack open like the skin on an old woman's heel.

The temple itself is about a thousand years old, a little older than Angkor Wat. To my untrained eye it is clearly of the same general style as some of the earlier temples in the Angkor complex. It lacks the giant faces of Bayon Temple with their famously serene smiles, and the exultant jungle vines and fig trees that strangle the ruins of Ta Prom and make it the darling of photographers, but I've met few tourists here, and none at all at dawn. Only the monks from the living temple whose chants welcome the day. In the golden daybreak their orange robes glow against the rusty red bricks of the temple. Atop this mountain I find something closer to my dream of Angkor Wat than the actual experience of visiting that vast temple complex allows. There are simply too many tourists in Angkor now, too many five-star hotels. Here is the chance to be alone with the ancient stones, to arrive, breathless from climbing all those steps, and to feel the universe burst open into vistas of clouds and rice and lakes and the chanting monks and the quirky little flags offering their patterned prayers to the rising sun.

In a rough stone corridor, its roof long gone, stands a large yoni, a concave hewn form embodying the divine feminine. The Shiva linga, the stone pestle formerly mounted in the crevice of the yoni and re-ifying the divine masculine, now leans forgotten in a nearby corner. Yet when devotion flowed through this sanctuary, and for centuries infused these two sculptures with spiritual life, they were wedded and worshipped. On the pitted tufa walls of the corridor you can still see the black splash stains of thousand-year-old anointings of curd, ghee, milk and honey. But in this Kali Yuga, said to be the fourth and darkest of the long ages in the Hindu cycle of the spiritual and moral degeneration of creation, here, as elsewhere, they lie apart.

A boy and his younger sister have followed me up the mountain. Wordlessly, the girl poses here and there along the way, inviting me with her eyes to photograph her. Barefoot, she climbs on top of the yoni and arranges herself unself-consciously. Three times I press the shutter.

Thinking I won't understand their Khmer words, the boy urges her, in a stage whisper, to press me for money. I catch the word *"loy"* — money — but she shakes her head, clearly enjoying this adventure of posing for a photographer. Her dress, threadbare and patched, echoes somehow the precise tan and gray of the stone, and also the pale celadon green of the lichen that clings to the corridor walls. She is of that place, a daughter of the mountain, of the temple; she is stunningly at home.

A few women who sell snacks struggle to haul their wares up the stairway as the children and I descend. I stop one of these ladies and buy drinks and food for the two children. The little girl happily guzzles her canned juice, but the boy saves his Fanta to resell, already conscious of want and responsibility. At the bottom of the mountain, the people who run the little thatched snack stand are arriving for the day. Fresh-pressed sugarcane juice mixed with lime and ice is the perfect restorative for walking home in the sweltering late-morning sun. I have stopped worrying about germs and have never felt healthier. The young woman who operates the hand-cranked sugarcane press wears a lime-green knitted beret and a rosy-cheeked smile. Her little brother pulls out a chair for me and insists I sit and rest. His *yei* welcomes me and chews her betel nut with her few remaining teeth. We sit side by side, holding hands, a couple of old ladies, teasing the children and happy to be alive. I nibble some *num,* glutinous rice with a sweet coconut center, steamed in banana leaf. I will get home too late for breakfast.

16
An Exclusive Club

This morning, Wayne tested a little girl of seven, Miss Phally, for HIV. I was drawn to Phally the first time I met her because she looks like I did at that age, a round-faced, high-waisted little thing with a Prince Valiant haircut. Her mother, worn out by her own illness and burdened by responsibility for three children, is often cross with the kids, and Phally shoulders her share of the load, carrying her little brothers on her hip, keeping them out of trouble.

Phally had been living with her grandmother while her mother was at Wat Opot with the boys, one of whom is HIV positive. When Phally herself fell ill, her grandmother, fearing the girl was infected and overwhelmed by the thought of raising a sick child, sent her to live with her mother at Wat Opot.

Today, Wayne placed a drop of Phally's blood on the paper test strip and watched with a sinking feeling as the first red line appeared. He prayed that a second line, the one that confirms that the test is not defective, would not appear. But it did, and in that moment a child's reality changed forever.

The morning Miss Phally was diagnosed with HIV I walked over to the big tamarind tree that is the central gathering place of Wat Opot. Phally was there with her brothers and mother and two other women, who looked at me questioningly to see whether I had heard the news. One lady, skeletally thin, has been ill for years. Normally she keeps to herself, sitting under the tamarind with her knees tucked under her chin, her eyes watery and her gaze turned inward. This morning she smiled at me, gestured with her head at Phally and drew with one finger on the taut skin of her palm what I first took to be a cross, and then realized was a plus, for "positive." My mind flashed back to a day I once spent in Cairo, where a Coptic Christian man, believing me to be a fellow believer, discreetly revealed on his inner forearm a tiny tattoo of a Coptic cross. Without her knowing it, without her fully understanding the implications, Phally has been abruptly initiated into a secretive club — but this is a club that no one joins by choice.

17
SINGING KITES

At the end of night, in the sudden equatorial dawn, a thousand pink lotuses yawn and push their toes into the cool mud, raise their stems up through the water and stretch open their petals to the morning sun. Because it rises from decay, the lotus has come to symbolize the transcendence of desire and suffering. Ancient sages speak of a fine, pure filament inside the stem of the lotus, and liken it to the golden thread that channels our spiritual energies from the base chakra at the bottom of our spine to the thousand-petaled crown chakra that opens finally into Oneness.

The lotus pool at Wat Opot Pagoda offers its waters to monks and villagers alike. When the monsoon comes, rain floods the tank and the fields freshen with new rice. In the dry season, when water levels have fallen and creeks have turned to dust, and fish have burrowed deep into the mud to hibernate until the next monsoon, villagers climb down the mossy steps to the pool and plunge old paint buckets through the masses of pink lotus blossoms that cover the water.

From the steps of the temple your eye travels south, past a railing whose balusters are shaped like the eagle deity Garuda, across the pool of lotus blossoms, past the white crematorium and the gilded mausoleum of the Wat Opot Children's Community, and finally to the distant mountain, Phnom Chisor, with its temple to the ancient Hindu gods. It is the dry season, between the Water Festival in November and the harvest, and you may see the children flying kites over Wat Opot, little square kites, like boys anywhere might make from discarded paper and sticks and knotted string. But in Cambodia there is also an ancient tradition of kite flying, and every year some of the boys build singing kites.

Opening my eyes in the middle of the night, the moonlight is so bright on the tin roof across the yard that for a moment I imagine it has snowed and I am back home in Maine. Naked and confused, I reach for a blanket, but then I feel the heat of the Cambodian midnight, smell the faint mildew of the sweat-soaked bed, remember where I am and throw off the light cotton

sarong I use for a sheet. I hear a deep thrumming, and I see from my window the moonlit silhouette of a singing kite, wheeling like Garuda over the rice fields.

It is said that when the eagle god flies, the wind through his wings chants the hymns of the Vedas, the ancient Hindu scriptures. The enormous singing kite, the *khleng ek,* sings prayers to the God of the Wind. The *khleng ek* sings a hymn of gratitude: for the harvest; for the sweet air that brings rain for the crops; for the wind that turns in its season to blow the rains away, allowing the sun to ripen the rice and men and women to bring in the harvest and lay it to dry and winnow the grain in their dooryards.

By tradition, singing kites are only flown after the rainy season. To fly them during the rains might cause the winds to shift disastrously and blow the rain away from the crops at the wrong time.

Kite flying in Cambodia is a grateful act, a miracle of survival. The *khleng ek* sings of freedom, as all kites do, but this ancient, sacred art was forbidden by the Khmer Rouge. Many of the old craftsmen, who could make a kite sing seven tones, perished during those terrible years. But today people all over Cambodia build and fly kites of all kinds, and the singing kite once more offers prayers for the harvest.

The *khleng ek* has an abstract, humanoid shape, broad-shouldered, narrow-waisted, flaring again to a fringed, vaguely fallopian tail. Its frame is made of bent bamboo, and, depending on its shape, the kite is said to be either male or female. For ceremonial kites fine cloth or elaborately patterned paper is stretched across the frame, but our children find whatever is handy: old cement bags, salvaged tarpaulins, plastic bags. They tie fringes to the shoulders and hips of the kite, and double tails that trail many times the length of the kite itself. These can be nothing more than strips the children cut from the colored plastic sacks that blow and catch on trees and bushes by the side of the road. But they dance and dip and brush the sky in a glorious calligraphy.

How does a kite sing? In some countries there are small clay whistles or gourds attached that catch the wind on chamfered edges, but in Cambodia it is the horns of the kite that sing. Mounted at the head of the kite is a broad bow, like an archery bow, and across that bow is strung a single ribbon of fiber, like a reed, tied to the bow by a string at each end. Pitch is determined by length of bow and tautness of string. At the points where the reed and the strings are joined there is a bole of beeswax. By varying the size and tautness of the bow and the mass of the wax, the craftsman may fine-tune his instrument. To test the sound a boy will tie a cord to the center of the bow and twirl it around his head, like an Australian bull-roarer. The kites our boys made were about two and a half meters high and perhaps two meters wide, and took five boys to launch and others to manage the tails. Some kites can be twice that large.

The *khleng ek* is flown all night long. By day, when the ground is warm and the air is cooler than the earth, the kite's song rises to heaven and is heard only faintly on the ground. But at night, when the earth cools, the sound bounces off the warm upper layers of air and villagers can relax after their day in the fields and savor the beauty of the kite's song. The singing kites the boys made usually produced three to five tones. I never heard a kite with seven tones. Perhaps that art has been lost.

When Chou Sarab died of AIDS, she was forty-one years old. Everything she owned, two sarongs and a few tops, fit in a bundle tied up in one bath towel. Wayne dressed her body in fresh clothes, and the monks came to the hospice to chant. Four other AIDS patients carried the white wooden sarcophagus to the crematorium. Sarab's daughters, Miss Da and Mary, were there. No one else from her family. Only Miss Malis from Wat Opot came to her funeral, because she and Da were friends. Rebecca had helped nurse Sarab, rocking her in her arms and singing Christian hymns, and pleading with her to say the name of Jesus before she died. Rebecca did not come to the funeral. She said she was allergic to incense.

Wayne swept the tiles at the crematorium and loaded the wood and charcoal, tucked the bundle with Sarab's belongings beside her body, struck the brass gong seven times and lit the fire. Finally, he closed the crematorium door and everyone went away.

I did not know Sarab well. She was a woman from the village who spent her short life working in the rice fields. She kept to herself and died modestly in the hospice, and I stayed mostly with the children. Da was living at Wat Opot with her mother when I arrived, but Mary came from the village when Sarab was dying. Mary looked about sixteen. She was big-boned and subdued and unsure.

The day Sarab was cremated, the children

were playing with Barbie dolls on the porch outside my bedroom. Mary wandered over and sat awhile after the funeral. Her long hair hung down uncombed. She wore a mis-buttoned plaid shirt. She had been up for days taking care of her mother and her face was puffy from crying and lack of sleep. There was a Ken doll on the table, and Mary picked him up and held him absent-mindedly.

I had noticed the children playing with Ken earlier. Mister Ouen held Ken and Barbie in what would have been a compromising position had they been anatomically correct, and the children were tittering and pointing. They burst out laughing when I walked by, then shushed each other and tried to hide what they were doing, but when they saw I was laughing too they relaxed and we all laughed together and everything was fine. I made a mental note to remind Wayne about the sex education program we had discussed.

Now here was Mary, facing a future with no family to protect her and a little sister to take care of. Wayne offered to let her stay at Wat Opot for a while, but she seemed hesitant. She was older than the other children, and much younger than the adult patients, and she and Da are both HIV negative. She told Wayne she was trying to decide whether to go up to Phnom Penh alone, to try to find a job in a garment factory. Getting a job might require a bribe, and Wayne worried aloud that without money she might wind up having to sell herself.

Mary listened. She held Ken by nothing more than his little plastic feet.

Unlike more affluent temples, Wat Opot Pagoda does not have its own crematorium. The earliest cremations of people who died of AIDS at the hospice were carried out by the village headman. He would arrive with a few other men from the village. Sometimes they had been drinking. The men burned the bodies in a shallow pit. Before antiretroviral drugs were available in Cambodia there were sometimes two or three funerals in one day at Wat Opot. Some families had little money for wood and charcoal so the corpse might be only partially burnt. Animals could be seen carrying off pieces of the bodies. Vandin and Wayne were troubled by the lack of respect shown to the dead, so they agreed to build a seven-story *pa cha,* a proper crematorium for family members who died of AIDS.

Vandin had once wanted to be an architect; Wayne, son of a baker, had built ovens to bake bread when he was doing medical work in Honduras. Together they designed and built the *pa cha* for Wat Opot. Like those Honduran adobe ovens, the *pa cha* had walls two feet thick made of unfired brick. Over time, the clay bricks were fired by the heat of the cremations. The whole structure is painted white. Smoke escapes from a seven-tiered chimney. Around the base of the *pa cha* is a tiled platform that stays cool in the shade, perfect for napping on a hot day.

Each cremation uses fifty kilos of charcoal and a pile of wood. These cost about 60,000 riel, or $15 — half a month's earnings for a rural farmer. When villagers cannot afford cremation they must bury their dead. Chinese people in Cambodia bury, building earth-bermed tombs shaped like horseshoes and oriented according to the laws of feng shui. These can be seen here and there, incongruously tidy amid the scrublands along the road to Phnom Penh. But burial is not the Khmer custom. So, as a kindness and a compassionate offering, Wayne will cremate the bodies of neighbors who die of AIDS in the villages.

Mister Bott, one of the older boys at Wat

Opot, is building a singing kite. He has cut green bamboo with a hand-forged egret's-neck knife, and bent the bamboo to an elegant frame, larger than a tall man standing with outstretched arms. He is anxious to get it flying and asks me to buy plastic sheeting and heavy-gauge fishing line from the local market in Bati. I'm game, excited to see this marvel in the air, but Rebecca tells Bott he must do *echai* duty, garbage pickup, to earn his supplies. It's fine with me, but I admit to a secret admiration for the boys who are too busy doing something creative and visionary to bother with earthly chores. They focus on what inspires them, and the rest merely dissipates their energies. Of course, they may grow up to be difficult men, and Rebecca's discipline is good for them. But oh, how I love the kites and the boys who dream of flying them!

Finally the kite is ready. Mister Bott has lashed the sheeting onto the frame and cut up plastic bags for a tail that stretches thirty feet or more across the field by the community school. Five boys carry the kite, stumbling along and holding the frame as high as they can above their heads. Some of the little kids follow, minding the tails to keep them from tangling in the underbrush.

Mister Bott runs on ahead, with the string wrapped around a pair of crossed wooden slats.

Suddenly a freshening breeze catches the kite and wrenches it from their outstretched hands. Everyone keeps running for a moment, as if they do not realize the kite is gone, and then they stop and just stare into the sky as Bott begins playing out string and the kite shoots higher and higher. Mister Kosal does a headstand, looking at the kite upside down, and some of the little kids jump up and down or do cartwheels, too exhilarated to stand still.

Bott maneuvers the kite toward the center of campus, and the community gathers round, laughing and pointing, listening for the first song. The kite has risen high now, and to everyone's relief it is beginning to chant a prayer, a harmonic hymn of gratitude for the ripening rice.

From a low humming, the song jumps an octave, halves the interval, then splits the gap again, reverses to a shaded trill and, in a seesaw of notes of almost vocal timbre, touches down again momentarily where it began before tumbling in a cascading melisma to a tone half an octave below and bounding back again, never duplicating a cadence.

170

Mister Bott has played out most of the string, and allows three of the younger kids to hold the spool. Everyone is excited, and the kids begin horsing around, hooting and tickling each other.

I see it coming.

A sudden gust of wind seizes the kite and snaps the spool from their hands, and the kite careens upward, the wooden spool bobbing after it through the treetops. The kids freeze, in openmouthed, shocked futility, but Bott lunges after the spool, vaults a barbed wire fence and hightails it across the rice fields, chasing the kite toward Phnom Chisor. For an hour we watch the kite in the invisible updrafts, floating higher and higher above the fields.

Eventually Bott returns, wet and bedraggled. He has chased the kite through streams and ditches, but in the end it disappeared into the sky above the ancient Hindu temple of Phnom Chisor. It was a beautiful thing to see it flying and know it was free to go as high as the wind would take it. And when we could not see it anymore, we imagined we could still hear it singing.

Mister Bott is philosophical. Sometimes when you make an offering to the gods, the gods accept.

■ ■ ■ ■

Miss Mary laid the Ken doll back on the table. She rose from her place on the porch outside my room and wandered slowly back toward the crematorium, where her mother's body was being consumed by the fire.

A little boy from the village, with muddy knees and wearing a torn T-shirt, was flying a kite nearby. It was not a singing kite, nothing fancy. Just the kind of simple white kite that children in much of the world still make for themselves from discarded newspaper and knotted string. The sun was low, and in the warm light of early evening Mary watched the little kite fly in and out of the smoke from her mother's cremation, like a spirit, or a pure white lotus rising from the mud on a thread of golden light.

■ ■ ■ ■ ■

PART TWO:
TRANSFORMATIONS

■ ■ ■ ■

18
Pilgrimage

People ask me, "How did you get to Cambodia?"

How do we wind up anywhere? Do we really know? One corner is turned instead of another in a life left open to possibilities. One time a friend of mine, delivering a boat to the Caribbean, pulled alongside another sailboat to discuss a port they were both approaching, and he saw a girl on board. Later there was a wedding, and babies. Meetings like this are unavoidable, even at sea.

For me, it also began in water: bathing in the River Ganges in Allahabad, India, on a cold January morning in 2001, among thirty million pilgrims.

Chances are you have never heard of the Kumbh Mela. Any coverage of the event on Western television is usually given short shrift, the name translated with a shrug as "The Festival of the Pot." A crowd shot, and some mention of how many people attended, given in millions. Indians themselves record the numbers in *lakh* or *chror* — for in a country of over a billion people isn't it more useful to count in multiples of a hundred thousand or ten million? On the television screen you might see ten seconds of local color: hordes of Naga Babas, warrior ascetics with streaming dreadlocks, storming into the waters clad only in marigolds and ashes. And you think, "How exotic!" but you can have no notion of the event itself.

The Kumbh Mela is a vast pilgrimage, a Hindu revival meeting, a gathering by the confluence of three holy rivers, a celebration of faith. Yet it is also a chance for living human beings to participate in re-creating an ancient cosmic event, nothing less than the renewal of cosmic rectitude through the joined efforts of the ancient gods and demons of India, good and evil, when they came together to churn the Ocean of Milk.

I had traveled twice before to India, first as a tourist, later as a seeker, but I wanted to go deeper. So when my friends and I were invited to the Maha Kumbh Mela, the largest gathering of humanity in history, invited to stay in the ashram of a local guru with a talent for needling the authorities, in a building that had been partially demolished when these same officials, it was rumored, caused a wrecking ball to be swung against it "accidentally" three times, we agreed to travel together to Allahabad, a city in north-central India. Our contributions would help shore up the ashram's crumbling facade, and we would bed down on straw pallets, on a rise overlooking the floodplain where three rivers come together to form the auspicious bathing place called the Sangam. In winter the rivers retreat to their broad dry-season shallows, and the sprawling rainy-season floodplain turns into a landscape of fine silt, where every twelve years a city is built, complete with roads and privies, electricity and housing, markets and banks, to accommodate the millions who come, when the stars are right, to take the holy "dip."

■ ■ ■ ■

I wasn't thinking particularly profound thoughts about a pilgrimage when I decided to come on this journey. I loved India, its smells and hues and complexity, and had not been back for many years. And it would be fun to travel with my friends, one of whom had never been out of the United States. But once you make a commitment to take a pilgrimage, a pilgrimage has a way of taking *you.* And so it happened that on a December night, about a week before we were scheduled to fly to India, I found myself in the emergency room of Mount Desert Island Hospital, my heart beating out a peculiar syncopation that took several electric shocks to set it pumping smoothly again.

My doctor is explaining the procedure to me, and I am telling him with a casualness that surprises us both, "Just get on with it," because I'm leaving for India in a week to bathe in the Ganges with millions of pilgrims. My physician, a sober Canadian who looks like a very young John Denver, shoots me a look that tells me he is not entirely sure whether to cardiovert me or have me fitted for a straitjacket. I finally agree to postpone my trip, but only by a week, and only until he can get me on some meds that will, I hope, prevent this arrhythmia from recurring when I am far away from familiar Western medical care. But what is really happening inside me is the realization that, unlike the millions of Indians who are traveling to the Kumbh Mela by train and bus and on foot across the subcontinent, as a Westerner I am insulated from that kind of pilgrimage. If I were walking across India and got a blister, there would always be a credit card and a night in a comfortable hotel. So the question arises: Of what does my own pilgrimage consist? Is it not this moment of sitting on a gurney in an emergency room, wired to an electrocardiogram, with the eavesdropping universe asking, "Okay, kid, how badly do you want this? Do you long to go with your whole heart?" And in this same moment comes a resounding YES! and I understand on what feels like the deepest possible level that whatever happens in India, whether I live or die, I will be, *I am,* perfectly all right.

As an Indian friend later tells me, all pilgrimages are internal.

The legend of "Churning the Ocean of Milk" is told in many of the Hindu scriptures. Stone carvings adorning temples from India to Angkor Wat show how the gods and demons wrapped the giant snake Vasuki around a holy mountain, and how, pulling back and forth, with the gods arrayed on one side and the demons on the other, they spun the mountain like a butter churn until the primordial ocean offered up its treasures. The greatest of these was the Kumbh — not a pot, really, but a vessel, brimming with Amrit, the Nectar of Immortality.

The story begins in a time of spiritual malaise, when the gods and demons had been locked in war for eons, a time when neither was yet immortal. The war took an awful toll, and finally the gods went to Lord Vishnu for advice. He told them to churn the Ocean of Milk for the Amrit, which not only would make them immortal but also would reestablish righteousness and set all creation on a better path.

But there was a hitch. The gods, weakened by war, could not do it alone; they needed to enlist the help of the demons. But under no circumstances could the demons be allowed to partake of the Amrit, lest they too become immortal.

The gods strained and the demons cursed. After much effort the vessel emerged from the deep. In the ensuing scuffle the demons grabbed the pot. The gods were frantic, but Lord Vishnu tricked the greedy demons and escaped with the Kumbh, flying all over the universe and hiding the Amrit at various holy places. In his haste Lord Vishnu spilled a few drops here and there, including at Allahabad, at the place where the three rivers meet: the muddy Ganges, the blue Yamuna and the mystical underground Saraswati, river of faith and deep knowing. And every twelve years, when the stars are right, millions of people make a pilgrimage to this very spot to bathe in the meeting rivers, which, they believe, briefly flow with the Amrit of Immortality.

In my journey to the Maha Kumbh Mela I traveled with Matthew and Laurence, two old friends from Maine. Matthew and I traveled light, but this was Laurence's first trip overseas and he had packed for all contingencies. Bunion pads and bungee cords, duct tape, combination locks, journals, tarps, cameras, Luna Bars, dried fruit, four hundred rubber bands and an elaborate water purification system. I tried to explain that there was bottled water in all but the remotest villages in India, but he wouldn't hear it. He had alfalfa seeds, and jars for sprouting them — Laurence had spent years as a raw-food vegetarian — shoes for any situation, sweaters, pants long and short and in-between, pliers, pushpins, a pink mosquito net, red suspenders and a hammer and nails. A can of nuclear bug spray promised to purge every crawling, stinging thing from our bedrooms. Beardless, he'd brought a beard trimmer, and Band-Aids, granola, toothpicks and cotton swabs for cleansing his ears and nasal passages. Toilet paper, Kleenex, grapefruit seed oil and a huge brick of Callebaut chocolate, which he surreptitiously nibbled to console himself on bad days. He had pills for malaria and Delhi belly, and herbal tinctures and tiny vials of homeopathic remedies to take in case the other pills failed, 180 pairs of Groucho Marx eyeglasses, a sack of molded rubber finger puppets incarnating the Hindu deities Brahma, Ganesha and Kali, two dozen blow-up globe beach balls and a staple gun. Finally, in a small plain box, tied with string and hidden among his socks and underwear, was a Ziploc bag containing a portion of the ashes of his daughter, Kira, who had died at twenty-one, ashes that he hoped to scatter in the Ganges if the spirit moved him.

Everything he carried was shoehorned into an immense duffel bag, which often forced us to hire a second taxi. On those occasions we were not kind to Laurence. As experienced travelers, Matthew and I prided ourselves on living off the land. Yet more than once we found ourselves sheepishly begging some strategic item from Laurence, to his immense satisfaction. Not once did he offer us any chocolate.

The place of the meeting rivers in Allahabad spread out before us, glittering in the morning sunlight. Looking closely we could see the actual spot where the muddy yellow shallows of the Ganges meet the blue depths of the Yamuna. The waters of the Saraswati we could not see, but we felt her, coursing beneath everything. At any hour, the Sangam was marked by a line of little rowboats, hired to carry pilgrims to bathe in the exact spot where the rivers meet.

At different times of day we would wander down among the crowds of pilgrims, a vast living nation that had come together for this occasion. Because this was the first Maha Kumbh Mela of the new millennium, it drew an unusually large and varied crowd. Over the course of a month seventy million people passed through Allahabad. Farmers in dhotis, village wives in faded cotton saris and urban high-tech workers sporting trendy Western fashions were joined by spiritual seekers from East and West. Movie stars from Bollywood and Hollywood arrived with their retinues. The foreign press published photographs of bathing women in wet saris and were severely chastised. Celebrity gurus held flashy media events to demonstrate their spiritual powers. Rolex babas held court. The Dalai Lama spoke. Madonna took a dip. I declined the kind offer to marry a nattily turbaned Rajasthani gentleman with a gold brocade kaftan and silver walking stick. Colorful sadhus from all over India wandered the grounds, their foreheads anointed with endless permutations of white ash and the scarlet powder called kumkum. One old man, carrying a trident, his matted hair falling to his waist and his pupils dilated with ganja or perhaps cosmic astonishment, stuck his face close to mine and demanded, "Are you *fine*?!" "Yes, Baba," I answered, "I *am* fine." And he blessed me and melted back into the throng.

Well-to-do pilgrims slept in tents, the poor outside on their bedrolls; the poorest, who live their whole lives on the streets of India, shivered in the dampness on frayed straw mats. Meals were cooked over small fires. Babies were born. Old people were abandoned to die. Some days we wandered through the acres of temporary temples, built of lashed bamboo and painted cloth, where famous teachers received their followers for *darshan* — the gift of beholding and being beheld by God — while loudspeakers broadcast their spiritual discourses. Devotees offered sacred food first to God for blessing, and then to crowds of hungry pilgrims. Some sects served dal with rice and vegetables, while at the sprawling Hari Krishna tent we feasted on carrot halva and milk fudge and rice pudding, delicately scented with rosewater. Naga Babas, renunciates who some believed had flown through the air from their Himalayan retreats, presided over smaller enclaves lit by crystal chandeliers, and offered us hits of Lord Shiva's intoxicating *prasad* from clay chillums. These yogis are naked but for the ashes they gather from the cremation grounds and rub on their bodies, making their skin the color of the sky before the monsoon. Some have spent many years performing extreme austerities, such as holding one arm raised until their muscles atrophy and their fingernails grow long and twisted as vines.

Some days we just sat by the river and watched the faithful wade into the waters and perform their ritual ablutions, then gather holy water in little vessels to carry home with them. Always people thronged to the Sangam. Even late at night groups of young men, too stimulated to sleep, congregated by the water, chatting and drinking.

It was on such a night that Laurence woke from a deep sleep and knew it was time to carry Kira's ashes to the Ganges. He dressed quietly, and found the simple brown box in his duffel bag, all the while trying not to wake any of the travelers who shared our room. Matthew stirred under his mosquito net in the next bed and asked Laurence in a whisper whether he would like company, and together the two friends headed out into the darkness.

It must have been between 3 and 4 a.m., the meditation hour, because that was the only time the broadcasts ceased. Otherwise, all day and all night loudspeakers blared the sacred and the profane, *bhajans* and sports car promotions, mantras and ads for toothpaste, to villagers who had never before traveled more than a few miles from their homes, and who still cleaned their teeth by chewing on twigs of the neem tree. After a while you noticed only the cessation of sound. It was too quiet.

■ ■ ■ ■

A predawn fog had risen from the river, mixing with the particulate smoke of a million tiny dung fires. Laurence and Matthew drew their shawls over their mouths and noses as they picked their way among the sleeping pilgrims. Already we had all developed deep coughs from the smoke and dust and dampness and the powdered DDT that was sprayed from trucks to keep down the malarial mosquitos.

Arriving at the water at this unlikely hour, Laurence and Matthew were a novelty that drew the attention of a group of young men, who had passed thus far an uneventful night. Half challenging, half jocular, and just a little drunk, they besieged the two Westerners with the usual banalities. At first Laurence answered politely, but as each new fellow arrived, asking the same question his friends had just asked, Laurence began to doubt whether he could actually accomplish his solemn errand. Finally, he turned to the oldest and pleaded in a voice clipped with emotion, "Please. I am trying to put my daughter's ashes in the Ganga."

The man started, suddenly sober, and a little ashamed. "Oh sir, I am so sorry.

Please. If there is anything I can do . . ."
And he spoke softly to his friends in Hindi,
and the young men's boisterous demeanor
changed to one of quiet reverence. They
drew back and made a path, and Laurence
carried Kira's ashes into the meeting rivers.

Standing alone in the darkness, Laurence
scooped water and let it fall through his
hands and prayed for Kira, who had died
suddenly, hardly more than a girl, and for
his infant son, Elijah, who had been born
prematurely, his lungs too tiny and weak to
survive, and had died without ever seeing
the sun. Into the dark river, Laurence
floated the little leaf cups, stitched together
by thorns, that carry candles and prayers
and offerings of marigolds and rose petals.
They floated first as flames, then as halos,
growing ever fainter in the mist, until finally
their glow dissolved into nothingness. Then
he sifted a portion of his daughter's ashes
into the river, keeping yet a little for himself.

"It is done," he told himself.

Matthew joined Laurence as he emerged
from the river, and together, turning toward
home, they saw how the young men were
standing, silent now, in a semicircle, guard-
ing the sacred space.

Laurence and Matthew climbed the river-
bank and walked back to the ashram, past

wakening pilgrims huddled around their tiny dung fires, and, as Matthew told the story, they knew that Kira walked with them.

Our month at the ashram passed slowly. There were cold morning showers, laundry washed and hung to dry on tree branches and a succession of chapati and ghee and dal and *subji,* a traditional dish made with cauliflower or potatoes. Visitors came and went, staying for a few days or a week. Shantji, our host, found Western youngsters wandering around the Mela grounds and invited them home. One night, Laurence led a fire walk that ended with Shantji's Indian devotees dancing in the flames, utterly unafraid of burning their feet on the coals. Watching their fearlessness and joy, we realized that these modest men were devoted yogis who had, for our benefit, kindly taken on the guise of cooks and cleaners. We felt humbled.

There were nights spent chanting and singing *bhajans.* Along the vast midway that grew up on the margins of the grounds we foraged for familiar Western dietary comforts like chow mein or chocolate chip cookies. Each new traveler we met was embraced: a young Japanese girl who tearfully told of meeting the Dalai Lama; an Indian scientist who had abandoned his career to wander the streets singing the mystical love poems of Rumi and Hafiz; a visiting teacher who spoke to us for one evening in Hindi and sang the scriptures in Sanskrit, and who was so miraculously eloquent of voice and gesture that even though we spoke not a word of either language, we felt that we understood. After a time, we transformed from a collection of errant travelers into a close community.

And so when the night of the great dip arrived — the most auspicious moment, when the planets were precisely aligned and the Amrit would once again flow at the confluence of the meeting rivers — it was as family that we walked to the Sangam. To be thus cocooned was comforting. For days people had streamed into Allahabad, by some accounts fifteen thousand a minute. NASA satellites broadcast pictures of vast crowds visible from space. Trains, backed up as far as Delhi and Calcutta, stood stalled on their tracks. The city, which had already been closed to cars, now began turning away pilgrims who arrived on foot. With thirty million people on the grounds there was simply no room left, and that morning every one of them was headed for the same narrow stretch of beach.

It was still dark when Laurence woke me. We dressed quickly, and our little group fell in with the crowds migrating toward the Sangam, millions of us, wrapped tightly against the morning dampness in woolen shawls the color of saffron and clay. We walked slowly, together with the vital and the infirm, many with bundles on their heads and babies in their arms, fingering worn prayer beads or carrying brass pots and plastic bottles to gather the precious waters, and chanting, "Hare Ram Hare Ram." We were leaves in a stream, twigs in a flood, water seeking its own level in Mother Ganga, hoping to merge our spirit with hers and set our souls aright for all eternity.

With so many people converging on such a tiny area, the Indian authorities had taken extraordinary measures to protect us from the deadly panic-driven stampedes that sometimes happen at such immense gatherings. Everyone had heard terrifying stories from past Melas, and although concerned, they seemed to be determined that this moment would not be desecrated by such a tragedy. Another fear was terrorism. Although this was January 2001, eight months before the fall of the Twin Towers, the Indian government was nonetheless alert to the potential for a disaster of enormous scale. Security was high, and both up- and downstream giant filters had been installed to try to intercept any explosives that someone might try to float into the Sangam on the main bathing days. To protect the pilgrims from the crush of their own numbers, an elaborate slalom of barricades had been set up at the approach to the bathing area, with guards stationed at every switchback to prevent violence that could result from people trying to jump the line.

It is one thing to consider such perils in the abstract, quite another to clear the disciplined order of the barricades and find ourselves at last on the narrow beach at the Sangam, with the energy around us changed. Some of us were moving toward the water, while others, who had finished their immersion, were climbing the banks from the river, pushing with equal vigor in the opposite direction. Chaos reigned as the great crowd congealed and moved at odds with itself. Beneath our feet lay gelatinous seaweed, ropy and wet and ready to trip us. Many might have slipped and fallen, to be trampled by the crowd, but there was no room to fall. From time to time I felt myself lifted entirely off the ground and carried, forward and backward, or spun like a leaf on the ocean, a legion of damp bodies pressing onto mine. Finally, there was no choice but to surrender to the dance of limbs and torsos, to trust this multimillipede of which I had become a tiny part. And in truth, when I forgot about the numbers and focused on the eyes of the people closest to me, there seemed no threat at all, only supreme goodwill, for we were all here with the same intention. It seemed there could be neither malice nor fear.

Under my feet I felt the earth and seaweed give way to water, and suddenly the world opened up and I found myself standing alone, in silent privacy, breast deep in the meeting rivers. I felt a warm breeze blowing gently over my bare shoulders. Then a garland of marigolds floated by, and I became aware that I was standing in a sea of drifting gold, offerings from the innumerable pilgrims with whom I shared this moment, and I relaxed completely into gratitude, stillness and love.

Somehow we friends found each other, climbed the slippery embankment and made our way back toward the ashram in the pale predawn light. A cold wind picked up, and groups of pilgrims, drawn together tight as lotus buds, waved us over to warm ourselves at their fires. Just ahead of us a young father held his small son by the hand, and as they walked they chanted, "Ram Ram Hare Ram."

And somewhere in this multitude wandered a tall American photographer named Bennett "Buck" Stevens, whom I had never met. Plagued by an acute case of Delhi belly, he was trying to photograph the Naga Babas as they bathed, the same Naga Babas who notoriously do not like their pictures taken. And it was through the intervention of this same Buck Stevens, whom to this day I have never met in person, that I would arrive at last in Cambodia.

Returning to the States after months of travel in Asia, life seemed to quicken, and destiny spilled out like grain from a torn sack. My mother had lived for many years with cancer, but suddenly an ominous new tumor near her spine required surgery. And so I found myself moving again, this time from Bar Harbor, a pretty tourist town on the Maine coast, to my mother's apartment in New York City. It was mid-September of 2001, only a week after the attack on the World Trade Center.

My mother was in the hospital for several weeks, and every day, after visiting hours were over, I wandered around Manhattan. The familiar streets of the city where I had lived as a child were muffled now by a pall of sadness. Hundreds of little shrines appeared along the sidewalks. Xeroxed photographs of confident executives or hopeful young restaurant workers, immigrants with foreign names, were taped to walls and hurricane fences, along with pleas for information on their whereabouts, as if they had simply wandered off, briefly distracted, and might at any moment reappear, happy to be home again among the living.

Burning candles guttered before small memorials on street corners. They reminded me of the roadside shrines I'd seen in India: a statue of a god, a photograph of a saint, sometimes just a rock painted red with kumkum and given piercing glass eyes, so its resident spirit might bestow on a passing believer the precious gift of *darshan*. Here in New York City people left the same flowers and burned incense, but there also were teddy bears and photographs of children and purple and black buntings on firehouses and police stations. Yet the eyes of the missing drew you in, staring out from the tattered handbills, riveting as the eyes of the

197

gods of India.

Uptown, in my mother's neighborhood, people still dined outdoors at sidewalk cafés, but the sense of normalcy seemed forced, like lipstick on a corpse. But as one went farther downtown, nearer to Ground Zero, the atmosphere changed. You might ask a policeman for directions, and while his mouth spoke the names of streets, his eyes told of sights he could never speak of. And on a still Yom Kippur evening, approaching the ruins of the Twin Towers for the first time, I thought I heard the bellowing of multitudes of souls, those who had died in fear.

Sometime in all this I Googled the Kumbh Mela. I longed for my friends, and for the spiritual optimism I had felt during my time in India. On Bennett Stevens's website I discovered a story he had written about his experiences, and some of his photographs of the Naga Babas. His writing was cheeky and irreverent, yet at the same time deeply respectful. I wrote him a fan letter and sent him a short piece I had composed at the ashram right after my own dip in the Sangam. He wrote me back, and now and then we exchanged emails, a quip, a photograph, a squib of writing.

■ ■ ■ ■

Meanwhile, my mother grew weaker. Our time together was fraught. In our differences of temperament we seemed always to love past each other. I marveled at her bravery in the face of excruciating pain, the birthday parties and Seders she presided over from the bed where she lay half paralyzed, holding court for the many friends who gathered by her bedside. Every day for months they came, young and old, drawn by her skill at making each feel as if he or she were her best beloved. I watched as one by one impending death stripped her of the last remnants of the worldly image she had so keenly cultivated: the rugged independence she had insisted upon since my father's death, her vanity and stunning sense of style that allowed her to make grand entrances but always keep people waiting. These were replaced by fierce determination and deep gratitude, and ultimately by a kind of spiritual translucence, an inner radiance, as if all the illusions that had sustained her in this life were finally dropping away, leaving only a momentary flash of what is pure and true about us all. Even so, when the end came I was aware that part of my mourning was for the relationship we both wished we could have shared, but never did.

A hundred people attended my mother's funeral. And even here there was a sense of the surreal. Her rabbi, a close personal friend, began the service by announcing to the congregation that we were gathered to celebrate the life and mourn the death of . . . and here he pronounced my name instead of hers. The audience gasped, and he was mortified and flustered, but I smiled at him, knowing how he had loved her, and excused him, saying, "It's all right, Rabbi. I know you still can't let her go."

Yet there was something oddly fitting in this. Like Tom Sawyer and Huck Finn imagining their own funerals, I felt that a part of myself *was* being buried that day. And as Laurence told me when he heard about it, in every spiritual journey there comes a moment when one's soul must pass through the shadow of death.

After my mother's funeral, after dismantling the apartment where I was born, there was nothing left for me in New York City. I returned to Bar Harbor.

Winter was coming in my small Maine town. There was record cold: twenty below zero for most of January. The foundation of my hundred-year-old house heaved. Doors would not open. I watched mesmerized as cracks marched across the plaster of my living room wall, a few inches farther every day. I sunk into depression, but even more chillingly into a sense of uselessness. Sad memories of the hard times with my mother, the futile attempts at real contact between us, were deepened by the grief we all shared after September 11. I don't drink, but I entered the sort of state I imagine brings longtime drinkers to join Alcoholics Anonymous. It was perhaps that same sense that one has done everything one can do, and is fresh out of ideas, and can only offer oneself and one's problems to the universe. So I prayed for *seva,* as the Hindus call selfless service, for something outside of myself and my problems, some way I might do something for someone else, even a very small something. Mine was not a particularly generous or high-minded surrender. I needed to save my life.

It took the universe exactly twelve hours to concoct a solution and offer it to me through the agency of Buck Stevens. His email began, "You know how you are always looking for a service project?" Buck was now in Cambodia, photographing an orphanage for children with AIDS, and they

201

needed volunteers. One did not have to be a doctor or have any special skills. The only requirement was that you like kids. I was stunned by the efficiency of this generous universe. I wrote a letter to the director, Wayne Dale Matthysse, listing anything that might lead him to think I would be a good catch. I needn't have bothered. Little did I know that Wayne has a soft spot for people on a journey.

Wayne's reply was simple. "Come."

19
WAYNE

Wayne traces the beginning of his own spiritual journey to an incident in his childhood, in a small town in Michigan. Most of the families in his neighborhood were conservative Christians of Dutch descent, except for one Polish family who lived across the street. They had a son named Gordy, some years older than Wayne, who was mentally handicapped. Wayne did not know nor did he care about any of that. At four years old all he knew was that this large, lumbering boy was willing to play with him. It felt to Wayne as if he had his own pet Goliath, benign and protective.

Maybe Wayne was thinking of the biblical story of David and Goliath the day he threw a stone at Gordy. Gordy threw one back; it's the sort of thing kids do all the time, only Gordy's stone opened a small artery in Wayne's forehead and there was a lot of blood. Someone called the police. A crowd of neighbors gathered, and amid mutterings about "Polacks" and "retards," the grown-ups decided that Wayne should not mention that it was he who had cast the first stone. He knew it was wrong to lie, but he was just a little boy who felt powerless to go against the crowd of adults feeding him what to say. He barely managed a nod when the police asked him to verify the story and then retreated in shame to his room, hoping it would all go away. The very next morning Wayne watched as a chain-link fence was installed around his friend's house. From that day forward Gordy lived under house arrest, and at eighteen years old he was sent to an institution. Wayne walked past that fence every day, and sixty years later he still speaks of bearing the weight of Gordy's imprisonment, the links of that fence as palpable to him as the chains forged in life by Marley's ghost in *A Christmas Carol*.

After high school Wayne took a job in a psychiatric hospital. He decided to enroll in a one-year psychiatric nursing course to see whether he wanted to pursue a college degree in the field.

Meanwhile, the Vietnam War had begun to escalate. Wayne joined the Navy in 1966, so anxious for a tour of duty that he managed to swap orders with another medic who did not want to go. At twenty-one he shipped out, convinced that God was on America's side.

Wayne wrote of leaving for Vietnam:

I was given a White Bible and a Congregational Prayer Book when I left my protected world of Christendom to join my fellow compatriots in battle against those Heathen Asian Communists. I was told, it was GOD'S Will that we fight them so that they could not spread their Atheistic views to others around the world.

But once in Vietnam he began to see things that disturbed him deeply. He wound up stationed near Da Nang in 1968, shortly after the calamitous Tet Offensive. This was in South Vietnam, and the local villagers were the same people we were supposed to have been saving from communism. But in the midst of battle it was never clear who was friend and who was foe, and it was said that some of these villagers had helped the North Vietnamese inflict stunning casualties on American soldiers and their allies. Threats now came from all directions, and for the thousands of U.S. soldiers who had seen their friends slaughtered during Tet, it was payback time. Wayne felt these sentiments mounting around him:

And when we burned what was left standing of South Vietnamese villages that were bombed just moments before our arrival by US heavy artillery, and I questioned my Commanding Officer "Why?" he said, "Because the Mother Fuckers were suspected of helping the GOD Damned Viet Cong during the TET Offensive and therefore deserve it . . ."

And when the mother of a severely wounded child came pleading for me to help stop the bleeding, I was told by my

CO not to do it because it was not my responsibility; someone else would be there in a moment to help them. But no one came in an hour and the child died, and when I asked him "Why?" he said, "It's none of your fucking business . . . !"

And when the lush green rice fields suddenly turned brown overnight from Agent Orange and the people were in tears because they had lost all their crops and I asked my CO "Why?" he said, "Because they might use some of it to feed the Fucking Viet Cong and so we had to do it . . ."

And when we captured a 14-year-old boy who was wearing a green colored shirt which he said he took off of a dead soldier because he had no clothes of his own, and the Captain ordered the Sergeant to take him away, which he did and returned a few minutes later without him, and I asked him "Why?" he said, "Because the little shithead could be a spy and if we let him go he could give away our position." And I said, "But, Sir, we marched in here with six tanks firing heavy ammunition and flame throwers shot hot gas on the homes that left smoke billowing hundreds of feet into the air. Do you really think they don't know WHERE we are?" And he said, "Shut your fucking mouth, Doc!"

Through it all, Wayne tried to maintain a sense of himself apart from the others, that he was there as a medic, a healer, not a killer, and that this justified his taking part. But one day that illusion too was shattered.

As we were leaving the village, a woman with a small child in her arms stood defiantly on the dike in front of us. She was forced to one side to wait in the knee-deep water until we passed. As I came close to her I smiled compassionately and I sensed that she understood that I was not the same as the others. She fixed her eyes directly on mine and then spat in my face.

As I was wiping the spit and tears from my eyes I became nauseated, not because of what she had just done, but because I realized that I had gone over to the enemy, without even changing sides.

Two incidents that happened on the same day back in 1968 changed my life forever and set in motion a conflict that has been raging inside of me ever since. It hit me harder than any bullet ever could have and caused more internal damage than all of the bombs and mortars that were dropped around me. It ripped the innocence from my soul and forced me on an endless journey of recompense, for a debt that cannot be repaid. I witnessed the murder of two children. And I did nothing to stop it.

Wayne's tour of duty in Vietnam ended abruptly on a battlefield near Da Nang. Crossing a field of tall grass, his company came under fire and one of the men was wounded in both legs. Wayne ran out to help him; his men set off some smoke bombs for cover. But as Wayne and two other soldiers struggled to move the wounded man, a mortar shell struck close to them and hurled shrapnel and glass into Wayne's face and eye. The sergeant called for a medevac. Wayne protested that the helicopter would give their position away, but the sergeant insisted that he would not let them die. Later, Wayne learned that the rest of his company had been overrun and that no one had survived. The medevac had, in fact, drawn fire to their location. Wayne's rescue had cost everyone else their lives.

From that day on Wayne would ask himself the question, *For what was I saved?*

After some time in a Veterans Administration hospital in Bethesda, Maryland, where an attempted cornea transplant failed, Wayne was released from the military with a partial disability. He was virtually blind in one eye. He returned to Michigan, but like many Vietnam War veterans Wayne found he could no longer fit into the family and job and community he had left.

In Vietnam, Wayne had been the only white soldier in an all-black company, a dramatic departure from his parochial upbringing, and it was these soldiers who had died in battle after he was airlifted to safety. He owed his life to their sacrifice, and when he came home he continued to associate with people he would never have known before.

It was during this time I met up with people who were every bit as much American heroes as any I knew in the military. They were draft dodgers, deserters and people willing to risk their lives and their futures because of their beliefs, but very few of them were Christians, and I began to realize that the world was made up of many kinds of people who saw things from different perspectives than I did. . . . What confused me most was the fact that I could see more Christlike behavior in many of them than in most of my previous friends, who called themselves Christians.

In 1972, Wayne used his savings to buy a used Thunderbird and drove to the Southwest. He was twenty-seven years old. Still hoping to find an authentic expression of his faith, he joined a Christian commune in Arizona but became disillusioned with the leaders. He wandered, knowing he was lost. He picked up a hitchhiker in Arizona and, as a favor, drove him to Iowa. Then he drove to Minneapolis to look up a fellow medic whom he had known briefly in the war; the man barely remembered him. Along the way, and more and more often, Wayne would perform some small kindness for a stranger. After a while, he recalls, his wanderings took on the quality and feeling of a guided journey, with each new encounter preparing his heart for the ultimate realization: that the love he needed could only come to him if he offered his own heart to all he met.

Wayne told me these stories so I could begin to know him, to understand his journey and the source of his compassion, and perhaps to prepare the way for me to reveal myself to him as well. He does this for many volunteers.

He also wanted to shed light on his impatience with public opinion and his profound distrust of authority. Like many of us try to do, he has arranged the incidents of his life into a coherent narrative, a legend of himself. Perhaps he also tells these stories in order to model a way we can contemplate our own journeys. In my time at Wat Opot I met a number of volunteers, and each of us left a part of our life behind and had come here seeking some lost piece of ourselves, whether we knew it or not. Sometimes we were permitted to stay on, not so much for what we could offer the children, but because I believe Wayne could sense that we needed space and time to find that missing fragment, or perhaps just needed to rest awhile before we continued our search. In allowing us this respite, Wayne does us a great kindness. First, because we need a pause, and second, because to be truly compassionate to the children we must learn to see ourselves clearly enough to accept our generosity into our own stubbornly troubled hearts.

Wayne is a large man. He has dark hair and a full beard, and the lightly freckled skin of someone of northern European ancestry who has spent many years in the sun. As director of Wat Opot, he has an uncanny ability to accomplish many things while not appearing to move very much, a fact that leads some eager new volunteers to imagine with some irritation that the director is not doing anything at all. He is slow, he is deliberate, and he manages his energy in such a way as to seem at times almost remote, yet Wayne has the capacity to be totally present.

For many years Wayne has worn only black, a choice he attributes to the vow of celibacy he took at a young age. People often question him about his vow, such a curious choice in our secular society, but it is not at all unusual in cultures that honor the channeling of sexual energy into spiritual practice. He tells several stories about it, the primary one being that he decided early on to dedicate his life to God and service, and never wanted to disappoint a wife or family or neglect those he had promised God to serve.

Wayne speaks enough Khmer to take care of the children and, he explains with a twinkle, he understands rather more than he lets on. But it is English-speaking visitors who provide a rare sounding board for his deepest thoughts. Until recently, he has lived mostly among foreigners. His available circle of Anglophone friends has consisted primarily of missionaries and Evangelical Christians, those same friends who began over time to become uncomfortable with his spiritual direction.

Often, late at night, I would find him at his computer composing an email to an old friend who had written an urgent letter expressing concern for Wayne's soul. These letters he receives are written with deep conviction, but although there was a time when Wayne might have written those very words himself, now, after years of contemplation, he tries to explain in his replies that the God he believes in would not deny Heaven to an innocent, unbaptized child, nor to people of compassion and good deeds whatever spiritual path they choose to follow. Sometimes his Christian friends describe the rivers of fire that await Wayne if he persists in believing that he can be saved by good works alone. Wayne believes that it is not enough to profess faith, but that when the Spirit enters into someone, good works will by their nature manifest.

I believe we should judge a tree by its fruit but they say that requires making a judgment and only God can judge.

To me, Salvation comes with compassion, and that can only come when we look at ourselves and realize that we are not perfect, that we are not good. To become compassionate there has to be an awareness of self, and so Christians would like to put that in a box: you must say these words, you must ask for forgiveness, you must accept Jesus as your Saviour. That's fine and good, but I want to see the works. If the Spirit enters into a person's life there has to be works, there must be works, and it must start immediately.

Wayne stands in two worlds, and that footing gives him both the insights and the burdens of binocular vision. Because he grew up in a conservative Christian community, he feels he has special insights that might allow him to open the minds of his old friends. So even after a long day with the children he will stay up late writing letters that try to break through, open a dialogue, spark something more vital than harangues, than threats of fire and brimstone.

During my second winter at Wat Opot, Wayne told me that he was disgusted with what was being done in the name of established religion and had stopped calling himself a Christian. He preferred to think of himself as a follower of Jesus. Rather than preaching, he told me, he aspires to embody his understanding of the life and message of Jesus, to follow the two commandments of the New Testament: to love God with all his heart and to love his neighbor. It is an enormously practical approach, rooted in works and manifestation. Wayne sets an example for the children and for all who come to Wat Opot with open hearts. He allows for the validity of other beliefs.

> I believe that the one called Buddha possessed a great deal of Universal Knowledge, as did other great thinkers, including the one called Jesus. It is not their teachings, however, that I follow . . . but the way in which they chose to live their daily lives. . . . For the true message of any Teacher is not their words . . . but how well they practice what they teach.

These days, Wayne tells me he doesn't talk much about his spiritual life.

> I believe that it is more important to live the life of Christ than to preach it, to help others develop their own Spiritual Life rather than forcing them to experience mine. My goal is to lead people to be

good, to lead goodly lives, to learn compassion for each other and to live in peace. If they become Christians, great. If they become great Buddhists, great. If they become great Muslims, fine. If they become great atheists I don't really care. If the improvement of life changes them I believe God is working in them.

During my first winter in Cambodia, Wayne received a letter from his own congregation in Michigan, an important source of support, informing him that they were withdrawing their funding for Wat Opot, effective immediately. They justified their boycott by saying that Wayne and his family were no longer technically members of their congregation, but to Wayne the real reason was obvious. He had made it clear to them that he did not consider it his job to convert the children to Christianity, and, as he once told me, "If God wants someone to be a Christian it will happen. That's not my department."

I was with Wayne the evening the news arrived, and he was disturbed not by his congregation's inability to accept his views but by their callousness. We wondered how people could be so dismissive of the traditions of other cultures. Was it not the same arrogant disrespect that led people to support America's attempts to impose its spiritual and political beliefs on the rest of the world? Here was Wayne, with a hundred children and adults depending on him for all their needs, and these good Christian folks had cut them off without any warning at all!

We had just returned from the crematorium, among the day's most peaceful moments. Inside the family room of the *pa cha,* surrounded by photos of our Wat Opot family, Wayne, a Christian, and I, a Jew, had sat quietly with the children, who are Buddhists. In the cool of evening we had sung a Christian hymn and chanted a Buddhist invocation, meditated together and offered incense to the souls of our parents. The children saw no discord in our worship. Had the children understood the doctrinal tug-of-war over their souls, they would have laughed at such adult foolishness.

Wayne and I both found it incomprehensible that people should punish the children for his evolving beliefs. He composed an email in which he thanked the church leaders for their past support and pointed out to them that, although he would now need to search urgently for new funding to feed his children, he could not and would not bring himself to beg them to reconsider, or even to allow him perhaps one month to find a new source of support. He told these church leaders he could not bear to imagine the closed-door meeting at which they would try every possible rationalization for turning him down.

From the beginning, Wayne and cofounder Vandin San envisioned Wat Opot as nonsectarian. Wayne was a Christian and Vandin a Buddhist, and the logo they designed depicts both the cross and the Buddhist flag. Wat Opot was to be open to all, whether believers or not, and pictures of Jesus and the Buddha hung together in the original hospice. Even today, although Wayne no longer considers himself a Christian, the evening ceremony in the crematorium still incorporates both Buddhist and Christian elements, as a way of emphasizing that all faiths are honored and welcome.

Still, some Christian visitors find it difficult not to proselytize. Wayne makes it clear that they are welcome to visit, but that out of deference to the Buddhist wat, which gave the community this land, and out of respect for the Buddhist majority of the residents, any efforts to convert anyone are strictly forbidden. When the hospice was filled with dying patients, before the advent of antiretroviral drugs, visitors would sometimes ask permission to sing hymns and pray over the sick. Wayne allowed this, but he once remarked to me how seldom he saw anyone in these groups try to comfort the patients, or even touch them.

Midway through my first season at Wat Opot I gave Wayne a collection of the poems of Rumi, the Sufi mystic who wrote, "There are hundreds of ways to kneel and kiss the ground." I knew reading was hard for Wayne. He was blind in one eye and still had a cataract in the other. But the next night I came to the office and found him sitting on his stool holding up the copy of Rumi a few inches from his "good" eye, the one with the cataract.

"Wayne," I said, "I'm glad to see you like Rumi."

Wayne looked up at me, his face aglow with amazement.

"Like him?" he answered. "I *am* him!"

I realized then how intellectually isolated Wayne's life at Wat Opot had been. He seemed to me like a figure in a myth, near blind, seeking truth but cut off from the companionship of literature or enlightened discourse. His cloistered existence had turned him inward, churned his soul and led him to insights that were firmly his own. For many years he lived surrounded by people who demeaned his search because it threatened their own beliefs. So, like the butter churn in the Hindu myth of the Ocean of Milk, the central metaphor of the story of the Kumbh Mela, Wayne continued to spin on his own axis, and, supported by a powerful faith, he churned up his own truth from the ocean of his soul.

For many years Wayne meditated alone, his eyes too weak to read, drawing from his memories of scripture and from lessons learned in battle or from caring for the sick and dying. Now, holding this copy of the poems of Rumi, he saw his own love reflected and affirmed in the words of a thirteenth-century Persian mystic who founded the order of whirling dervishes, and who composed his poems while turning "as the earth and the moon turn, circling what they love."

Like the demons tugging against the gods in the Hindu myth, straining against the doubts of his friends and colleagues clarified Wayne's understanding and strengthened his resolve, a struggle Wayne likens to "sharpening steel on steel." Over time it became clear to him that you can actually learn to understand the demons, even to love them. You can be grateful to them, moreover, for affording you the energizing push and pull that allows you to make spiritual progress. You can even admit that there are demons living in you. But you must have the discernment and fortitude never to turn your children over to them.

These days, Wayne and the children go to the temple every Saturday, where the monks give them instruction in Buddhism, and they share a weekly meditation.

One of the points I am trying to understand for myself and get across to the children is the purpose for our Saturday worship service. The chanting is the same each week and it is boring unless you realize the importance of the discipline the monks are teaching. The words have no meaning, the chant has no power, the Buddha is dead . . . but by doing the chanting we are gaining control of our mind, even if it is for one hour a week, and as we learn to control our life, the Buddha (Universal Knowledge) awakens within us and we begin to realize all that He did, and our life becomes meaningful as a result.

■ ■ ■ ■

In 1972, Wayne's postwar wanderings took him to Gallup, New Mexico, where he began visiting prisons with a missionary group. Ultimately that work grew into a counseling center for Navajo and Hopi youth, but he had no thought of that when he first arrived. He was just looking for somewhere to serve.

I worked on a construction crew for a few months and started going to the jail in Gallup on Sunday afternoons with some of the missionaries. They would pass out tracts and tell the men and boys in the jail that JESUS loved them but warned me not to give them my name or contact information. I thought that was strange. I met a lot of young people in the jail; most were Indian and some were only twelve years old. Curfew violation was the main reason for being in jail and some were there for two or three weeks before being released. I asked the public defender why they held them so long and he said it was because legally they could only release them to an adult. I asked if it could be any adult and he said yes.

Wayne started going to the jail every day to get the kids out. He would drive them home, sometimes all the way to the reservation, which took half a day. He spent less and less time working construction. He struggled with finances. His car broke down in a snowstorm and he had no money to repair it.

> I walked home in the blizzard because I had to pay my last $10.00 for the tow truck. I had no idea of how I would get the money for the repairs and no place to go. When I got to my room I collapsed on the bed and cried.
>
> In a dream state I awoke and saw Satan at the foot of my bed laughing at me. I struggled to get away but couldn't. I started shouting "JESUS help me!" and Satan disappeared. As I tried to clear my head I realized that I was being put to a test. That is when I said to GOD that if He would take care of my finances, I would give Him my life to be used as He saw fit.

Wayne's work with Native American boys in prison attracted the notice of the local newspaper. A church offered him a small building to start a counseling program for young people, and so with two friends he began the Ford Canyon Youth Center. Wayne had begun to receive his veterans' disability payments, and they all lived cheaply and did good work on a very low budget.

Wayne continued with the center until they applied for state funding, which required hiring a board of directors and licensed counselors. At that point he found that he was no longer considered qualified to run the program he had started because he did not have a professional degree. In the end he was fired for opposing the director over allocation of funds.

I have always opposed corruption and dishonesty and unfortunately in every program I have worked in it was there. When I found it, I confronted it, and in so doing had to pay the consequences, but it was always worth it because I knew in my heart it was the right thing to do.

My journey, however, had started and although times would get rough again, I never looked back.

In 1984, Wayne traveled to Honduras. He had wanted to return to Vietnam or Cambodia, but those countries were still closed to foreigners. Of his possible choices, he picked Honduras because he had read that it was one of the poorest countries in the Americas. With little more than his medic's bag he settled in Yocón, a small village four hours from the nearest hospital.

It was like the Wild West. Everybody carried guns and machetes. Often in the middle of the night someone would come banging on the door, to fetch me to remove a bullet or sew up a machete wound or amputate a limb nearly severed in a bar fight.

He also began to care for a group of homeless boys whose mothers had remarried and whose stepfathers did not want to raise another man's children. As some of the boys reached college age, Wayne rented an apartment for them in Tegucigalpa so they could attend university.

He bought a little house in the village, fenced the yard and planted grass and a garden. As he would years later at Wat Opot, Wayne created a beautiful and harmonious environment. Wayne told me that he used to complain that the boys would never do any work around the house. He had to clean and wash and pick up and do all the cooking himself. But a few years ago, on a trip to see his mother, Wayne was invited to visit some of the boys who had immigrated to the United States. They were all doing well and had immaculate homes. When Wayne joked with them that he wondered how they could be living so nicely when they had been such slobs, they answered that Wayne had set an example of how things should be, and when they were able to have homes of their own they remembered how they wanted to live. Sometimes when I watched Wayne working around Wat Opot, setting an example by doing work he could have asked others to do, I thought of this story and understood that he chooses to teach by example, and he takes a very long view.

Wayne honed his instincts in Honduras for twelve years. One morning he started out on a short trip to Tegucigalpa, but as he walked to the bus, people in the town approached him to say goodbye. "I'm only going for a day or two," he insisted, but the emotional farewells persisted. He was puzzled, but by the time the bus reached Tegus he realized that the townspeople were right. It was time for him to go. He went to the apartment where the boys were living near the university and drew up a contract dividing the money from the sale of the house in the village among the boys. They said goodbye, they wept, and then Wayne got on a plane and flew back to America.

For a few months in 1996, Wayne went to the Philippines to work with the indigenous Aeta people living around Mount Pinatubo. Then he returned to Vietnam and tried to start an aid project. He wanted to offer his atonement to the people of Vietnam, but he discovered that the government was not allowing Westerners to live in the villages. He might have administered a project from the city, but he saw many frustrated Western aid workers sitting for hours in bars in Ho Chi Minh City, the former Saigon, drinking beer, and he knew that would not suit his hands-on style. At last someone suggested he go to Cambodia, which had recently reopened to foreigners.

And so it happened that on Valentine's Day of 1997, Wayne found himself in Phnom Penh with one slender carry-on bag holding a change of trousers, a fresh shirt and two pairs of black underpants.

Noise. Filth. Piles of rubble. Homeless amputees, emaciated survivors carrying starving children on their shoulders. Phnom Penh was terrible in those days. Wayne rented a small apartment and began getting to know children who were living on the streets. The kids dropped by when they needed to feel safe or have a little something to eat and Wayne took care of them when they were ill. He had to register with the police, and sometimes they questioned the children as they left Wayne's house. Once the police were thoroughly convinced that he was not one of the sexual predators who descend on vulnerable countries in the aftermath of disasters, the patrolmen would drop over now and then for tea and a chat.

The children were living in slums, and, then as now, there was a lot of urban renewal going on. Wayne remembers a night when several children wanted to sleep over at his apartment.

> They were afraid that someone would set fire to their slum community. They told me bulldozers had moved in during the afternoon. The following morning fire broke out and burned the whole place down in minutes. The new Casino now sits near where their home used to be. Two young children who were trapped in their home died.

Wayne's first jobs in Cambodia were with the Catholic Office for Emergency Relief and Refugees (COERR), and for a small Phnom Penh orphanage. At COERR he met Vandin San, a quietly charismatic young Cambodian who was training monks to educate villagers in AIDS awareness, prevention and patient care. One day, Wayne remarked that he had seen scant evidence of an AIDS epidemic in Cambodia.

"Why would they tell you?" Vandin asked. "What do you have to offer them?" Because of the fear and stigmatization faced by people with AIDS, most kept their illness a secret. "Come," Vandin said. "I will show you AIDS in Cambodia."

Thus began a collaboration between an American Christian and a Cambodian Buddhist that was to evolve into Partners in Compassion, a nonsectarian organization dedicated to caring for people affected by HIV/AIDS. Building on five acres of land donated by a Buddhist pagoda named Wat Opot, Wayne and Vandin opened a small clinic and hospice for people dying of AIDS. When COERR left Cambodia they offered Wayne and Vandin some of their supplies and a little money that was left from their operations.

At first Wayne continued to live in his apartment in Phnom Penh and traveled once a week to the clinic, but soon the growing AIDS epidemic drew him to move full-time to the rural village of Sramouch He. Here he and Vandin trained Home Care teams consisting of monks and laypeople who traveled through villages teaching about AIDS and bringing medical care, food and emotional support.

Wayne was fortunate to have Vandin for a partner. As a Cambodian, Vandin moved easily in official circles. He worked well with local people and Buddhist monks, and knew far better than Wayne how to engage the many layers of government regulators and bureaucrats. Wayne once told me that Vandin might have been a government minister, but chose instead to work with people with AIDS.

One day over lunch Vandin told me about his life, and a little about the early history of Wat Opot. Vandin grew up in Cambodia, but during the Khmer Rouge regime he escaped with his parents to live in Vietnam. After the war he returned to Cambodia and took a job with COERR, and they trained him to work in their HIV program. Thailand had a big AIDS problem, and Vandin spoke Thai, so COERR was able to send him to workshops and conferences in Thailand.

In the early days, Wayne and Vandin worked side by side, caring for the sick and training the monks. Vandin told me that in the beginning the Ministry of Cults and Religion did not approve of the monks' participation in the AIDS training programs. Traditionally, it was not considered proper for monks to talk about sex. So Vandin lobbied district and provincial governors, who then petitioned the ministry to support the project.

As a young man, Vandin had hoped to become an architect, and he studied for two years before his money ran out. He designed and built the *pa cha,* Wat Opot's crematorium, and the beautiful central dining hall and kitchen, but over the years, as their

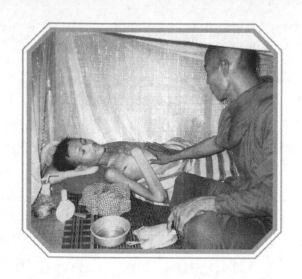

work grew more complex, Wayne and Vandin assumed different roles in the organization. Vandin's title is executive director of Partners in Compassion. He has nearly ninety staff members, and today his projects extend beyond the community and beyond HIV/AIDS.

Wayne tells me that he himself is "just an adviser, but my voice is heard and [Vandin and I] do most of the program planning together. My work responsibility is only to the Wat Opot community," a self-supporting project. "Vandin carries a much bigger responsibility than I do. He is well known and respected on a local and national level as an honest and very efficient leader. We are equal only in our respect for each other and our commitment to the needs of the

Cambodian people."

I asked Vandin about how the AIDS epidemic crossed into Cambodia. "Before the United Nations came," he told me, "Cambodia was mostly a closed society. Only a few people traveled. Before the war, the government inspected prostitutes weekly. AIDS in Cambodia came through Cambodians living on the Thai border, in refugee camps and from UN troops who came with UNTAC."

UNTAC was the United Nations Transitional Authority in Cambodia, the UN peacekeeping operation. They arrived in 1992 to replace the Vietnamese army that had beaten back the Khmer Rouge, and to help Cambodia prepare for elections. The UN forces came from many countries. By local standards their salaries were enormous. Cambodia was in ruins. Between the American bombings and the reign of the Khmer Rouge nearly a third of its population had perished. Those who remained did anything to survive.

UN troops went to Thailand for R&R and returned infected with HIV, and Cambodians say that Vietnamese camp followers also brought AIDS. The disease travels with armies and refugees and is still spread to the interior by truckers who are far from home and visit prostitutes along their routes. In the end UN troops carried AIDS home to their own countries as well.

The problem with this version of events, however, is that, according to the Cambodia National AIDS Authority, the country's first cases of HIV were reported in 1991, a year before UNTAC arrived. As it takes years for a patient to manifest symptoms, this suggests that the first infection in Cambodia preceded the arrival of United Nations forces. For most people, contracting HIV was a death sentence. Vandin recalled the cremations in the early days of Wat Opot: "Sometimes two or three patients, adults and children, died in a day."

Whatever the sources of the AIDS epidemic in Cambodia, the picture changed radically in 2003 when the Belgian branch of Médecins Sans Frontières opened their clinic in Takeo. Because Wayne and Vandin already had Home Care teams operating in the villages, MSF could rely on them to support their patients with food and information, and to provide patients with transportation to the clinic.

Because people with AIDS have weakened immune systems, they are more likely to develop full-blown tuberculosis as well. So it is crucial to ensure that patients and their families understand and follow the drug protocols. Missed doses can quickly breed drug-resistant strains of both AIDS and TB, so MSF requires that patients have sponsors, someone competent to supervise their care. Sometimes the Home Care team just helped to train the families, but in some homes there were greater challenges. In families that were too fearful of AIDS or simply too poor or unwilling to invest any effort in a child they were certain would die, it seemed better to take the children to live at Wat Opot.

One day Wayne showed me several looseleaf binders filled with patient histories dating from the early days of the community, long before antiretroviral drugs were available in Cambodia. Each page contained notes about the people Wayne and Vandin treated when they first opened the clinic and hospice. There were records of hundreds of patients, all of whom are now dead. I leafed through the pages, staring at snapshots of modest men and women, posed with their children in front of stilt houses. Sometimes there was also a cow, or a prized possession like a motorbike. Sometimes there was a baby. Wayne told me that many of those babies were infected and later died

of AIDS. It was the beginning of the epidemic in Cambodia, and these unfortunate people did not understand what was happening to them or why. The women were good wives and mothers. Perhaps the father, a hardworking farmer, had traveled to Phnom Penh and spent a little of his rice harvest money on a prostitute and brought the sickness back to his wife. The baby would have come before either of them knew they were infected. I contemplated this plague arriving in the wake of all the other horrors Cambodians had already suffered. It was all unspeakably sad.

Wayne and I talked about this sadness one afternoon. We were sitting at Chhang's Place, a small outdoor eating pavilion at Wat Opot named for Brang Chhang, a beloved little boy who had died in Wayne's arms, calling his name.

Just prior to our conversation Wayne had been writing a piece to send to his former congregation who had cut off funding because of his "heresy." I was helping him with proofreading. We had been talking about duality, and I had asked Wayne whether he believed that everything really was *of* God when there are terrible things like war and AIDS and children dying.

Wayne had replied, "Most people think of AIDS and say, 'Oh, that's terrible. How could you stand all the people dying?' But when you are in the middle of it, it is also beautiful. So it is not the caring and love that people are thinking about, only the sadness and pain."

Wayne had written,

I believe that GOD is Love. From a distance pain and suffering can appear to be acts of an unjust and unloving GOD but when one realizes that those who have suffered the greatest are often those who appreciate life the most, then one begins to understand that pain and suffering are actually gifts from a loving creator. Perhaps your question should be: Why does GOD allow some people to live in comfort?

For those who live in the greatest of comfort are often those who find no meaning in life.

I remembered how my own preconceptions of what Wat Opot would be like had vanished the moment I arrived. Yet the idea of seeing this terrible illness as a gift from a loving God unsettled me at first. Perhaps it is not so much a question of how we see the origin of events, but of how we receive them into our lives. As Holocaust survivor and psychiatrist Viktor Frankl wrote in *Man's Search for Meaning,* "We who lived in concentration camps can remember the men who walked through the huts comforting others, giving away their last piece of bread. They may have been few in number, but they offer sufficient proof that everything can be taken from a man but one thing: the last of the human freedoms — to choose one's attitude in any given set of circumstances, to choose one's own way." A few years later when I was diagnosed with cancer I would discover how seeming disasters can bring gifts I had not imagined possible, gifts that bring joy and love and open the heart. But sometimes I wonder, had I not spent this time with Wayne and the children, would my heart have been open enough to receive those gifts?

Wayne tries to instill in the children a sense of their own worth, that being HIV positive does not make them unlovable. He teaches them that they are beautiful, that AIDS is something they can live with, among the many afflictions of humankind, and still live lives full of aspiration, accomplishment and joy. And he strives to help them develop a sort of moxie to face their trials: "That is what I want, for them to be able to say, 'Ya, I got AIDS. So what? You got a big nose!' " As the first generation of children to grow up with AIDS, they will, he hopes, be the ones who go out and challenge the way the world sees them.

Wat Opot has a reputation among many other aid organizations as an unusually effective program run on very little funding, and it is a model for raising children infected with HIV and uninfected kids together, as a mutually supportive family. One day, Wayne was visited by a group of high-level program directors from a large international NGO.

One Vietnamese woman tearfully said to me as she left, "The work you are doing is so great, your children are so blessed to have you. Our HIV children in Vietnam are isolated from the rest of society. If only our leaders could see your program maybe they would change things. Hopefully some-day you will come and help us too."

A few years ago Wayne attended a UNICEF convention for AIDS workers and NGO staff. It was held in a fancy hotel in Thailand and dozens of organizations sent delegates. Each group was given three minutes for a presentation. Of course, no one stuck to three minutes, and the meeting ground on and on. The presentations were mostly about numbers: numbers of patients served, numbers of staff trainings held — bang for the buck.

When his turn finally came, Wayne showed a short film he had prepared called *Got AIDS?* Wayne made the film to show to HIV-positive children, to encourage them and to let them know they are not alone. It is a simple little film, about four minutes long, only a slideshow with captions and music. A boy and his little sister arrive at Wat Opot. "My little sister got AIDS," he is saying. "Our mother is sick and cannot take care for us. . . . So they sent us here." One by one, the children tell the brother and sister that they too have AIDS and are orphans. Other kids reassure them that "having AIDS is not a problem if you take

care of yourself, eat good food and take your medicines on time every day." Two of the older boys with AIDS then invite the newcomers to talk out their problems. And Miss Chan Tevy, as winning as ever, adds, "And if someone causes you a problem . . . come to me and I will teach you how to charm them." A group of kids is turning somersaults in a haystack: "The important thing is not to worry about your tomorrows, just enjoy all of your todays!" In the final frame it's the two new children again, looking relieved. The older brother is saying, "Thanks, guys! I got a feeling everything is going to be just fine."

When the film was over, a woman in the audience stood up and began shouting at Wayne.

"This is precisely the sort of thing we are trying to prevent. These children are orphans. They have no guardian to protect them. And you are exploiting and exposing the ones who have AIDS!"

Taken aback, Wayne said nothing until the moderator urged him to respond.

"First of all," he said, "these children have a guardian. I am their guardian. And I am trying to teach them that they do not have to be ashamed that they have AIDS. It seems to me that your work is with the people who think that AIDS is something to be ashamed of, the ones who would ostracize them. I am trying to teach my kids to live in this world, and to speak for other children with AIDS."

Wayne speaks sometimes about the problems facing NGOs. He takes for granted a certain amount of corruption and that officials everywhere expect to find a little money in their palm after they shake your hand. The bigger issue, as he sees it, is waste. While he does not expect everyone to live as he does, a lot more of the funds raised could go to useful projects rather than being spent on fancy offices and oversized SUVs or luxury sedans. He speaks ironically of "international conferences where delegates discuss world hunger while dining on filet mignon."

However, some of the greatest day-to-day waste results from duplication of effort and the lack of organizational coordination. Take, for instance, the many different AIDS education pamphlets distributed by NGOs in Cambodia. Each of the hundreds of organizations designs and prints its own version of the same material. Wayne points out that if they would just get together and design one pamphlet with a strong message, and share the costs of printing, they could save a lot of precious funds. "Then they would have a unified approach where they could really concentrate on printing a message that was needed for *this* country, in its *own* language, and it would work well," he explained.

Wayne is fond of telling visitors and new volunteers about the early days of Wat Opot. I listened to these stories for months, and the more I heard, the more aware I became that Wayne has a unique skill: the ability to create something from virtually nothing. Unlike many well-intentioned people who are stymied by a lack of funds or institutional backing, Wayne begins modestly, and he tries not to let his projects grow any bigger or more complex than he can manage. Perhaps he has large plans — for instance, he does speak of a master vision for Wat Opot — but he is perfectly happy to tinker along the way, enhancing, beautifying and bringing his corner of the world gradually closer to the image in his mind.

Unlike programs that depend on imported technology, Wayne tries to base his solutions on labor and materials that are readily available locally. That way, if villagers wish to adapt, emulate or replicate something he has done at Wat Opot, they will be able to do so for themselves.

Take clean water, for example. It is one thing to come into a village and tell people they ought to drink two gallons of clean water every day. But what if your drinking water comes from runoff from a rusty tin roof and must be stored for months in concrete jars during the dry season, until it turns green with algae? And what if firewood is so costly that people can hardly afford to cook their rice, let alone boil their drinking water?

So you need to understand what the people have to work with before you can come with suggestions of how they can change their life.

My advice for people who want to do some good would be to go into a village, live at the level of the local villagers in the same kind of environment that they have, and then make changes and let people say, "Hey, I like the way you're doing that. That's good," and then they can change too. This way you're doing things with products they already have, rather than importing stuff from America, solar panels and things that they have no access to.

This may seem a modest approach, but

how many ambitious foreign aid projects have foundered because after expensive imported technology is installed, poor countries cannot afford to buy parts or hire foreign technicians to maintain them?

Wayne's past experience has also made him wary of becoming dependent on large donors. Although Partners in Compassion, the original organization founded by Wayne and Vandin, receives money from the Global Fund and other philanthropic organizations, the Wat Opot Children's Community is an independent project, and draws its own support from many small donations and from money raised by volunteers. This way, Wayne hopes to avoid the scramble for funding that can happen when a large donor decides to pull up stakes. Sometimes, in the middle of a project, it becomes clear that it is not working as originally intended. If Wayne has accepted a grant, he has few options. He can continue to carry out the terms of the contract, or abandon the project, return the money and account for funds spent. Either way, he is jeopardizing his relationship with the donor and wasting energy and money.

Wayne is also keenly aware of the law of unintended consequences. One night he told me about an email he had received from a fund-raiser. A wealthy, anonymous donor had offered to build houses for families with AIDS. They were willing to donate five thousand dollars for each house, a fortune in a country where a farmer's wage averages a dollar a day. Wayne wrote back that in his opinion five-thousand-dollar houses would cause problems. It seemed clear to him that the donor, though generous and well intentioned, had no sense of what money could buy in Cambodia. Such a house would incite envy in the community and bring misfortune to its owner. As soon as construction was completed, every relative the family ever had, and many they did not know they had, would seek to move in with them, and before long someone would find a way to force the original family to move out. Or perhaps someone from the village, somebody with power, would remember a large unpaid debt and, again, the family would find itself homeless. Wayne suggested to the donor that he could build a perfectly adequate house for three hundred dollars. But the donor had other ideas and was never heard from again. Still, Wayne was convinced he had done the right thing.

Ever since his time working with Navajo and Hopi youth in New Mexico, Wayne has trusted that he will be given what he needs to live and do his work. Although Vandin is paid as codirector of Partners in Compassion, Wayne takes no salary and donates his military pension and Social Security check to the Wat Opot general fund. When money is scarce, Wayne's faith often leads him to search for a deeper message. He has occasionally had to borrow from his staff or even from the children's savings to buy food for the community. But hard times can bring people together, and they remind Wayne that his staff is also committed to the children's welfare. And for the children to pitch in from their modest savings accounts teaches them that they too can participate in taking care of a large family.

I am responsible for the daily needs of over 70 children and still live on that simple Faith that GOD will supply all that I need for each day . . . and He does! . . . I believe strongly that GOD wants all of us to be totally dependent on Him. Just as He delivered Manna one day at a time in the desert, He wants us to trust Him one day at a time with our livelihood, and the best way of showing Him that we really do trust Him is by living without a protection plan, content with whatever He gives us each day. I know this goes against everything the Western society teaches, yet I truly believe that if one wants to fully experience the miracle of GOD'S love in their life, it is the only way that it can be done.

God will Bless us in His own time and in His own way and I am content with that.

Still, there are moments when the strain begins to show. At the height of the Iraq War, he wrote,

It would be nice, for just one day, not to have to worry about feeding the 100 people who depend on me for their daily bread. It would be nice to know that all of my children will continue to get their medicine even after MSF pulls out. It would be great to have the resources on hand that would guarantee that all of the 1,000 families who now receive World Food Programme rice in our program will still be fed when we get dropped from the WFP in a few months. Dropped because they have run out of funds and the USA cannot pay its dues because it is too busy fighting a three-billion-dollar-a-week war against an enemy who spends far, far less and has far better results because the people of Iraq are not fools.

To a well-to-do American visitor who wrote that he had so many blessings in his life that "sometimes I think they are just sitting around in Heaven having some fun with 'Let's just see how much good stuff we can pile on this guy and watch how he reacts,' " Wayne replied that he hoped the man would take a closer look at what he considered a blessing,

because the life you are living can only be made possible by your country's continuance of its present course. Are your blessings truly from Heaven or are they really only the spoils of WAR! A war that is causing death and destruction to millions of people around the world, and is taking food out of the mouths of my children as well.

To me he added, "If ignorance was an illness I think I would have to perform Last Rites for a majority of the American people!"

■ ■ ■ ■

Over time I began to trust, as Wayne did, that things would work out. After Rebecca left Wat Opot and took her funding with her, I turned to my friends and neighbors in Maine. Wayne told me that their generous donations kept food on the table for most of that winter. So I was a little worried when I decided to return to Cambodia the next winter, concerned about who would take over the fund-raising. I wrote to Wayne with my fears, and characteristically he reassured me.

> I wouldn't worry about where the money will come from. I find it more enjoyable to look back on how you were given the financial baton for a while and now it will pass to others and that is what makes living on faith great. Watching how things work out without ever having to worry about it.

And he was right. Over time new volunteers came, and when they returned home they often raised money or recruited other volunteers. Like the branches of a great growing tree, even faraway friends and family did their part to support the people of

Wat Opot.

Yet money continued to be tight. Toward the end of my second visit, Wayne's mother became seriously ill. His family wrote that he should come home if he wanted to see her again. Airfare was fifteen hundred dollars, and Wayne had virtually no money. He wrote to his family that he could not make the trip unless they sent him a ticket. They agreed, but there was still not enough in the bank to buy food and pay the bills for the month he would be gone. He needed another thousand dollars. I considered donating enough to cover expenses, but something told me I shouldn't. I'm not sure why, but it did not seem this time to be my place to do that, and I walked around in a kind of agony as Wayne talked about canceling his trip. I checked in with myself again and again, but the answer was always, "No, not this time. It's not your job." Three days before his flight, Wayne went to Phnom Penh to cancel his ticket, but before he went to the travel agent he checked his bank balance one last time. Two donations, totaling exactly a thousand dollars, had just arrived.

We talked about this afterward, and I told Wayne how conflicted I had been.

"I'm glad you didn't do it," he said. "I need to believe in God, not in Gail."

"I wish I had your faith," I replied.

Wayne laughed, just a little exasperated, and said, "What more proof do you need?"

Wayne is the second oldest of a family with nine children, and the oldest boy. From his responsibilities as a child he learned how to be a leader. At first his parents would leave him alone with his younger siblings, and he tells of trying to get them to do chores. Usually this resulted in tantrums and chaos.

I don't remember how many times I had to remind them that when Daddy got home they were going to get theirs. I do know that by the time the car drove in I was really looking forward to them getting their butts spanked and sent to bed. What I wasn't prepared for was my father's reaction of disappointment after surveying the disaster area. "Wayne, I left you in charge. What happened?" I was speechless. How did I turn out to be the bad guy?

Within minutes, Mom had a work crew going and the same brats that defied my leadership were busy cleaning up the mess that they had created and although it didn't sink in right away, I began learning a valuable lesson:

Good leadership is not about being the

boss. It is about getting people you love to work alongside you.

A big part of leadership is learning to take responsibility for what happens on your watch, even if someone else is the cause of a problem. To threaten my brother and sisters with what would happen when Daddy got home was a sign of poor leadership on my part and to be looking forward to their punishment was not a sign of love and concern for them but a sign of weakness and self-centeredness on my part.

So when there is work to do, Wayne begins and the children immediately gather to help,

not because of threats or even rewards, but out of love and a sense that they are part of a family. And because Wayne makes it fun to do things together — even picking up the trash.

Wayne sometimes speaks of Wat Opot as the loving family he always wanted. Sometimes families of choice can offer a kind of love and acceptance we yearn for, but never manage to achieve, with our families of birth. And now Wayne has gone from being the big brother to being father to his many children, and to a few adults as well — both patients and volunteers. Wat Opot *is* very much a family, a place for the children to grow up, for all of us to grow in compassion and understanding, and when the children are old enough to leave, Wayne wants them to know that this is a place to which they can also come home again.

Wayne wrote this poem about Chay, a little boy, and his mother, Yeang Lab, a woman with AIDS who brought him to Wat Opot so she could die knowing there would be a family to love him.

INTO THE ARMS OF STRANGERS
Yeang Lab and Chay.
She would never let him
out of her sight
but day by day withdrew
more and more
into the shadows of his world . . .
watching with Motherly pride
yet with tears in her eyes,
as he won over the hearts of others,
and showered them
with the hugs and kisses
once meant for her alone.
She left his life quietly . . .
with no word of farewell,
requesting to be taken to the hospital

while he played in his new world.

20
VOLUNTEERS

Between the time I heard about Wat Opot and when I actually left for Cambodia, half a year passed. I've written in Chapter 10 about spending some of that time taking a course on teaching English as a second language. I didn't know any Cambodians, but I read up on their country and its history, and learned a few greetings in Khmer from the sweet couple who run a restaurant in my village in Maine. Unconsciously, though, I was stalling. The orphanage seemed just the *sort* of place I was looking for. A place *like* that. Hadn't I begged the universe for service? And hadn't the universe promptly offered me Wat Opot?

I didn't recognize it yet, but in those days Cambodia was consistently portrayed in the media as a terrifying place moving backward from an ancient glorious past to a hopeless future. Every story I read, every image I saw, perpetuated the stereotype of Cambodians as impoverished, emaciated or mutilated by land mines. Moreover, as an American living in a relatively safe community, I was afraid to expose myself to the risks I was convinced were rampant there. I longed to travel, to offer service to the poorest of the poor. But in Cambodia?

My own journey to Wat Opot was not unique. Most volunteers stumble through its gates by accident, or after a series of coincidences that some describe as "guided." Many people visit, but for those who stay on for a time, or who upon returning home are gradually engulfed by a powerful call to come back, Wat Opot is our own Brigadoon, a place that exists in a universe parallel to our normal lives.

People who hear about Wayne sometimes call him a hero or a saint, and he has joked that I paint too rosy a portrait of him. Perhaps so, but there is a lot of just plain labor involved in running Wat Opot. Time that might be better spent with the children is eaten up by record keeping, corresponding and fund-raising. Staff must be trained and managed. Volunteers arrive with more baggage than just their backpacks, and the kids know exactly how to push their buttons, so on top of everything else Wayne needs to be *our* counselor too. Year after year, it is a matter of persevering, remaining committed to the children, doing what's needed.

Even before they arrive, some visitors speak of wanting to leave their mark on Wat Opot, of "creating a lasting institution." Sometimes it sounds almost like a military occupation. Aid programs and AIDS and Cambodia itself are changing. Being nimble and able to adapt may be more to the point. Wayne was able to build a small, efficient program for a manageable number of people by devoting virtually round-the-clock attention. Wayne shows us what a person can do, and knowing his own limits and the limits of his program is part of his genius. He accepts his own finitude and has built only as much as he can keep alive and perhaps pass on to his successor. Although other people may learn from Wat Opot, Wayne's operation is on a small, very human scale.

Friends have said to me, "How *painful* to be with all those sick children." But a vital part of what we are doing as volunteers is simply bearing witness to it all — the joyous and the heartbreaking alike. As my friend Luke Powell wrote to me of photographing land mine victims in Afghanistan,

When little girls have told me how their

259

legs were blown off or old women told of losing large families and being left alone, when men talked of picking up the pieces of close friends, I find that I had no problem hearing what they said, bearing it. It is always so chillingly clear that one must stand hearing about whatever the other has endured and was brave enough to recount.

In truth, daily experience at Wat Opot is complex and chaotic. I wake up early in the morning and someone comes running up to me for a hug. Often there are several kids hanging off my arms on the way to breakfast. Most of the day it is kids playing, running in packs, sulking, hugging, laughing, dancing, studying, doing what children do. You play with them, pick them up when they cry, let them nap on your shoulder. It is easy to forget that some are HIV positive. If you give one kid a candy, word spreads, and suddenly you are besieged. It's totally normal in some ways, while at the same time it is exceptional. A child bursts into tears — who knows why? — and then you remember that these are very much special-needs kids. Or is it just a normal reaction, as might happen in any schoolyard where kids are testing the pecking order? In any case it is all happening so fast that interpretation must wait until later, because at the same time something else is happening. Some visitors slept last night on the porch, and the children have discovered — *air mattresses!* You cannot imagine how much fun thirty kids can have with a couple of air mattresses if you have not seen it for yourself, and there is simply no way to translate, "Don't bounce on that thing!" into Khmer. So you just sit back and enjoy them enjoying life.

Sometimes the energy of the children overwhelms and exhausts me, but what better time to appreciate their life force than when overcome by its passion? The great miracle of Wat Opot is how it heals the spirits of these children so that they can manifest that vibrant, living energy. And here I am, sitting in the middle of that chaos, folding an origami crane or cradling two sleeping children, smelling their hair.

I am tempted to philosophize about all this, but just as music is made of sounds and silences, and paintings are composed of colors and light and line, maybe helping comes from being available to whatever is happening, and not from theories. A lot is accomplished simply by showing up and being happy, and the more you go back the deeper you can go, like a funny old auntie who comes every year for the holidays.

Without question, volunteers with specific skills are badly needed. Nurses, teachers, someone to manage the crops and animals. Right before I visited in 2009, Wat Opot was hit by an outbreak of measles. At that time Wayne had only one volunteer, a French-English nurse named Caroline. One by one, thirty kids developed high fevers.

It would happen suddenly. A child would be playing and the next minute they would just go down, laid out where they fell. Wayne and Caroline picked them up and put them into bed and there they stayed, with no argument. These kids have been sick a lot in their lives; they know the drill.

Some volunteers concentrate on special projects or on activities for the kids: a water storage and filtration system, craft projects, a bus trip to the zoo or to a mountain waterfall. Deb, a nurse from Maine, bought mattresses for the children, and then sorted through all their clothes, got rid of the worst of them and took a pickup truck full of kids to the market to shop for new outfits. Caroline donated a commercial washing machine, a huge improvement over small children washing their own clothing. Other volunteers involve their friends and home communities in a variety of creative ways.

Wayne says he can tell a lot about a visitor by watching how the children respond to them. Do little ones circle warily, or hang back, or just make a beeline for their laps? Wayne trusts the children's intuition as he trusts his own.

Of all the volunteers I've known, I learned the most from Molly. When I first arrived at Wat Opot, Molly had already been there for a few months. She belonged to the same congregation back in the States that supported Rebecca's work at Wat Opot. Once a year Rebecca went home to America, and while she was there she gave talks at her church to raise donations for the children. Sitting in the audience, Molly listened raptly to Rebecca's stories. To Molly, Rebecca seemed like Mother Teresa, compassionate and saintly, and in Molly's mind the thought grew of journeying to Cambodia to offer service.

Molly was large and enthusiastic, a mass of curly red hair and goodwill and freckles. The children clung to her like iron filings to a magnet, and melted into her capacious warmth.

When she was younger, Molly had ridden with a motorcycle gang. Her body was a tattooed memorial of dates and names and crucifixes, all dedicated to dear friends who had died or been killed.

Recently she had been born again.

For Molly, volunteering offered a fresh start in a new place, free from the complications of her past. Here, she could love simply and be of service, and the kids would welcome and embrace her. From her friends and congregation she raised enough money for a ticket to Cambodia. It would be the first time Molly had ever been out of the United States.

From my first tentative days at Wat Opot Molly had helped me to settle into this large confusing family of children with unpronounceable names. I took photos of everyone, and she wrote the children's names on their pictures and told me what she knew about each one. And she knew a *lot.* In her short stay she had learned their names and ages and medical histories. She knew which adults were related to which children, which women were the paid caretakers of which orphans and how some children were related to each other. She knew their stories, and she explained to me some of what they had been through in their brief lives. But most of all she knew *them,* knew that Mister Sampeah always teased Miss Malis, knew that Mister Ouen had massaged his dying mother even when she cried out in pain, knew who woke up afraid in the middle of the night. Molly had the beginnings of a basic, working knowledge of Khmer, and she had many Cambodian friends. She spent her days with the women and children of Wat Opot. She nursed the very small and very ill Mister Wat when he was dying of AIDS, so that he could feel happy and loved in his final days. At night, like Wendy in Neverland, she visited each dormitory in turn to say a comforting goodnight to the children. Sometimes a quiet voice — I think it was Ouen's — would whisper back, "May God bless you."

Molly arrived at Wat Opot just as Wayne was leaving for a month to visit his family in America. Rebecca would be in charge. Taking care of both the children and adult patients was exhausting, and when her duties were over, Rebecca spent much of her time in her room. This left Molly on her own, and the children, missing Wayne, came to her for love and for reassurance that Wayne would return. To be more available to them, Molly moved her bed from Rebecca's apartment to the screened porch outside.

The Pagoda Boys also loved Molly. These were kids from the villages who had repeatedly gotten into trouble and were sent to live with the monks. Some had probably been abused, or had lived on the streets, and each had committed a series of petty crimes and, if unchecked, could eventually get themselves into serious trouble.

Nor did the monks treat them kindly. The boys were ragged and dirty, and they were always hungry. Molly seemed to be the only person who could reach their hearts. She gave them food and, when Rebecca was in Phnom Penh, let them visit with her on the porch. Sometimes they would creep by her room at dawn and whisper her awake through the screens. Once she even let Mister Da, the oldest boy, take a shower in the shared bathroom in the holiest of holies, Rebecca's apartment. She gave him shampoo and rinse and sweet-smelling bath gel, and a brush to scrub off the dirt, and a huge soft towel with Bible verses on it. When he emerged she gave him fresh clothes she had bought in the market, trimmed his hair and doused him with powder until he smelled like a flower garden. Mister Da gazed in the cracked mirror of Rebecca's armoire and was amazed.

A month after I arrived, Molly went back to America. Before she left she gave away everything she owned to the women and children of Wat Opot. To me, she confided that with all she had given away, she had never given anything to a monk, but we agreed that she had come some distance from believing that all Buddhists were going to Hell.

She hated to leave, and we all missed her terribly. Every evening after dinner, when the flight to Singapore headed south over Wat Opot, the children would point up to the sky and call out, "Molly go *Amérique!*" Then they would look sad and ask me whether she would ever return, and I would tell them that I knew she would try her best, because she loved them.

"Wayne," I asked one day, "how come Molly was such a natural with the kids, especially with the Pagoda Boys?"

Wayne grinned, and replied, "Molly *is* a Pagoda Boy."

It's Christmas Eve, my first at Wat Opot. Rebecca is having a small gathering on her porch. We share some lychee juice and a bottle of Bailey's Irish Cream. Here we sit, four seekers, none of us comfortable in our home cultures. Andrew, a young Australian, whose friends told him, "Why bother to travel, and anyway no need to stay very long." Rebecca, who admits that "Jesus is the one man who never betrayed me." Wayne, always the outsider, his new haircut making him look all the more like a penitent on a Dutch altarpiece. Me, feeling alone again amid all these people. Molly had the key. She never locked her door.

Sothy and his younger brother Rith are watching TV. Their mother recently died of AIDS, and they have come to live at Wat Opot. It's raining and cold tonight. Rith has fallen asleep beside his brother on the floor of the new dorm. Sothy moves Rith's hand under the blanket, tucks the blanket up around his neck, bundles him up to keep him warm. Such a brave little boy! Later he carries Rith to bed, and then, wearily, he comes and lays his head on my shoulder, and it's my turn to keep *him* warm.

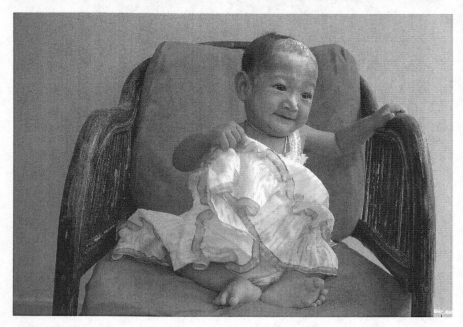

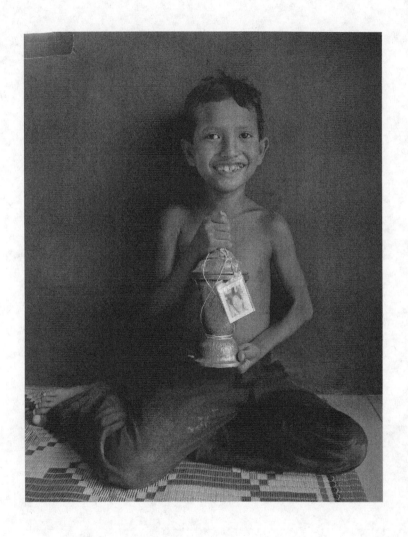

■ ■ ■ ■ ■

PART THREE:
CONFUSIONS

■ ■ ■ ■ ■

21
THE RAPTURE

It was December 2006. I was going back to Cambodia for the second time. I was excited; I missed everybody, all the children, Wayne, the adult patients who were part of the community. I'd been there for five months the first time, and it was wonderful, but it was hard. I never had children of my own, and I often laughed that being there would take care of my kid karma for lifetimes to come. But deep down I also felt that I wasn't very good at being with the children. Too often I would just do the wrong thing, or try too hard and muck things up. This time, I told myself, it would be different. I knew I must stop thinking that I had to *do* things or *teach* things. The first month I had been at Wat Opot I didn't know what I was supposed to be *doing*. As I've said, I wasn't good at teaching English, or teaching anything really, to scores of children ages four months to sixteen years old who wouldn't sit still. One day at supper I told Wayne I didn't know what I had done all day. I'd gotten up, eaten three meals, read a book, napped and hugged Miss Srey Mom. And Wayne thought for a moment and said, "A day when you hug one child is a good day."

I expected Wayne to meet me at the airport in Phnom Penh. But the day before I arrived I got an email that said, "Probably we'll be there to pick you up, but if not wait half an hour, and if we haven't come, you'll know we've been Raptured and you didn't get to go." Wayne called himself a Christian then. He used to be an Evangelical, but he'd come to believe that when he gets to Heaven there'll be Buddhists there, and other people of compassion. So his mission group labeled him a heretic and kicked him out because he wouldn't try to convert anybody. They said he was going straight to Hell and taking the children with him. I was only the second Jew Wayne had ever known, and he used to kid me about it, and I would kid him back about his celibacy. "You know, Wayne," I'd say, "you're going to get to Heaven and God is going to take one look at you and He's gonna say, 'Wayne! WHY?' "

Wayne told me he'd been celibate all his

life, and I got the feeling celibacy wasn't easy for him. He said he took his vow seriously, in part because he had met so many people along the way who didn't. Although he wasn't a minister he wore all black; even his jockey shorts were black. I used to see them drying on the line. He said that he wore black shorts because if he ever found himself giving in to temptation, if he ever got stripped down as far as his underwear, he'd see the black color and he'd remember his vow.

We had rabbits we were raising for food, but they wouldn't have babies. Do you know how hard that is to do — to get rabbits to *not* have babies? Wayne said someone had told him it was probably because the cage had a concrete floor. He said he couldn't see what difference *that* made. And I said, "Wayne, you've obviously never been on the bottom!"

I think Wayne secretly thought I was a loose woman, but he never said anything. That's the kind of relationship we had. I trusted Wayne, more than just about anyone I've ever met. In fact I made it a practice that any time I had a problem that I didn't want to talk to Wayne about I'd go right to his office and tell him about it. And he never disappointed me or made me feel stupid.

Wayne's a contemplative man, and usually he keeps his energy focused inward. But once, when I was leaving for America, I looked deep into his kind gray eyes and he looked back into mine, and all the way to Phnom Penh, every time I thought of Wayne's eyes I would find myself weeping, and realized I had been given a glimpse of something rare. I'd looked into the face of a truly good man.

It's afternoon now, and I'm playing on the bamboo bed with a bunch of children. We're wrestling and laughing and rolling around — a whole puppy pile of us. As Wayne walks by he says to me, "You know, some of the volunteers would be afraid to do what you're doing." And that makes me feel good.

And Dara is there. He's nine, a skinny kid with chopped-up short hair, like someone had shaved his head and his hair hadn't come to a consensus yet about how to grow back. And though he has two living parents — unlike most of the other kids, who are orphans — both of his parents have AIDS. Dara and I have been hanging out and getting to know each other, and he's been playing all afternoon with a toy car I brought from the States, when a four-year-old boy — the son of one of the Home Care staff —

comes over and starts crying, *"Lan! Lan!"* —
"Car! Car!" He wants to play with the car
too, and he's really annoying, and he won't
stop whining. I ask Dara to *please* give him
the car for a while and Dara shakes his head
no. And it's so hot today. And the little boy
is insistent, *"Lan! Lan!"* Dara is stubborn.
"Dara, you've had it all day," I say. "Just let
him play with it for a little while. Share it
with him, okay? It's good to share." I take
the car from his hands and give it to the
little boy, who grabs it and runs away with
it. Dara shoots me this look of pure loath-
ing and throws himself down on the bed
and starts to cry real tears. I can't understand what I've done that's so terrible. I try
to apologize, but he isn't having any of it,
won't even look at me. He just keeps wail-
ing and sobbing.

At dinner that night, I ask Wayne what I
did wrong, and he says, "Well, Dara's got it
rough at home. His father drinks and hits
him sometimes. So he makes friends with
you and he's having a great day and he's
opening up, and then you take his toy away
and give it to that spoiled little kid who gets
whatever he wants anyway."

"So what do I do now, Wayne? I think I've
lost him."

"It'll be okay."

"It's hard, Wayne. I'm used to being able to explain, to talk about things. But we don't have any words."

"Just do something nice for him. It'll be fine."

"At this point I don't know what 'nice' would look like. Dara won't even look at me."

"Don't worry. Just watch for a way. Just love him."

We're sitting in the walled garden out behind the kitchen having our dinner. A few of the kids come back to keep us company, and sure enough, there's Dara, pretending not to look at me. Normally he never comes back here. I pick out a nice big orange and walk over and offer it to him politely in the Cambodian manner, using two hands, and he gives me a great big smile and accepts it politely with both hands. Then he hugs me, and from then on I've got a buddy.

There's a little girl named Miss Punlok who recently came to Wat Opot. She's about two years old. She and her mother were found living on the streets of Phnom Penh, and were brought here because her mother was dying of AIDS. For two months, while her mother lay dying in the hospice, Miss Punlok never moved from the foot of her mother's bed. Punlok had a permanent look of horror and shock on her face, and although she could not have known what was happening, she could tell it wasn't good. Probably she had never known her mother when she had not been sick. What's more, we'll never know what her life was like on the streets. But even here with our family she was so terrified that no one could come near her without her bursting into tears and starting to scream at the top of her lungs. And peeing. After her mother died, I tried to make friends with her, but any time I came near, her eyes would get big as saucers and she'd start to scream. So I would always say, "Hello, Miss Punlok," when I saw her, and I learned just how much distance to keep between us so that she wouldn't cry. But I secretly hoped that sometime before I left for America I might see that little girl smile.

It's evening now, dusk, just after dinner, before the children get their meds and before the generator goes on for our two hours of electricity. I'm going to leave for America soon, for the second time, and I'm feeling sad, and watching everything and everyone carefully so I'll remember the details. We're all just sitting around and the

kids are playing jump rope with looped-
together rubber bands, and running back
and forth with pinwheels they've made out
of twigs and twisted green mango leaves.
I'm lying flat on my back on the still-warm
concrete near the bamboo benches, and
Mister Kosal walks by looking so cute, and
I grab him and lift him up over my head
and he throws his arms out and starts laughing and making airplane noises. Suddenly a
whole bunch of kids are crowding around
me and they all want to fly, and someone
points up to the sky; the evening flight from
Phnom Penh south to Singapore is just going way high overhead, and Miss Punthea
says, "Madame Gail go *Amérique*!" and I

say, "Not yet, sweetheart, not yet," and grab her under the arms and throw her up over my head. At first she's not quite sure about it and keeps her arms tight to her sides, but after a minute she starts laughing and spreads her arms wide and starts moving them up and down like a little bird.

Way off on the side I see Miss Punlok. She's standing all by herself, watching us with her serious face and wide eyes. But I see something new in her eyes. Maybe she's thinking, "Ooh, those kids are having a good time, I wish I could do that, but maybe I don't trust that *barang,* that foreign lady, but those kids are laughing and having so much fun, but I don't know about that *barang . . .*" I look over and am feeling so good I'm suddenly not afraid to take a chance. So I wave for her to come over, and she walks slowly, cautiously, never taking her eyes from my face. I take a deep breath and pray, "Please don't let me blow this," and catch her and up she goes! She throws her arms open wide and starts giggling and squealing and soaring, and it's amazing, because it's the first time anyone has seen Miss Punlok laugh and she doesn't even pee on me.

I put her down and she sits on the warm concrete and looks so happy, and I go on playing airplane with the other kids. Then I see Dara, off to one side, watching. He walks over to Miss Punlok and looks right at me, and then, WHACK!, he slaps her in the head with the palm of his hand.

Miss Punlok's face contorts, and she opens her mouth to start screaming. Inside me a voice is roaring, "Damn it, it was perfect. You've ruined everything!"

"Dara!" I yell out to him. "Why did you do that?" And he smacks her again. WHACK! Still looking straight at me. WHACK! Making sure I see him. WHACK! "Dara! Don't do that! She didn't do anything to you!" WHACK! "Dara!"

Before I know what I'm doing I jump up, and I'm tasting blood in my throat. I grab him by his solar plexus and then I have him pinned on the bench with one hand, and my fist is pulled back to punch him. He is staring at me and his eyes are wide and I am staring down at him, and everything stops, and the world goes away, and I'm yelling, "If I ever see you touch her again you'll be one sorry little motherfucker!"

In that moment I understand precisely how someone could beat a child, and that knowledge terrifies me.

Everyone has stopped moving and nobody's talking and they're all staring, waiting to see if I hit him. I stand over him for another minute, and slowly I lower my fist and release him, and he squirts away fast; all the energy drains out of me, and I retreat slowly toward Wayne's office.

"Wayne, I think maybe it's time for me to go home. I almost punched a kid just now." And I tell him what happened. "I'll be on the first plane home if you want."

Wayne sits there for a long moment, thinking slowly, like a black glacier. Finally he takes a breath and says, "Well, you didn't hit him. And Dara needs to learn that his actions have consequences and bring out reactions in other people. I think it will be okay. It might be a good thing. Don't be too hard on yourself."

But I'm still upset. Later that night I'm in my room talking with Papa Steve the Giant Tasmanian. Steve has a joyful, easy way with the kids, and he always seems to know the right thing to do. He's a compassionate listener and I just need to talk and try to figure out what happened. I'm still shaken by my anger. Suddenly, a tentative little tap; someone's at the door, and I open it. It's Dara. He looks so shy and timid — looks sort of how I'm feeling myself. And I know he's come to see if we're still friends.

"Pencil?" he says. He's always asking Wayne or me for something, a pencil, a comb, a Band-Aid. He comes to the office twenty times a night. Just to get some attention, just to be with us, just to be sure. And I open my arms and hold him, and he holds me back. And then I give him a pencil and a big stack of paper. And there's not enough of the same language between us to say what we're feeling, but I tell him anyway that I love him, and I know he's a wonderful artist, and I promise to pay more attention to him because I know he needs it, and to please, please bring me all his drawings to look at. And I give him an extra box of crayons, and he hugs me again and he runs off to draw pictures.

We who volunteer must constantly be aware of the enormous and unearned power we take on simply because we are part of an aid organization. This power can be very subtle, so subtle that we may not be aware of it unless someone points it out to us. When I told an American Buddhist friend in Phnom Penh about what had happened between myself and Dara, she pointed out that when Dara came to my room that night he really had no choice. He was a little boy who lived at the kindness of strangers. We housed and fed him, and he was dependent on us for sustenance and for love. He had behaved badly, but only because he was needy in a way he did not know how to express, and I had reacted in anger partly because of what he did, but also because of my own ego attachment to having things a certain way. But in our equation of power and need, a breakdown of relationship was so dire that it was he who had to come to me to mend fences.

We have this power from the moment we arrive, because we immediately join the hierarchy at a certain level, even though we have no clue what we are doing. Simply because we are Westerners we are treated differently, and with such power comes the responsibility to at least try to be conscious. We each bring emotional baggage to whatever we are doing, and the children are forgiving of our bumbling, in part because they have suffered greatly and are compassionate and have seen others like us and have probably survived much worse, and in part because they must be tolerant to stay in the good graces of strangers.

Still, even aware of these complications, we feel called to volunteer. We arrive, and when the first child looks into our eyes we fall in love from the center of our being.

Then we must do everything we can not to betray this small human being, to be aware of our contradictions and attempt the impossible, in all humility, to humbly love with pure compassion, in a way that allows the child and our self both the bewildering complexity of our natures, and our simple need to love and be loved in return.

22
"WE DID NOT KNOW YOU"

Some of the most important things that happen for me at Wat Opot come from stillness. When I am not busy *doing*, I have time to notice the child who needs a friend and I am free to focus my attention completely. I cherish the moments when just sitting still creates the occasion for a child to approach me for companionship or simply for comfort, the sort of comfort they might have sought from their own parents.

It's a hot afternoon. Once again I am trying to nap on the porch outside my bedroom. For three days and nights, *pleng ka,* traditional wedding songs, have been blaring from speakers in the village, speakers mounted high on poles and aimed in the four directions. Cambodians make a gift of their nuptial happiness — a gift of music to their neighbors. They scatter it broadly like seeds in a field. That is all well and good, but I haven't slept for days now, and I'm feeling poleaxed.

Miss Jorani approaches, softly. Usually she is remote and primped, in the manner of pretty thirteen-year-old girls the world over. But today she has a fever, and her illness makes her vulnerable. Her long brown hair falls uncombed in tangles about her face. She snuggles in beside me, but the relentless music and the intense heat of the Cambodian afternoon make it hard to sleep. After a while she rolls over and whispers, "I miss my parents."

Miss Jorani came here a few years ago with her older brother Pesei and their mother, who was dying. Their father had already died of AIDS. For a year the children took care of their mother. They washed her, fed her, massaged her as she wasted away. When I told Pesei I admired how they had cared for their dying mother, he stiffened. "I took care. Jorani played." He had been eleven then, Jorani only nine.

Jorani and I talk for a while. I tell her that my parents have also died, and that I miss them too. This is not a dramatic moment, unless you consider that a young girl who has never spoken to me about her life or her emotions decides it is safe to open herself, just a little.

She leaves for a moment and returns with a small collection of photographs — one of those paper folders with plastic sleeves for snapshots given away free by the photo-processing houses in Phnom Penh.

In one image, Jorani's father stands bare-chested before the stone ruins of Angkor Wat. He is slim and handsome, a man at ease, on vacation with his family. In another picture he wears a jacket and tie and check-ered pants and stands beside her mother. He looks young and self-conscious, a coun-try boy in city clothes. Her mother is smil-ing, pretty. She wears a red party dress. The field of tulips behind them is only a painted backdrop but they seem happy, secure, liv-ing a middle-class dream. Finally, there is a photo of Jorani with her brother, taken before the same unlikely landscape. Pesei's hand is draped about his little sister's shoulder, and they are dressed alike in im-maculately pressed white shorts and flow-ered tops, and red-and-white candy-cane socks. Jorani looks about four years old. I remember an almost identical photo of myself with my own older brother, taken around the same age.

Her final picture shows her father standing next to his truck. Did he contract AIDS from one of the many prostitutes who cater to men on the road? Was he infected even then? Had he carried the virus home to his wife?

The photos are faded and cracked, and already dark stains from the tape holding them together have begun to seep through the paper. In a few years these pictures too will be only memories.

We talk a little about our lives. Finally, I remark to Jorani that her English is much better than I remember from my first visit. "Have you been studying," I ask her, "or were you perhaps just a little shy before?" She answers, "We did not know you."

Rajana is eleven years old. He has two younger sisters. About a year ago his mother left Wat Opot with one of the male patients, leaving her three children behind. Recently she gave birth to another baby. Rajana rarely hears from her, and mostly it is only when she needs money and tries to pressure her children to give her what they have saved from their allowances. In my two seasons at Wat Opot, Rajana has rarely spoken to me. It is not that he doesn't like me; he is simply aloof. Wayne thinks he is missing his mother, and holding out hope that she will come back for him. To allow another mother figure to get close would be to admit he has given up hope.

Wayne tells me that Rajana asked him once whether we grow up to be like our fathers. Wayne asked him why he wanted to know. "Because my mother had three husbands, and none of them was any good." Wayne assures him that if he can ask such a question, he will not grow up to be a bad man.

One day, shortly before I am to leave for America the second time, I am having lunch with Wayne and a group of children. I mention that I hope to come back again, perhaps next year, and Rajana looks over at me and then remarks to Wayne, "I think Gail really loves children."

Later he presents me with a hundred-riel note, his ice cream money for the day. "Here," he says, handing it to me with both hands in the polite Khmer manner. "So you have *loy* when you go *Amérique*." In this small ceremony, I can see that Rajana has taken on the role of provider and protector. This boy has decided what kind of man he wants to be.

What is our real work here? We say we hope

the children will bond with us, but what are we actually offering them, we who come and go between worlds? More than anything I have done, or tried to teach them, or carried from America to give them, it is the mere act of returning here that has made a difference, that has let them know that I care enough about them to come back. The more times I return, the more the children will understand that they have truly become part of my life, that these quiet moments we share are the things we go through together, the things that make us a family.

23
"GO, AND SEE!"

Before I arrived in Cambodia most of my contact with Wayne had been through Wat Opot's nurse, Rebecca. She was now in the States for a few months, fund-raising and visiting family, and in several long phone conversations she tried to prepare me for life at Wat Opot.

Rebecca clearly loved the children, but her stories of their going to church on Sundays and praying nightly on their knees before bed seemed strikingly at odds with Wayne's description of Wat Opot as nonsectarian. I wondered how they could see their world so differently, but figured all would become clear in time.

Rebecca told me what clothes to bring — nothing sleeveless, out of deference to local sensibilities — and to be sure to bring as many bras as weeks I was planning to stay, because hers were always being stolen from the clothesline. Had I not lived in Africa and India and traveled for years in developing countries, her stories might have intimidated me. Illness and theft figured large in her accounts of life in Cambodia: heat, bad water, the risk of contracting malaria or rabies, of catching tuberculosis, which was more prevalent than AIDS. Even walking in the village could be perilous. Gangs of boys roamed the roads, ready to rob you — or worse! But when she spoke of being born again her voice changed. As she recounted her oft-told story, she would slip into a mesmerizing, rhythmic whisper, as if she were speaking to Someone Else, and you were only eavesdropping.

Over time, Rebecca told me about her life — going from darkness and sin to the light of her religious salvation. For her there was only one choice, between a loving Savior and "the one who walks the earth." I was fascinated. In my own world the choice between good and evil has never been so clearly drawn, but I listened and did not argue. I reasoned that Rebecca and Wayne must share the same basic beliefs, and I wanted to understand them both as well as I could before I arrived. After much wondering and second-guessing I recalled some simple advice applicable to situations like this: "Go, and see!" And then I went ahead with my plan for five months in Cambodia.

Rebecca was a brave woman who had also been a frontline nurse in the Vietnam War. She was short and compact and still wore her hair in a military razor cut. After the war she had worked in a pediatric ward in the States, so by the time she moved to Cambodia she was well trained to care for the growing number of children who would come to Wat Opot.

For six years Rebecca had helped Wayne build Wat Opot from a simple hospice to a home and community for a hundred people. She told me she missed the early days, when it was just the two of them and a handful of patients. There had been long talks at night after work, and a sense of companionship and mission. They brought children back from the villages, many of them orphaned, wasting away with the same new and terrifying disease that had killed their parents.

I have already told you about Miss Chan Tevy, found sewn into a hammock while her aunt worked in the fields. Other children lived in boxes in the open ground floor, barred from the upstairs living quarters, feared, fed minimally and left to waste away. Wayne and Rebecca took these children to Wat Opot and nursed them. Many died, but a few survived long enough for the anti-retroviral medicines that reached Cambodia to turn skeletal, hopeless pariahs back into children.

The first week at Wat Opot I stayed with Rebecca in the apartment she had built for herself. It was an L-shaped warren of beds and wardrobes, mementos and Bibles, and the still air inside was scented with moth-balls and mildew.

I soon discovered that Rebecca and Wayne had serious differences over the mission of Wat Opot. Although they shared a deep love for the children, over time it became more difficult for Rebecca to accept Wayne's refusal to proselytize. For Rebecca, bringing souls to Jesus was of overwhelming urgency, and their differences became more and more pronounced. Late into the night, sometimes for hours, Rebecca would tell me about Wayne's shortcomings, and how the children, who knew nothing of God, only Buddha, would lose all chance at Heaven. She was especially indignant about the tinsel-backed glass painting of the Buddha that hung in the hospice, right alongside a Renaissance-style image of Jesus praying in the Garden of Gethsemane.

"Jesus should be above," she insisted. "He is so much more."

Whenever Wayne went to Phnom Penh, Rebecca would move the picture of Jesus to a nail higher on the wall, above the Buddha, and when he returned Wayne would move it back. So it went.

One day I watched Rebecca caring for a woman on her deathbed. She held her and rocked her and sang her hymns. She implored her to be saved by uttering the name of Jesus before she died so she would be welcomed into Heaven. Rebecca sat astride her patient, gripped the dying woman's face in her hands and keened, "Jesus, *Jeeesus!*" But the next day, Rebecca chose not to attend the woman's funeral. As the monks prayed and chanted the Buddhist funeral service, there arose in the distance the sound of Rebecca's stereo, turned up to full volume, broadcasting Christian hymns over the entire campus, a wail of protest, a dirge for the soul of a woman she had failed to convert.

A few years later I would be reminded of Rebecca beseeching the dying woman. As a breast cancer patient, I encountered a radiation technician who lectured me about how my soul would be lost forever if I died without accepting Jesus Christ. I had just described my time in Cambodia, and she asked if I worked for a mission organization. Wat Opot, I had explained, was nondenominational and honored the Buddhist traditions of its residents.

"I could never support that," she snapped, and began a harangue that dismissed both Buddhism and my own Jewish heritage. Here I was, bald and weakened from months of chemo, my thoughts turning daily to my own mortality. Lying naked, exposed and furious, beneath the vast technology that this zealot commanded, I simply could not summon the strength to confront her. Staring upward, I remembered that woman dying of AIDS with Rebecca straddling her chest as she struggled for her final breaths, and thought, how desperate she must have been, and I felt terribly close to her.

Wayne explained that he and Rebecca had spent years disagreeing about how best to raise the children, whether they should go to church, what the proper attitude toward Buddhism should be and whether they should try to convert them to Christianity. But lately they both seemed exhausted by their endless debates. Although Wayne told me they had never been romantically involved, he and Rebecca sometimes seemed like an old married couple, fighting the same battle year after year until it ground them down into indifference. Wayne said he hoped that he and Rebecca could find a way to work well together again, but in the end she decided to leave Wat Opot to start her own health care project for women in the provinces.

In the beginning I was afraid to venture into the village. I had been subtly influenced by Rebecca's account of being threatened by a gang of bad boys and only saved by the little children who formed a phalanx, prepared to "fight to the death to protect" her. Her message was clear: Don't walk alone! I knew there had been some problems between Wat Opot and the villagers. Peering through the gates at the Wat Opot grounds, our poor neighbors might well feel envious. Ducks and chickens disappeared, and once somebody tried to butcher a mother pig, an audacious crime that was foiled when the sow herself sounded the alarm. But these were rare, stealthy acts, carried out on moonless nights. Wayne believed they were mostly the work of one small group of teenage troublemakers.

Gradually, as I became more confident, I began to explore the several nearby villages. I'll never know what happened to Rebecca and the children that day on the road, but whenever I walked outside the gates of Wat Opot I found only smiles and a warm welcome. As with so many other experiences in Cambodia, it is the graciousness of the people that is their offering to you — their pure, welcoming humanity.

But Rebecca's story made me wary at first, as did her insistence that I bring along a huge supply of brassieres. One look at the relative size of our endowments compared with those of the slender Khmer women convinced me that if anyone was stealing our bras it would not be for the usual purpose. I brought the matter up with Wayne and we speculated wildly about other possible uses for D-cups, but in all my time in Cambodia the only things that ever disappeared from my room were a small pocketknife and a large partially eaten cookie.

For months I lived happily at Wat Opot, sharing the children's lives but unsettled by the dissonance between Rebecca's stories and what my own eyes told me. From time to time she would issue an edict. Once, she attempted to ban children from visiting the hospice, which was mostly filled with adult patients, some of them their parents. Rebecca believed that the kids were catching illnesses there. Wayne thought this simplistic. Everywhere they went, he reasoned, the children were exposed to germs and viruses: at the village school, in the marketplace and even in their own dormitory, where they liked to sleep several to a bed. Wayne's own office was in the hospice, and he loved having the children run in and out freely. He felt it also did the patients' hearts good to have the children near them. Sometimes when Wayne sat with a patient, the smallest of the kids would hang on his chair or crawl up on his lap for a hug. Meanwhile, in Wayne's office, the older boys would be slicking down their hair and strutting before the mirror and dousing themselves liberally from his bottle of Chaps.

Another time, Rebecca proclaimed military discipline and *echai* (garbage) patrols. There would be no more allowances if children did not pick up the trash that blew around the compound. Wayne's approach? If he saw candy wrappers or other litter he would simply grab a large bag and begin picking it up himself, and before he knew it a couple dozen kids of all sizes would be laughing and playing and tumbling down the banks of the canal to fetch every last scrap. In the end, Wayne would hoist the littlest child and give him the thrill of emptying the big bag of trash into the fire pit. Wayne knew how to turn even housekeeping into a game, and the kids joined in because it was fun to do it together, and because they loved Wayne.

I began to examine whatever Rebecca told me very carefully, and to double-check everything with Wayne. Sometimes it was a story about one of the children, usually one promising older boy, someone I knew to be bright and diligent, searching for a way to get an education so he might take care of his younger sibling and have a good life. In Rebecca's stories he would be transformed into a little con artist, exploiting the sympathies of volunteers. Similarly, one of the mothers who went off to the city to try to open her own business was clearly leaving to work in a den of prostitution. Wayne explained that these were poor people, only a few years removed from one of the greatest of human catastrophes, and totally dependent on strangers for food and shelter. If a mother hoarded soap it was because there might not be any soap tomorrow. Or if she sold her rations in the village, maybe she was saving money toward a day when she might start a small business of her own and move back to an independent life. And if there were another national disaster and the NGO closed tomorrow, surely she would need a little money tucked away to feed her children.

Rebecca opened a small shop and began charging the residents for necessities like soap and toothpaste, dispensed from a padlocked cabinet. Rather than pay from the allowances they saved for snacks, some of the children stopped brushing their teeth. The patient in charge of the shop had trouble keeping track of the money and was accused of stealing. The little business sputtered soon enough, but not before there were lots of hard feelings.

When our youngest baby became very ill, Rebecca announced that the child was going to die and accused her caretakers of shaking her. This gave rise to bewilderment and doubt between the two sisters who watched over her, each knowing full well it was not she who had done anything wrong.

In fact no one had, and the little girl was fine again after receiving an IV drip. As babies do, she had become dehydrated from persistent diarrhea.

When I questioned her dark scenarios, Rebecca insisted she knew something because she had prayed about it and God had answered; there was no leeway for discussion. The door slammed shut.

Still, we shared some light moments. After a small New Year's Eve gathering at her apartment I stayed behind to help wash the dishes. Electrical storms had treated us all that evening to a magnificent light show. Approaching slowly from all sides, they unleashed at last a massive, thunderous rain. Three storm fronts collided right over our heads. Lightning burst everywhere at once.

Rebecca and I hunkered down, waiting for the barrage to end. She poured us two glasses of warm lychee juice and we sat on the floor playing Old Testament Bible Dominoes. Every time Rebecca won she would shout, "Yay, Christians!" and pump the air like a cheerleader. And whenever I beat her I would call out, "Jews win!" and we'd both laugh. It was so dumb and funny. I just wish we could have been the friends we both needed.

Things came to a head between us one night over the issue of sex education. Several of the Wat Opot girls had clearly come of age, and a few of the older boys had begun prettying themselves up and staying out late at dances in the village. Molly and I brought up the subject at lunch and Rebecca said she would ask one of the Khmer mothers to talk with the girls. That was good as far as it went, but we were concerned about the larger issues. I worried that the orphaned girls might be especially vulnerable to offers of intimacy. We needed to talk with all the children about self-image, disease and pregnancy, and Molly and I also thought we should talk about the happier aspects of healthy sex and relationships.

Most of the adults the children knew had been impacted by HIV/ AIDS. Wayne's lifelong celibacy complicated things, and we sensed it was difficult for him to accept that these children he still saw as babies were growing up. The children needed healthy role models, people who spoke Khmer.

Rebecca had said she would look for someone suitable to counsel the kids, but for a long time nothing happened. One evening, as Rebecca sat in her room playing computer solitaire, I asked her whether there had been any progress on a sex education program. She replied that she thought the children had too much on their plates at the moment, and she had found a Christian Khmer group whom she would invite when she thought the time was right.

"What will have to happen for the time to be right?" I asked, surprised that she wanted to put it off.

"It will happen when I say it will," she spat back.

"It's just that I'm worried that if we delay too long it will put some of the kids in jeopardy," I told her.

"They ought to know right from wrong by now," she stated, and flipped another card.

I felt a chill; it seemed as if she were waiting for a disaster to befall one of the children to help her make a point about sin, punishment and damnation. "Which of these children are you willing to sacrifice to make that point?" I demanded. She did not reply. We glared at each other for a moment, and Rebecca turned another card. I was shaking as I left her room. Through the air vent between our rooms I heard the gospel music begin. It grew louder and louder and played for the rest of the night and Rebecca sang along with it in her shrill vibrato.

■ ■ ■ ■

In Cambodia millions of land mines lie partially buried. Decades after the war people still trigger the shocking loss of their own limbs, or lives, nearly every day. The Khmer Rouge had controlled the area around Wat Opot so it was never mined, though now and then the children unearthed a stray bullet. Hyperbole aside, sometimes living and working with Rebecca felt nearly as scary as knowingly walking through a minefield.

Maybe it was my fault for not understanding that faith does not like questions, and that my badgering signaled to Rebecca that I did not respect her beliefs. But it was not her beliefs I objected to; it was her hiding behind what she claimed God had whispered to her personally to avoid having to explain her opinions and actions to anyone else. After all, why *should* she have to justify anything at all to someone like me, someone with no commitment to Wat Opot and so little to offer? On the other hand, maybe she was just now realizing that Wat Opot was changing, and she would never again know the clarity of mission and intimacy she and Wayne had shared in the early days.

I'm sure Rebecca was disappointed that I couldn't be the friend she needed, and that I didn't respond to her witnessing, didn't accept Jesus as my Savior. If I could have made her understand how deeply I did respect the work she had done, things might have been different between us. She had worked exhausting hours, been mother and grandmother to hundreds of children, only to lose many of them to this terrible disease, to suffer through their dying and still to care for the ones who survived, to love and to touch those whom family and society had abandoned.

Reading over my journal from that first winter at Wat Opot, I find the story of Rebecca woven through my impressions of this new world of AIDS and children and Cambodia. Many times I recorded some puzzling event, trying to understand what I was seeing. I wondered why Wayne allowed someone who undermined him and caused ill will to remain at Wat Opot, but as I grew to know him better I began to understand that his reasons were both deeply compassionate and quite human.

The evening after Rebecca and I argued about the sex ed course, I asked Wayne whether my staying at Wat Opot was causing problems. Might it be better if I returned to America? I had hoped he might try to dissuade me, but his response was frank and practical. He explained calmly that except for himself, Rebecca was the only other fixed point at Wat Opot. Whatever their issues, he knew she would get out of bed at three in the morning to care for a dying patient, and once every few weeks, when he went off to Phnom Penh for an uninterrupted night's sleep, he knew he could leave the children in her care. She was a capable nurse, and there was no one else willing to make the commitment.

Rebecca was also a determined fundraiser, and Wayne was responsible for feeding a hundred people every day. Rebecca wrote glowing newsletters that she sent to her congregation back home, and through them she raised about half the budget of Wat Opot. But Wayne told me that she kept the money from her supporters in a separate fund under her own control, and if she disagreed with him about a project, or if he did not consult her, she withheld the money. Wayne worried about how he would feed the children if Rebecca left. His own supporters, who up until that time had mostly been Evangelical Christians, had begun labeling him a heretic, and many had withdrawn their support.

Wayne also worried about Rebecca, as a friend about a friend. He was concerned about her state of mind and what would happen to her if she left Wat Opot. Wayne and Rebecca had worked side by side for years. They shared a rich history, and I am sure they had many unspoken understandings, as old friends always do. Wayne hoped that sooner or later Rebecca would become less riveted to the idea that only Christians can enter Heaven.

As an outsider I was troubled by the incredible amount of energy we all spent worrying about Rebecca, complaining about or ignoring her unpredictable reactions, apologizing to Buddhist visitors when she refused to leave her apartment to greet them. All this took a palpable toll on Wayne's energy, and her control over the purse strings made him feel vulnerable and angry. And that anger, unexpressed, mutated into depression. I observed to Wayne that even if Rebecca left, even if he lost her help and her funding as well, the amount of energy that would be released would more than make up for whatever she was providing, and he would find new and creative ways to take care of the needs of the community. This was to prove true, though it would take a little time and precipitate a major shift in the mission of Wat Opot.

Rebecca began to go away frequently to work with her missionary organization. A weekend would turn into a week, and she would return, only to leave again in a week or two. Clearly she was feeling called in a new direction. Finally she decided to leave. The first months were hard on Wayne. Rebecca sent a newsletter to her congregation decrying Wayne's lack of commitment to taking the children to church on Sundays. She said that although her decision to leave Wat Opot was painful, she would still be supporting the children through a "secret fund," given to one of the employees behind Wayne's back, to buy gas for the truck so the children could go to church. I received a copy of this email when I was back in the States. It seemed to me a profound betrayal of Wayne and the children, a way of telling the people who had been feeding them for many years to abandon them. I did not want Wayne to be hurt, so I kept the email to myself. Instead I set about doing my own fund-raising, at least until Wayne found some new resources.

After Rebecca left, Wayne took on the grueling job of tending to the needs of the entire community. For the first few months he hardly slept. Often he would spend the entire night in the hospice with a sick patient, followed by a full day of taking care of the children. There was the twice-daily regimen of medication, the administrative duties and the moment-to-moment injuries, illnesses and personal crises of so many people.

The situation came to a head when Wayne received a call from Médecins Sans Frontières asking him to take on yet another very ill adult patient who would need intensive care. Already exhausted, Wayne felt himself nearing collapse. He prayed late into the night, asking God why He was giving him more than he felt he could handle.

The next morning, Wayne announced to the long-term patients that he was closing the hospice. The hospital in Takeo had recently opened an AIDS unit, and anyone who wished to be taken care of would be transported there. For the rest, he offered an option: get out of bed, take your meals in the kitchen with everyone else, begin participating in the community, and you can stay. To a person, they got out of bed and stopped living the lives of the ill. When I returned to Wat Opot the second winter I was amazed to see the same people who had been languishing on hospital cots now up taking care of children and looking much happier than I had seen them before. Wayne and the children seemed far more relaxed. A new chapter had begun.

24
HUNTING FROGS, HUNTING RATS

Viewed from the ruins of the ancient stone temple atop Phnom Chisor, the rice fields fan out to the horizon. At the first rain, even before the fields are planted, ripe grain fallen from last season's harvest takes root and begins to sprout. It grows up through the water, and for a week or so the little fields shine in a dozen shades of new green. The fields are separated by narrow paths of sun-baked clay that run like mullions through a stained glass window. Here and there a line of bushes or scrub or palm trees forms a windbreak.

Soon white humpbacked cattle, who have foraged hungrily for months in the dry, dun-colored paddies, will go to work turning the soil, and rice planting will begin. Months later, if the gods be kind, the golden harvest will be piled in mounds higher than your head, and people will labor all day at threshing and winnowing.

In spite of the exhausting work — sowing seeds, transplanting seedlings and bringing in the harvest — many people in Cambodia do not have enough to eat. In our region, with its fickle rainfall, fields rarely yield more than one rice crop per year, and with the changing climate even that single crop may be unreliable. During the war years the Khmer Rouge force-marched much of the population to slave labor camps, and long-held land titles were lost. As a result it has become difficult, often impossible, for many farmers to reestablish their legitimate claims to family land. Many who owned their own land before the war must now toil in other people's fields for a pittance, and even the strong are often undernourished. To make life even more difficult, open land, where people once foraged for edible wild plants or small game, is becoming privatized, cultivated or fenced, blocking access to vital food sources. For people with AIDS or tuberculosis, who may be too ill to work in the fields, there is never enough to eat.

Once a month a big white van from the United Nations World Food Programme delivers rice for the Wat Opot family and for families affected by tuberculosis and HIV/AIDS in the neighboring villages. Early in the morning workmen begin offloading sacks of rice. Villagers arrive by bicycle and motorbike, then wait for the Home Care staff to check their papers and give them their monthly ration. They chat and visit, or sit patiently on the ground or on piles of rice bags. Women come with plastic market baskets, their heads wrapped in checkered *kramah.* An elderly layman from the temple wearing a coarse white shirt greets me courteously, speaking the French of Indochine. Little girls, all dressed up for the occasion with red lipstick and painted fingernails, accompany their *yei.*

Soon vendors arrive, drawn by the crowd. One man sells steamed Chinese buns from a glass case on wheels. Another makes ice cream sandwiches — tutti-frutti cut into triangles and served on the Khmer version of French bread. Brightly colored fruit ices frozen into the bottoms of recycled plastic juice bottles sell for a penny. The children pick at them with tiny spoons.

A distinguished older man from the village opens one of the sacks, removes a palm full of rice and separates the grains with his thumb. He examines them myopically, sinks his face into his palm, inhales deeply and

313

nods his approval. The rice smells fresh.

In addition to rice, people receive rations of cooking oil and salt. Once, I was told, there was canned fish as well, but it became too expensive, or perhaps the donor country stopped sending it. Palm oil — the flag on the white tins tells us it is a gift from the people of Japan — is poured into small plastic bags or soda bottles through a funnel improvised from a rolled banana leaf. Moto drivers with their trademark baseball caps lounge about smoking cigarettes, waiting to sling the heavy sacks of rice over the back of their bikes. By noon, each groaning motorbike will carry two or three extra people with all their provisions home to the village.

On Rice Day, food was distributed to hundreds of local families. In other scenes like this all over Cambodia, thousands of people received food from the World Food Programme.

In 2006 and 2007, a massive shortfall forced the World Food Programme to reduce and then suspend food deliveries to more than a million Cambodians. For the Wat Opot family alone, this meant diverting scarce funds to buy rice to feed a hundred people a day. But our local problem barely scratches the surface. Some village children who had been drawn to attend school by the promise of nutritious meals stopped coming. People receiving drug therapy for AIDS or TB lost the extra nutrition they needed to grow strong. More insidiously, some patients with TB, no longer lured by the incentive of free food, did not come for medicine to complete their arduous six-month course of therapy, and thus began developing drug-resistant strains of tuberculosis. Treating multiple-drug-resistant TB is enormously expensive, and its spread threatens public health worldwide.

Except for a few such pauses, the World Food Programme delivered rice to Wat Opot and its neighbors for ten years. But in December of 2012 the program was suspended. At that time, the Wat Opot Children's Community decided to dedicate $250 a month of its own money to buy food for ten of the poorest families in the village.

During hungry times the children of Wat Opot turn to hunting to supplement their diets. From the first, I was impressed by the children's knowledge of their environment. English and math they may know only a little, and their education in their own history may be scant, but even the youngest are expert foragers. They know everything that is edible on their five acres and beyond, where to find it and when it comes into season. Children munch on grubs from the boles of trees. Bushes provide berries. There are tamarind trees and mangoes, the latter sliced into small woody shingles and eaten green, dredged in *ombeul,* a mixture of salt, sugar and hot chili pepper. Tall children boost little ones into the branches of trees to pluck a certain white flower whose stamen drips sweet nectar. At night, boys hunt frogs with flashlights and bamboo cages. They cast nets for catfish and minnows in the ponds and roast them over a fire on a metal grill. Older boys are expert marksmen, bringing down small birds and plump rice rats with their slingshots. The children's people are farmers, and fishing and foraging are part of their heritage. Their families had survived off the land whenever crops failed, and during the unspeakable hardships of the Khmer Rouge years. This knowhow is still passed from parent to child and, when there are no parents, from child to child. Everyone knows that the season after next may bring hard times and hunger.

Sometimes on the day rice is delivered Wayne has a party at Wat Opot for all the local children affected by HIV/AIDS. These can be children who are themselves HIV positive, or children whose family members are infected. While their families wait to receive their rice, the children gather at the dining hall at Wat Opot. There are greetings and snacks and Wayne gives them a few toiletries — shampoo, soap and toothpaste, and a new toothbrush. Sometimes there is a craft project, and always there are games and competitions: sack races, break dancing, singing contests and balloon blowing, with the children staring crosseyed as their balloons puff larger and larger until they pop or tear loose and rocket around the room amid cheers and laughter. But the favorite is always the dance contest. Five children at a time onstage, with the audience voting for semifinalists and then finalists and, finally, a champion. Almost inevitably it is the littlest child who charms us all. Standing onstage like a frightened field mouse, she is trying shyly to smile through a smear of red lipstick, twisting her hips to and fro, her arms held tightly to her sides, her hands turned out, fingers curled upward and fluttering like tiny fins. She moves sometimes with the beat but more often not, but with such innocence and optimism that the children burst into applause and such

317

hoots of delight that there is no doubt who is their beloved, and she easily carries off the grand prize of a few hundred riel.

One night after my first Rice Day, Wayne and I were working late in the office. He had finished giving out medicines at the evening clinic and was straightening the cabinets. We had managed to connect to the Internet for the first time in days, and I was writing an email to a dear friend in Paris, Luke Powell. Luke was important to me. His photography in the minefields and refugee camps of Afghanistan had inspired me to search for a way to offer service in the world. He was my mentor and my touchstone. I wanted to impress him, to show that I was learning the ins and outs of the NGO scene. I had already sent him newsletters about AIDS and the children, and today I had written him about the party, the balloons and the dancing. But in tonight's email perhaps some titillation . . . or even a whisper of scandal? While most of the rice we received was fine, now and then some of it tasted off, a little ammoniated. It might have been the rice itself, how it was stored, or perhaps the water in our own cisterns. Although this was 2006, I had noticed that the rice bags that day were dated 2001 and 2002. I wondered whether the rice retained its nutrients after four or five years in storage. The kids devoured mountains of rice without complaint. They were active and growing, ever famished. But to me the rice was sometimes inedible. I decided to play up the drama:

The truck came today with rice rations for the community from the World Food Programme. Two hundred bags of . . .

"Hey, Wayne," I called out. Socheat had just run into the clinic with a bloody knee, and Wayne was busy cleaning and bandaging as Socheat bawled. "How much do those bags of rice weigh, anyhow?"

"I dunno, maybe fifty kilos."

. . . Two hundred bags of fifty kilos each. People come in the morning for the distribution. I noticed the dates on the bags and asked Wayne how long rice is good for. He said about a year. The dates were from 2001 and 2002. Somewhere along the way it appears the fresh rice that is sent over is switched for old stock, and someone gets to sell the good stuff. Can't prove it, though. Some of the rice we get is decidedly second-rate and tastes ammoniated. It's hard to tell where the corruption starts exactly, whether it is in the purchasing or along the way. Saudi Arabia and Japan probably have good intent, but what sometimes arrives is a different story.

Did you see anything like this in Afghanistan?

I pushed Send and went on to other things.

The next evening there were two emails in my box. The first was from Luke:

I wrote to several people in the World Food Programme, in the publicity office in Rome, in WFP Japan, and the director for Cambodia; I forwarded them your letter. If nobody turns up to investigate then you can assume it to be common practice.

"Oh shit!" I said aloud. Wayne looked up at me from across the desk.

The second letter was from the head of the World Food Programme in Cambodia.

Your friend . . . has transmitted your message about the poor quality of rice . . . delivered to your NGO last Thursday. We are very sensitive about possible issues of diversion and would like to know more about the problem.

Would it be possible to have a meeting with you? Could we visit the area and meet with the beneficiaries? Would you have a sample of the rice that was delivered/distributed?

"Wayne," I said quietly. "I have something to tell you."

Wayne once told me that he had been fired from every job he ever held. Generally he was fired because he told the truth about something. He is a man of principle who perpetually holds out hope for the honesty of others, but he has frequently been disappointed. Over time, this has produced in him a tendency to hope for the best but to keep his head down, to take care of Wat Opot and to pray that the good he does will erect a shield between the children and the whims and political storms swirling around them.

I pulled my stool up to Wayne's, sat facing him, almost knee to knee, and confessed everything. He was very quiet. He looked like a man watching his life flash before his eyes. "Wayne," I said, "I will write a mea culpa. Anything you need." I felt panicked. For the third time since I had come to Wat Opot I offered to be on the next plane to

America. "You can tell them you threw me out." All I could think of was a thousand families starving, our children hungry, denied their rice because my foolish attempt to impress a friend had brought down the wrath of donor nations of the very program that was feeding us. It came home to me in that moment how incredibly fragile all this was; everything Wayne had built here, starting with five ragged acres and creating a small paradise of mango trees and ponds and children kept safe and loved. Everything could be demolished by a moment's thoughtlessness. *My* thoughtlessness.

Finally Wayne said, simply, "Well, let's see what happens. Maybe it will work out for the best." If I had not already loved Wayne and trusted his power of restraint before that moment, I did so now. He managed a twinkling smile and added, "I never figured you for the type who'd start an international incident."

I wrote to the director of the World Food Programme in Phnom Penh, backpedaling hard:

I wrote a personal note to a friend containing speculations not based on hard fact, and certainly not meant for publication. I had some questions when I saw the dates

2001 and 2002 on some of the rice bags, and wondered whether this was normal and healthy practice, and whether Luke had run into anything similar in his extensive field experience. But I certainly did not mean to accuse anybody of wrongdoing . . . mostly to shed light on a puzzling situation.

I aired my fears to Luke, practically shouting through the email that I could not believe he would forward something written privately without asking permission.

"Gail, Honey," he wrote back. Luke had never called me anything remotely resembling "Honey" before. I could feel him patting me on the head like a foolish child.

Nobody with any sense is ever going to criticize you for caring enough to write to me. I was the one who wrote to WFP, and I did so because I know that they want to know about such things. It is open lines of communication between the field and the main offices that keeps help flowing and corruption from taking over, as it is always THE primary threat to operations among the desperately poor. You are not going to anger WFP by writing to a friend who has worked for them about a concern, even if it turns out to be nothing. Most of the people back in the offices and positions of leadership have worked in the field too, and the purpose of their jobs is to deliver clean, fresh rice to places like Wat Opot. You are part of a huge team with WFP and a respected member, since you are the one actually serving rice to orphans in Cambodia. My short [photography] contract with them did not make me an expert, and I spent little time in the office, but when I got notes back immediately from them thanking me for passing your message along, I'm pretty sure they meant it.

Wayne and I hoped they did.

I had a bad night and woke up the next day with a fever. I skipped breakfast, threw up a dose of doxycycline I had taken on an empty stomach, and was hanging up my laundry on the line outside my room when an immaculate white Toyota Land Cruiser drove through the gate. It was blisteringly hot, the dry season that follows the harvest. It had not rained in weeks, and the only thing I could think of in that moment was how this World Food Programme vehicle — and nothing this large, gleaming and official could be called simply a car — had managed to make it all the way from Phnom Penh without picking up a mote of dust. The United Nations official, similarly immaculate in his pressed khaki suit, was the largest Cambodian I had ever seen. Massive. Think football lineman. Think Refrigerator Perry.

As this tidy apparition descended from the SUV's plush air-conditioned interior, my feverish brain was convinced I'd discovered where all the good rice had gone. Worst of all, he was smiling. The Khmer smile is famous. It graces the great stone heads of the Angkor temples, and beams from the faces of compassionate golden Buddhas. One discovers that Cambodians smile for all sorts of reasons, not all of them friendly. It is considered impolite if not deranged to strike aggressive poses. So when they are upset or embarrassed, or sometimes when they are angry, Cambodians smile.

I made a running dive for my room. Wayne should be the one, I rationalized, to make first contact. Hadn't I done enough damage already? He would call for me when he was ready.

A few minutes later one of the children conveyed the summons. Wayne had taken the official not to his cramped office, but to the conference room. It seemed a wise strategy, to discuss the situation in a room decorated with photographs of all the wonderful projects Wat Opot had done for the children and the community.

For the first twenty minutes we exchanged courtesies and tried to decipher each other's accents. Our visitor's English, while good, was imprecise. I kept trying to explain that it had all happened because Luke, my conscientious friend, had forwarded a bit of gossip meant for his eyes only. But our visitor seemed uninterested in this. He was mysteriously fixated, for reasons I could not fathom, on the concept of fifty-kilo bags of rice. As we talked, his voice grew tighter, the pitch perceptibly higher. He spoke rapidly, and he never stopped smiling. Finally he made us understand that our rice had been shipped in bags weighing thirty kilos, and that if the bags we received truly weighed fifty kilos, this fact alone was proof that the rice had been switched. As he himself was the shipping coordinator, his own job was on the line. Did we, he dared wonder, have any of the bags left from that shipment? After all the confusion, it came down to a simple matter of visiting the storage shed so he could tear off a few tags to show to the director in Phnom Penh confirming that we had, in fact, received the correct shipment, thus clearing himself of incompetence or complicity in any wrong-doing.

But why, he persisted, had we written that the bags weighed fifty kilos? Trying to paint the confused scene where I had asked a pre-occupied Wayne how much the bags weighed and he had answered "fifty kilos" off the top of his head almost outstripped our powers to explain and the official's to comprehend. But finally he got it, a comedy of errors. He smiled, and this time it seemed genuine. He was so relieved he took out his wallet and showed us the photos of two plump, immaculate daughters, whose papa's job was safe.

For me, this was a lesson in prudence and discretion, in what could go wrong if I did not rein in my flare for the dramatic. As for Wayne, he was vindicated in his faith that my indiscretion would perhaps have posi-tive consequences. He now knows that if there is a problem he is not alone in the field, and that the World Food Programme will probably be respectful and responsive. He found that reassuring, as his past experi-ences with bureaucracies is that they have not always been supportive. As for the batch of ammoniated rice, which was from a previous delivery, unfortunately we did not have any left to show the visiting official. But clearly the World Food Programme was concerned, and if it happened again we would know who to call.

By afternoon, as the antibiotics finally took hold, I was feeling a little better. It was late February and the rice fields had been harvested and the once-fresh green rice was now mere stubble. I sat on the cool tiles in the shade out back of the crematorium, writing of the day's events in my journal. Mister Kosal found me and slept in my lap with his arms and legs flung out wide like a rag doll. I watched him sleep, listened to him breathe, and the simple goodness of a sleeping child on my lap made me feel joyous and whole.

25
PAGODA BOYS

If there was one job that Wayne disliked, it was giving the children their daily allowances. Each evening before going home the teacher, Madame Sophea, handed Wayne a list of children who had attended classes that day, and those kids would receive a little spending money, the equivalent perhaps of twenty cents. While this might seem an insignificant sum, having any money at all set our kids apart from the village children. But Wayne reasoned that while a local child might be welcomed home from school with a snack prepared by his own mother, our children had to fend for themselves. For a few pennies a child could buy a colored fruit ice, and still have enough for a hardboiled egg and a small sack of glass marbles.

To encourage saving, Wayne set up a banking system where a child might save all or a portion of his allowance. Some kids, like Rajana, saved everything, and over time amassed a tiny fortune. Others saved to buy clothing at the market, and some kids spent every penny on sweets. It was their choice.

Wayne would sit on a stool with a sheaf of paper money of the smallest denominations, bills worn damp and dog-eared by circulating from hand to hand to hand. Giving out spending money seems a simple task, but in the days before Wayne's cataract surgery, reading lists written in Madame Sophea's minuscule script strained his eyes. I offered to take over the job. It was the beginning of my time in Cambodia and I figured it would give me a way to put names and faces together. Equally important, it would give me a chance to say hello to each child at least once every day.

The first few days were chaos. The waves of children overwhelmed me, and they knew it. Instead of queuing up politely as they did for Wayne, the children became a clamoring mob, jostling each other to get served first, then circling around behind my chair and draping themselves over my shoulders. I felt suffocated and panicked, but slowly I began to learn their names and faces. Over time I relaxed and so, therefore, did the children, and things became more enjoyable.

Except, that is, when Madame Sophea made an error. If she noted that a child had gone to school when he had not, the entire line of children would become indignant and set the record straight. But if, for example, she accidentally left Mister Kosal's name off the list, then he would draw himself up to his full height and demand his allowance. And the other kids would back him up in a way that permitted no argument. Their sense of justice was unassailable.

Of course, the Pagoda Boys would show up at allowance time too, right on schedule. They weren't really bad kids, but they had histories of petty theft, glue sniffing and general mischief. In the local parlance, they might eventually become "gangstas," small-time criminals who often as not wound up in street gangs or in prison. If they became too troublesome in the community, they might even turn up dead. In a last-ditch effort to straighten them out, their parents sent them to live with the monks. They were not studying for the monkhood, or even going to school. They just cleaned floors, washed clothes and did other odd jobs around the wat. Mostly they tried to stay out of sight.

Since Molly had left for America no one paid much attention to the Pagoda Boys. I doubt the monks gave them much beyond a place to sleep and a little food. Wayne let them line up for allowances, and they were grateful. I felt sorry for them; compared with our kids they were ragged and unloved. But in truth, a cagier and more disreputable band of little rapscallions you could never hope to meet.

Though their numbers varied, there were three regulars: Mister Ma, Mister Pa and Mister Da. They would insert themselves here and there in the line, receive their money and then change places, circle back, all sweetness and light, and, in a surreptitious do-si-do, dance right back round again. In the confusion of my early days, when I never knew who was who, I'm sure they succeeded often enough. But after a while I caught on and would scowl at them, and they would look me right in the eye, blink innocently and run off chuckling into the evening. When I complained to Wayne, he said, "Think of what you would do if you had absolutely nothing."

Rebecca was still at Wat Opot in those days, and not surprisingly she disapproved of giving money to the Pagoda Boys. They were not "our" children, and when Wayne went to Phnom Penh she counted out precisely enough money for the Wat Opot kids, but not a penny extra for the three hustlers.

I'm not sure how it came about, but one night Rebecca got the notion that the Pagoda Boys might be a fertile field for her proselytizing. She gave each boy an enormous bottle of shampoo, much bigger than our kids ever got, and instructed them to tell the monks, "This is a gift from Jesus."

We were all having dinner the next night when the Pagoda Boys showed up, Mister Ma, Mister Pa and Mister Da. They were completely bald. They grinned mischievously at Rebecca, put their hands together and bowed respectfully so she could inspect their freshly shaven heads, and announced, "Monks say to tell you, this is a gift from Buddha."

26
THE DANCE

In the 1960s, I spent a summer in Liberia, West Africa. This was twenty years before generations of child soldiers would be consumed by two tragic civil wars, and the capital, Monrovia, was still a sleepy town.

One afternoon as I was trying to glean a little content from the oscillating sibilance of the shortwave broadcast of the BBC

News, the announcement came that Robert Kennedy had been gunned down. They didn't use his first name, and for a few surreal moments my brain could not grasp what I was hearing. I had been a freshman in college the day President John F. Kennedy died, and my first thought was that I was hearing some odd temporal aberration, a radio signal that had become lost in space, bounced off a distant star, a round-trip of four and a half years, and had just now been picked up by a funky shortwave radio in a little cinder-block house on a beach in Monrovia, Liberia.

This was only two months after the stunning assassination of Dr. Martin Luther King Jr. I had been at the University of Michigan on that awful day. The black students had drawn together in a huge circle on the campus quadrangle. They stood, holding hands, heads bowed, mute, inconsolable, while the world held its breath.

Now Bobby was dead, another senseless loss. Later that day, coming home from buying groceries in the market, my Liberian taxi driver asked me, accusingly, "Why do all Americans carry guns and shoot each other?"

The next month, July 1968, was the anniversary of the Nigerian Civil War, the Biafran War. I was staying with a friend who had served in the Peace Corps in Nigeria. He was close to a number of Biafran expatriates, Igbo people from the tribe that was fighting to break away from the rest of Nigeria and form an independent state. Some of these expats, who were living in Monrovia, invited my friend and me to a celebration of the first anniversary of Biafran independence. We sat on a little dais watching the proud and poignant observance, knowing what no one would admit that night, that the war was beginning to go badly for the breakaway Igbos, and that this giddy moment might well mark their last anniversary as well as their first. We feasted from huge communal bowls of country rice and goat meat, but I cringed when I was presented with the dish of honor, a dark rich monkey stew. In the center of the broad cauldron protruded a tiny clenched fist, like the hand of the Lady of the Lake, but also too much like a human child's hand for my sensibilities. All night men in their embroidered finery danced and shouted, sang and drank Guinness Stout mixed with Orange Fanta, but it is the image of that little dark hand that haunts my memory, so evocative of the swollen-bellied, emaciated children who would starve to death before the killing was over.

When the Biafran War began, my Peace Corps friend was evacuated and reassigned to teach English in Liberia. We lived on South Beach, an area of Monrovia occupied mostly by squatters, a mix of local people and immigrants from Ghana, Senegal and the Gambia. One bad road ran the length of the beach, so rutted that after a rainstorm taxis sank up to their axles and people had to trudge home lugging their bundles through ankle-deep mud.

Several Peace Corps volunteers who lived down South Beach way approached their local program officer to see about paving the road. This supervisor had been in the country for years and knew a thing or two about how things worked. The volunteers told him they had arranged with army officers in the barracks at the end of South Beach to supply men and machinery for grading the road, provided the volunteers could scrounge up enough blacktop to pave it. The program officer let them know that he could make it happen, but he cautioned strongly against it. Many influential people lived in the sweltering downtown center of Monrovia. Some of them owned beachfront property, but they didn't pay much attention to what happened on unimproved land.

Fix the road, however, and the rich and powerful would descend, evict the squatters and erect fine homes, cooled by the ocean breezes.

This was my introduction to the concept of unintended consequences. Years later in Cambodia I would listen as Wayne mulled over the possible ramifications of each new project, always wary of the unpredictable. Some volunteers at Wat Opot would become frustrated with his caution, but my experience in Liberia had taught me that when you charge blindly into something new you may do more harm than good, despite your honorable intentions.

So we left well enough alone on South Beach, and the little woven mat houses continued to flood in the rain, and the rutted road continued to devour taxis, and rain pelted the bam-bam roofs, and we all lived peaceably together. Children played with kites made from sticks and newspaper. Small girls carried younger children on their backs and walked their swaybacked rhythms with full buckets of water on their heads, strengthening their sinews for the elegant carriage they would have as women. Ladies wore their brightly patterned sarongs and made small market, and the air smelled of smoke from plantain fried in red palm oil;

337

we all ate country rice and fiery soups simmered with greens and fish heads, and young men played volleyball on the beach at sunset, while old gentlemen palavered and drank palm wine.

Replace the red laterite soil with white clay, the scent of palm oil with the tang of lemongrass and fish sauce, and you have evening in Cambodia. No wonder Wat Opot felt like home when I arrived.

I spent my last afternoon on South Beach knocking on my neighbors' doors to say goodbye. One after another they welcomed me in and offered tea or Fanta and invited me to sit awhile. We had some memorable conversations, and on that day I felt as never before that I might have been a part of this gracious community. Each person I visited asked me why I had not come before. I had lived a whole summer on South Beach. Neighborhood children had run in and out of our house all day long. Why had I never made the effort to get to know my neighbors? I was very young and it was my first time out of the United States, so I forgive myself my shyness. But I regret the lost opportunity to have made friends with my neighbors. They never called on me, so I imagined they weren't interested and kept to myself. I suppose they saw me as standoffish at best, or perhaps indifferent. I was a city girl and unaccustomed to the ways of villages. I never understood that it was me who should have played hostess and invited them all for tea. It was a great waste not to have made friends with these marvelous West African ladies. How often do we go hungry in the midst of a feast?

Forty years later at Wat Opot I would recall this lesson. But not right away.

My first visit to Wat Opot lasted five months, and much of the time I felt overwhelmed. I stayed close to Wayne, reassured by his calm and compassion and looking to him as my role model. So for those first few months I rarely interacted with the other adults at Wat Opot.

Wayne pretty much allows people to find their own level, and though I am sure he noticed that I avoided the hospice, he didn't mention it. Like many people, I didn't know how to be with the very ill and dying. Where Papa Steve with his expansive personality might offer a vast smile and hold someone's hand or spend a few minutes cooling a patient with a small plastic fan, I simply wished I could sit by their bed and be present. Instead I always hurried past the hospice, and felt a numbing fear. It wasn't that I thought I would catch AIDS; I had no problem cuddling with the children. It was more visceral than that. Not long before I went to Cambodia I had helped care for my own mother for a year as she lay dying of cancer. Paralyzed from the waist down, hers had been an excruciating, attenuated death. Her body was so much my body, so close in form and texture, that there were some days when it seemed it was my own death I was watching play out before my eyes.

When I came back to Wat Opot the second winter I found the place transformed. Wayne had closed the hospice, and most of the patients had gotten up from their beds and were again involved in the life of the community. Wat Opot had become more like a small village. The children seemed encouraged by the adults' return to the world of the living. Deaths were rare now, and the children were beginning to believe that they might indeed have a chance to grow up. With the hospice closed, Wayne was getting more sleep and could concentrate on the needs of the children and on developing programs to enrich their lives. A new mood of ease and hope permeated Wat Opot.

Whenever Wayne was away, his assistant Mr.

Sary was in charge and the energy at Wat Opot would subtly shift. Suddenly it would feel like a small Khmer village. I would notice this shift late at night, in glimpses of a world that Wayne and I were not a part of. In the dry season, for instance, Khmer people nap during the oppressive heat of the day and stay up late enjoying the evening. With Wayne away, there were little card games and clusters of people chatting on the swings outside the clinic. Children would slip outside and spread their sleeping mats on the cool earth. The weavers would gather on the bamboo beds outside their quarters, and tease each other and look up at the stars, and sometimes late at night they would bake taro root in the coals of little campfires.

One night, when Wayne had gone to Phnom Penh, everyone decided it was high time they had a dance. The first I heard of it was when Mr. Sary began to construct the Tower of Power. A brigade of kids passed one loudspeaker after another from the dining hall to the pounded dirt courtyard right outside my window. As Sary built the wall, several speakers wide, he climbed atop each new level and one of the bigger boys would pass the next row of speakers up to him. In this way the tower grew to a height of twelve feet.

Any time I went to a Khmer wedding in the village I found a tower that reached the ceiling of the tent. The equalizer's sliders would be precisely adjusted to a maximum of excruciation, and the music itself, distorted beyond recognition, would resemble the bellowing of the primordial OM at the creation of the universe. As representatives of Wat Opot, Wayne and I were always offered the table of honor, right in front of the Tower of Power. We would politely demur, insisting that we were not worthy of such regard, and that we should surely sit *way over there,* with the children and poor relations. Wayne, characteristically insightful, countered my complaints about impending deafness by explaining that the noise was in fact a manifestation of generosity. If one is having a happy occasion, wouldn't one wish to share the joy with one's neighbors? "Even one's neighbors in Phnom Penh?" I grumbled, wondering whether wearing earmuffs would constitute a breach of etiquette at a Khmer wedding.

So when I saw what was taking shape in the courtyard outside my room, I fled, ready to bury my head under a pillow for the duration. I was not at all comforted by the knowledge that dry-season parties often last until three in the morning.

For about an hour I sulked. I tried to read or write in my journal, but nothing could exist in my brain in the same space as that noise. I was about to go bonkers when the thought came to me of that last day in Liberia, saying goodbye to the women of South Beach, and all the missed opportunities. "What are you *doing* here?" I asked myself. "Trying not to go deaf," I replied, abashed. "Well, deary, you make your own Heaven and Hell. You can either sit in here and complain and have a miserable night, or risk a little deafness and join the fun." So I took a shower, wrapped myself in my prettiest sarong and ventured out into the cacophonous pandemonium.

The claxon struck me full force when I stepped outside, and I almost lost heart, but then Sampeah spotted me, and soon a whooping mob of kids was running over and grabbing my hands and escorting me to the edge of the crowd. I lingered for a few moments, watching the circle of women perform their lovely line dance. They advanced with stately steps, swaying their hips and sculpting the air with their hands, the minimalist symmetry highlighting the pure grace of their movements.

343

Ouen took my arm, as he had that day at the eye clinic, gallantly playing the dutiful grandson, and guided me into the circle. The women took me up and began to teach me the steps and gestures, laughing at my awkwardness, but welcoming me all the same. Intoxicated with their open hearts, I danced with them late into the night, and for a few days after the party, whenever I ran into one of these women in the hall or on a path, they might begin moving their hands in dance gestures, and I would join them, and we would dance around and past each other, bumping hips and laughing.

As in long-ago Liberia, acceptance had been there for me all along, and once I began to offer myself, the friendships blossomed. Most of the women spoke little English, and my Khmer was likewise dreadful, but there was abundant goodwill.

I dreamed that night that I was by myself in my room. I was enjoying the peace and quiet when a Cambodian man entered with a transistor radio. He smiled at me and then turned on the radio, and played his music very loud. I looked at him, smiling sweetly, of course, as one does in Cambodia, not wishing to give offense, and said, "Shhh-hhh." He smiled back and nodded, and cranked the sound even louder. Suddenly I realized with that logic peculiar to dreams that "Shhhh" in Khmer means "Please turn it up louder." (Incidentally, the Khmer language lacks a "shhhh" sound, but dreams have their own rules, even their own linguistics.)

Some nights after evening clinic I would sit outside with the women, eight or ten of us crowded onto a bamboo bed, giggling and joking, poking at each other's breasts like a party of old bawds. They never tire of telling me mine were *tomaaaah!,* holding their hands apart like an old fisherman bragging about the biggest catch of his life. Clearly, they saw my melons as a marvel of nature, the Cyrano's nose of tits. We laughed for hours. The children came and went, leaning in for a quick hug before going back to play. Older boys wandered by with flashlights and bamboo traps, hunting for frogs. Insects sang and the moon rose in the clear dry-season heavens, and we all relaxed and enjoyed the evening until finally we hugged each other and drifted off to bed.

27
A Seventy-Two-Year-Old Grandmother

A seventy-two-year-old *yei* with AIDS came to the clinic. She told Wayne she had caught the disease from her husband. "He was playing around and I threw him out several times," she said.

"Well then, what happened?"

"I took him back . . . once too often."

28
A House with High Walls

Between trips to Cambodia I sometimes speak to groups about Wat Opot. Now and then someone in the audience feels moved to volunteer, and I help them prepare for their trip. After they return I am anxious to hear about their experience. I ask many questions, but short-term visitors, jet-lagged, inundated by a flood of children, can hardly give me the news I crave. Frustrated by their generalities, I have to remind myself how long it took me to learn scores of unfamiliar Khmer names. But if I listen carefully, I can begin to tease out news about specific children. As with adults, certain kids stand out in a crowd: Little Run with his huge ears and overwhelming need to be held, Pesei who is so personable and makes such an effort to interact with foreigners, serious Rajana, Ouen, Chan Tevy.

Sometimes two souls connect quickly and deeply, and the returning volunteer will tell a story of one child who has become a true loved one and how painful it was to leave her or him behind. But in the end these glimpses mostly set me to wandering through my own memories, and more often than not these are memories of Miss Srey Mom.

Most of the children do well at Wat Opot, even if they have come from dire situations. But children have some needs that cannot be met very well in a large, unruly community. For those who have grown up on the street or in abusive situations, Wat Opot can be a haven. But for a few children like Srey Mom, raised in comfortable, loving families, for whom the doors of Paradise have abruptly swung shut, life at Wat Opot can seem devastatingly lonely.

Hoping to marry after their parents died, Srey Mom's sisters abandoned her at Wat Opot. Yet underneath her trauma I sensed a little girl from a middle-class family who had been her parents' darling. She was personable and confident, even funny, but she had profound needs for the intimate, bonded relationship she must have had with her own father and mother.

To make matters worse, Srey Mom had tuberculosis as well as AIDS when she came to us, and she had to undergo six months of antibiotics before she could begin to receive antiretroviral drugs. The underlying disease weakened her, and she had frequent fevers and a recurring ear infection with a strong odor that made other children avoid her. Older girls, the pretty girls who might have been big sisters to her, shunned her.

Like other new arrivals, Srey Mom was assigned a "mother," one of the women patients who are paid a small stipend to look after the younger children. Wayne cannot afford to hire outside caregivers, and many women from the village would be afraid to care for children with AIDS. Most of the so-called mothers do a good job, but for a few it is primarily just a way to earn money. Many of them have children of their own, and all the women are patients, and are living with their own sadness.

Madame Ketmoni, who became Srey Mom's caretaker, is a shrewd market woman, a survivor. She set up a small business on the grounds of Wat Opot, selling snacks to the children after school. From the daily market in Chambok she brought fruit and sweets and cans of juice and soda and spread them out under the huge tamarind tree near the dining hall. Sometimes she boiled eggs, or cooked fish with green mango chutney. She hung her string hammock from a strong limb of the tree and there she spent her afternoons, suspended like a resourceful spider. From where she sat, she managed to intercept the major portion of the children's allowances before they spent them on the little colored ices sold by vendors from the village.

Ketmoni took care of Srey Mom when she was ill and looked after her, but she was not the nurturing mother Srey Mom needed. After a time Srey Mom went to live with Thida, a woman with four children of her own. Thida's two daughters, both teenagers, avoided the little girl, who had by then become depressed and had begun to neglect her body. Now and then her sisters would bring her a pretty new outfit, but these stayed in her basket, unworn. Instead, she wore the same soiled pajamas day and night for days at a time and resisted our urging to wash her hair or put on clean clothes. She began to have hair lice. AIDS made her vulnerable to skin infections, and now and then the women shaved her head to get rid of the lice and to better treat the fungus. Bald, her head smeared with white powder, she was mortified and became even more withdrawn.

First Wayne tried to treat the ear infections. Then an ear specialist in Phnom Penh gave her a stronger antibiotic, but the problem came back. Fevers came and went, sometimes lasting for days. One night I went to Thida's apartment to check on Srey Mom and found her asleep on the cool tiles. All the children sleep on mats, often with no padding, but when I saw her on the floor, wrapped in a thin blanket, feverish, with all life going on around her in a brightly lighted room, she looked as alone as anyone could be in this world. I wanted to pick her up and take her home with me and love her, and I knew that was impossible. I asked myself whether I should take her into my own room and take care of her for the rest of my stay at Wat Opot. But I was afraid of her great need, and perhaps of my own, and what the parting would be like when, in a few weeks, I left for America. In the end, would the promise of a caring parent turn out to be only another abandonment?

Wayne tells me that Srey Mom's AIDS has become resistant to firstline antiretrovirals. The doctors have put her on secondline drugs, and she is doing better, but Wayne worries about whether she will survive. In the end, we fear, it may not be the disease that takes her, but the sadness.

After lunch, fifteen or twenty children come to my porch to play with the Legos I brought from the States. Some play in groups, building fanciful constructs. Pesei works alone, often in my room, where it is quiet. His creations are intricate and cerebral: a building with an interior circular staircase that can only be glimpsed through a tiny door in the roof, flying machines with hinged, prehensile elements and unlikely functions. His conceptual abilities amaze me. He is the only one who has attempted to build any of the objects in the instruction books, but like the others he mostly has no use for the manuals and prefers to build from his imagination. In contrast to the complexity of Pesei's vision, Mister Vantha flies to the moon on a craft of two or three crossed pieces of plastic. For him it is enough to stretch this tiny suggestion of a spaceship toward the sky and he is off, careening through the stratosphere, buzzing

and spluttering as he inhabits the aircraft of his imagination.

Off to the side sits Miss Srey Mom, all alone, quietly building a house out of Legos. It is, with slight variations, the same house she built yesterday and the day before. Sometimes there is a pretty garden in front, with a symmetrical avenue of flowers and plastic palm trees. Other times there is no garden, but the house is still the same. She lays the first course of bricks around the periphery of the house and then installs the door. She opens the door, and then she closes it firmly, and builds the walls of the

house. Atop each wall, which varies in height from day to day depending on how many blocks she has managed to commandeer in the initial free-for-all with the other children, she places a plastic dinosaur or pterodactyl. These gargoyles face outward to the four directions, fiercely protecting the inhabitants inside; there are always three.

"You?" I ask, pointing to the tiny figure she has placed in a small bed. She looks up and nods. "And?" I point to the other two.

"Mama. Papa."

Then she drops her head and continues building walls, higher and ever higher.

29
AND YET . . .

One day I was telling a friend a story from Wat Opot about a girl and a boy who got into trouble together and were both expelled from the community. Wayne had been adamant that this expulsion was necessary; I was not so sure. My friend, who always listened well and took the long view on such matters, pointed out that the conflict between Wayne's viewpoint and my own was fundamental and even archetypal. Whereas I was acting the part of the mother, determined that no single child should fall by the wayside and be lost, Wayne was forced to make all decisions from a different perspective: What is best for the health of the entire community?

With my friend's insight to guide me, I grew more sensitive to the complexity of the demands Wayne faces every day. His decisions directly affect the lives of more than a hundred people, and sometimes there is no "right" decision but only what seems like a better choice, one with fewer potentially harmful side effects. I may at times still disagree with him, but never again will I do so without a profound respect for the agonizing choices he is forced to make.

What prepares a person to make these kinds of decisions? Wayne's whole life has trained him to ponder the meaning and consequences of his actions. His early religious training stressed stringent self-examination as a spiritual practice. He tells me that every year — and I reckon it is far more frequently than that — he has made a formal examination of conscience.

Wayne also carries with him scars of regret for some of his past decisions. When he tells the story of how, while on a patrol as a medic during the Vietnam War, he failed twice on the same day to intervene and prevent the deaths of two Vietnamese children, the listener feels compelled to forgive by reminding him of all the good he has done in the world since that time. Had Wayne directly disobeyed orders in the field he might have faced a court-martial. Wayne refuses to accept the listener's absolution, which in truth the listener has no right to offer. One has only to think of the excuses served up by Nazi war criminals to understand the full implications. Wayne's failure to save those children, even at risk to his own life, forces him forever to continually redefine the meaning of his life. When he states clearly that his work at Wat Opot has been and remains his atonement, this is not hyperbole, but his true and genuine soul offering: to spend the rest of his life making up for that one day.

And so whenever Wayne is faced with a decision that will profoundly affect the lives of other people, or even whether they will be given the antiretroviral medicines that will allow them to live, his moment of decision must be examined against the backdrop of a man seeking to probe and redefine the meaning of his own life and how he sees himself as a human being.

The following episodes may shed light on some of the excruciating moral dilemmas that confront Wayne every day.

HONDURAS

One night Wayne told me the story of a poor man who came to see him in Yocón, the little village in Honduras where he worked as a barefoot doctor from 1984 until 1996. This hamlet, hours away from any hospital, was as violent as the Wild West, and much of Wayne's work involved removing bullets or sewing up machete wounds after bar fights. But on this night a man from the countryside walked into Wayne's office carrying his daughter in his arms. She was about five, very ill, too sick for Wayne to treat. He urged the man to take his little girl to the hospital at once, but the father had no money, so Wayne gave him twenty dollars for fees and transport and sent him off.

A few weeks later the man returned with another child.

"How is your daughter?" Wayne asked.

It turned out that the man had not taken his daughter to the hospital that night. He had taken her home, where she had died.

Wayne was incensed. "So now you are bringing me *another* child, and I am supposed to help you? Or do you just want me to give you more money?"

The man sat meekly with downcast eyes and waited for Wayne to finish. Then, quietly, he explained that as he waited for transport to carry his daughter and himself to the hospital he had begun to think. His little girl was gravely ill, and he knew that if she saw the doctor she might possibly recover. And yet . . . there was a better chance she would die anyway. The man had ten hungry children at home, and with twenty dollars he could feed them all for weeks. So after agonizing over his choices, the man had made the terrible decision and taken his daughter home.

MISS MALIS

Miss Malis [*MaLEE*] was new to Wat Opot, but she was clearly not settling in very well. Wayne told me Malis had no social skills. That was an understatement. Her clothes were dirty, her hair unwashed. She slumped around with her head hung down and her shoulders hunched up. The other children clearly disliked her and treated her as an outcast; boys ran up and whispered things in her ear, things that made her cry. When she wasn't sobbing she mostly sulked or stayed far away from the rest of the kids. The kids said she was *ch'goo-ut* — crazy.

Miss Malis had been living with her aunt and uncle in the village and was ten years old when her aunt brought her to Wat Opot. The aunt told Wayne that Malis was retarded and crazy and she could no longer have her in her house. By the time I arrived, Wayne had concluded that Malis was not crazy and she was definitely not retarded. True, she didn't get along with the others, but he suspected that her behavior, like her posture, had been devised to protect herself.

But from what? The most likely scenario was that someone had been trying to abuse her, and she had kept him away by making herself as repulsive as possible. Wayne supposed that her aunt was afraid her husband would beat her or leave if she confronted him, so she did the only thing she could think of to protect her niece. She moved her to Wat Opot.

When Miss Malis slouched across campus I sometimes caught up with her. I would put my hands on her shoulders and gently straighten her posture. *"Srey sa-aat,"* I'd tell her. "Pretty miss, don't walk like a *s'waa.*" (S'waa means monkey.) Then we'd laugh and do monkey imitations and I'd launch into a routine that Papa Steve had, about monkeys eating mangoes, *"S'waa hoap s'wai."* Then reverse it to *"S'wai hoap s'waa,"* mango eats monkey. It was silly, but Miss Malis would laugh and straighten up, and I'd give her a few packets of soap and shampoo so she could wash the lice out of her hair. Over time she started taking care of herself, and she began to do well in school.

The older pretty girls, the three who might have been prom queens or cheerleaders in the States, did not approve of my paying attention to Miss Malis. Once, when she had a bad cold, I took her into my room and fed her some ginger tea. For a week the three girls refused to talk to me. I was livid. I had had my fill of girls like that in junior high school.

But one night I heard a commotion and ran outside to see Malis cowering on the ground, with the three alpha chicks hitting her, chanting, *"Ch'goo-ut! Ch'goo-ut!"* I broke up the fight and took the girls aside and gave them each a talking-to. They made a show of ignoring me, but I never saw them hit her again.

I spoke to Wayne about the incident. He said that he mostly tries to stay out of such things unless they get violent. He figures that with so many children there will be inevitable jockeying to establish a pecking order, and the sooner everyone knows where they stand the easier things will go for the newcomers. In his experience, interfering only prolongs the agony.

Wayne recalled being low man on the totem poll himself. He said it had strengthened his character and made him more resilient.

Maybe. But I wasn't satisfied.

I slumped in my chair remembering how low I had been in the pecking order when I was in grade school. It amazed me to see the same sort of behavior here in a Cambodian orphanage that I had experienced in a middle-class New York City public school in the 1950s. Amid all this misery and loss, to add the animal urge to cull the herd . . .

"I really hate this," I told Wayne.

"We gotta love 'em all." Wayne shrugged. "But we don't always have to like 'em."

During my first winter at Wat Opot the children mostly slept together in a small tin-roofed stucco building. The oldest boys hung hammocks and spread their sleeping mats on tables in the dining room on the other side of campus, but the younger boys and all the girls slept in the dorm. There was a ruckus one day, and it turned out that some of the boys had been bullying Miss Malis, had threatened to come after her in the night. Wayne called a meeting of all the children. He was solemn. First he promised that no one would be punished. He only wanted to be clear about what had happened. Then he asked those kids who were not directly involved and those who had not witnessed the events firsthand to leave. Then he locked the door and settled himself on a high stool.

"We have a decision to make," Wayne began. "We must decide whether we want to live our lives as human beings or as animals." Then Wayne asked the kids what was going on, and they told him, because they felt safe and trusted Wayne to keep his word that no one would be punished. In the end Wayne told the kids that they were getting to an age where it was better for boys and girls to sleep separately. It was all very calm, very quiet, but the kids got the message, and that was the end of that. For now.

When I returned to Wat Opot the second winter, Miss Malis seemed to be doing better. She had moved to the other side of campus, away from the older girls, and was living with one of the families. She seemed at ease; she had grown taller and stood straighter and she was near the top of her class in school. She had her own circle of friends. One evening, watching her dance at a party, I remarked to Wayne that she was growing into a lovely young woman.

Five months later I went back to the States, but kept in close touch with the doings at Wat Opot. One night just after Cambodian New Year I received an email from Wayne telling me that they'd had their "first sex episode." It had happened between Miss Malis and Samrang, one of the older boys; they are both HIV negative. With so many kids growing up together we had all been wondering when something like that might happen. Wayne's response was to have both of them leave Wat Opot.

Samrang, a big strong youth, was old enough to look for work in the outside world. He had not been applying himself in school and lately had not been getting along with anyone. Wayne felt "he wanted to fly, but he was needing a push." Samrang asked Wayne to allow Malis to stay. He argued that it was his fault because he had come home drunk from a New Year's celebration. But Wayne decided that since Miss Malis had approached Samrang she should be held equally responsible.

When the young woman's family in the village learned of the incident they wanted the kids to marry at once. Their marriage would, in effect, have made Wayne her father-in-law, because Wayne is Samrang's legal guardian. Then, regardless of what happened between the two kids, Wayne would have been responsible for Miss Malis and for any children she might bear.

Meanwhile, Wayne had discovered that this was not Malis's first sexual encounter. It was common knowledge — to everyone but Wayne — that she had been sexually active for some time. With so many boys coming of age, Wayne decided it would not be wise to allow her to remain as a full-time resident of Wat Opot. Wayne told me that even the younger children were aware of what had happened, and took it as a lesson. To have allowed Malis to stay would have set a bad example for all of the children.

Samrang went to Battambang to work in a gas station. Before long he realized how limited his options were without an education, so he asked Wayne about coming back to school. Wayne told him that if he studied and did well in his exams he would receive help with his school fees, but Wayne would not allow him to move back to Wat Opot. Samrang, Wayne decided, must live with the monks next door.

As I read Wayne's email in my study in Maine, I was troubled by his decision to force Miss Malis to leave Wat Opot. I wondered whether she was being punished for things that had happened to her when she was a child. Had Wat Opot somehow failed her? She had entered as a traumatized, very possibly sexually abused little girl. She had been ostracized and further brutalized at Wat Opot by a clique of older girls. If someone had asked me which of our girls might turn to sex as a way of gaining a sense of acceptance and love, I would have guessed Miss Malis.

I told Wayne that I worried that sending Malis to her uncle's house would expose her to abuse. Couldn't he make an exception? Here I was speaking as a mother, concerned only for the welfare of one child. And yet I could see that Wayne might need to make a different and far more difficult decision, one that he felt was best for the entire community.

Part of the problem lies in how few adults there are to look after all these children. I think Malis needed someone to care about her all the time, someone to shepherd her through her teenage years. At Wat Opot, volunteers come and go, and even if we are there for months it is never long enough to give the continuity the children need. We can grow close to a child for a little while and see them again if we return, but most children, like Malis, need more consistent guidance than that. Even if Wayne had the money to hire more help, it is hard to find adults in the village who are willing to be foster parents, especially to children with HIV/AIDS.

Wayne does his best, but Malis needed a mother, and ironically she is one of the few children at Wat Opot who actually has one. But her mother is away in Phnom Penh with a new husband, and they do not want her daughter living with them.

Miss Malis went to live in the village with her relatives and continued going to school. Wayne gave her an allowance and she took meals at Wat Opot. When I returned there in 2011, I learned that Miss Malis had had a baby by her aunt's husband.

About a third of the children at Wat Opot are HIV positive. Our oldest children with AIDS are only now reaching puberty. I know that Wayne is concerned about how his children — whether HIV positive or negative — will behave in the outside world, whether they will act responsibly and honestly. Wayne is also acutely sensitive to how Wat Opot is viewed by people beyond the walls.

In an extreme example of what can happen, one woman, an adult AIDS patient on antiretrovirals, had been having sex with an HIV-negative teenager from the village. His parents found out, and discovered that the couple had not used condoms. The woman was blasé, saying that "this was how he wanted it." Despite all the attempts at AIDS education in the villages, the boy did not understand how the virus was transmitted; as someone with AIDS it was her responsibility to protect him. The boy's parents were irate, and one night they sent a group of local goons with clubs to break windows and terrorize the campus. The woman was well enough to live and work outside, so Wayne made her leave Wat Opot.

One of the missions of Wat Opot is to encourage acceptance of people living with HIV/AIDS so that they are not feared or ostracized or shunned or even killed. If our children or adult patients are seen as endangering others, then much of the progress that has been made could be destroyed.

KIMCHAN

Kimchan was a pretty, vivacious young woman who had moved to the community with her three children, each by a different father. She was smart and capable and had a better grasp of English than most of the women, but she was also mercurial, quick to anger and, apparently, unwise in love. She found living at Wat Opot more frustrating and confining than did some of the other women, who seemed to relax into life here as a kind of refuge. Still, it would have been hard for Kimchan to leave. Wat Opot provided her children with food and shelter and education, and took care of their medical needs.

Of course, life in the outside world is hard for people with AIDS. Often they do not have the strength to harvest rice under the hot sun. The garment factories of Phnom Penh, faced with tight schedules, avoid hiring workers who might take sick days or need time off to visit a doctor, or who lack the stamina to work overtime when demand is high and deadlines looming. With three children, Kimchan knew that her options were limited. She settled into life at Wat Opot, but her angry outbursts made her unpopular with the other women.

Sok Mean [*sok MEE-in*], a large woman with a broad open face, came to Wat Opot with her husband. He was very ill with AIDS and she nursed him faithfully in the hospice, feeding him and cleaning him day and night for months. Over time he recovered, but as he regained strength he began to flirt with the other women. This enraged Sok Mean, and on several occasions she berated him for his ingratitude.

A rumor began to circulate that Sok Mean's husband and Kimchan had been spending time together. Sok Mean attacked Kimchan, leaving savage bite marks on her face and arm. It was an ugly scene, an overflow of frustration and violence. Kimchan retreated to the clinic, where Wayne tended to her wounds. I found her lying on a bed with an IV in her arm, deeply shaken.

Wayne tries to stay clear of what he calls "Khmer business," such as how parents discipline their children, and the endless back-and-forth among people living in close quarters. At Wat Opot actual violence is rare. I can remember only one other instance when people fought in earnest. Even the small children understand that *chee-um,* blood, carries AIDS, and that fights are dangerous and forbidden. After the fight between Sok Mean and Kimchan, it was clear that something had to be done. Wayne tried to put the decision off until morning, when he could talk with Vandin.

But around ten o'clock that same night one of the boys, breathless from running, came to fetch Wayne. When Wayne reached Sok Mean's house he found her naked, chasing her husband around the yard with a kitchen knife. She had managed to slice four long wounds in his back. Wayne walked quietly into the midst of this madness, removed the knife from Sok Mean's hand and wrapped her in a blanket. I was amazed by his calm presence, but he told me later that in his experience as a psychiatric nurse, people who do such things really want to be stopped. He said he could tell that Sok Mean was not trying to kill her husband, because she was using the length of the blade to cut shallow wounds, rather than plunging it point first into her husband's back. Wayne believed she wanted to punish her husband, to teach him a lesson, but not to kill him.

The children were quiet, shocked by the violence, and drew close to the adults for reassurance. But that incident decided things. As Wayne put it, "If this were a movie I would pull the video out of the player and destroy it. I would not let my children watch."

Now there was a hard decision to make: Who would have to leave Wat Opot? Sok Mean had been mightily provoked by her husband's philandering, but Wayne simply could not allow such violence to continue. Her husband's flirtations were clearly disruptive to the community, and it was only fair that he too should bear responsibility. Wayne was inclined to allow Kimchan to remain because of her three children, but when he put the question to the other residents they insisted that she leave. They reminded Wayne that this was not the first serious incident Kimchan had been involved in, and they saw it as only fair that she be held responsible as well. With so many conflicting interests and points of view it would have taken the wisdom of Solomon to sort it all out, but Wayne did his best. He told Kimchan that she too had to leave, but offered to keep her children at Wat Opot, and Kimchan agreed. And so three children became motherless that night.

Wayne gave each of the adults 30,000 riel (about $7.50), which is about a week's wage, for transport and to get started in their new lives. They could all continue to receive medical care through the Partners in Compassion Home Care services. Sok Mean headed for Phnom Penh. She had experience in the garment industry and could find work there. Wayne offered Kimchan a paying job in the Home Care division in another village. It would have been a good opportunity for her to begin to reenter the outside community, but she declined. She and Sok Mean's husband left together.

Late that night Wayne reflected ruefully on the day's events. He wondered whether it had been, at least in its endgame, a setup, in which Kimchan got to unburden herself of the responsibility for three children and run off with her lover, and Wayne had to give everyone traveling money.

Kimchan visits her three children now and then. Each time, she tries to pressure them to give her the contents of their savings accounts, and Wayne always refuses. A year or so after the incident Kimchan came back alone and pregnant. She asked Wayne if she could live at Wat Opot. Wayne offered to take care of the new baby, but the other women said Kimchan was too disruptive and they did not want her back in the community.

Kimchan's two daughters seemed to do pretty well after she left. The youngest adjusted quickly; the older girl missed her mother and lost some of her confidence. Wayne believed that Rajana, her son and eldest child, always held out hope that Kimchan would come back and be his mother again.

Rajana is an insightful boy, a good student, with a quiet dignity. He always held himself a little apart. Two years after Kimchan left, Deb, a volunteer nurse, visited for a month from Maine. She and Rajana grew close, and when she left, Rajana told Deb she had been like a mother to him.

When I returned to Wat Opot in 2010, Rajana was living with the monks. He had dropped out of school and planned to become a monk himself. Often in Cambodia a young man will become a monk for a few years before returning to society. Wayne gave Rajana money to buy his monk's robes. He thought Rajana would make a good monk.

NEW PATIENTS

One day a physician from Médecins Sans Frontières phoned to ask whether Wayne might accept a mentally disabled woman with no family to care for her. She was also going blind and needed more personal care than the hospital in Takeo could provide. MSF would not give her antiretroviral drugs unless she had someone to guarantee her care.

Wayne felt he was being blackmailed — that the woman was MSF's problem, Cambodia's problem, but not *his* problem unless he accepted her. On antiretrovirals she was likely to survive for years, and her care would take away a lot of his time and attention from the children. And yet, she was a human being in need of help, and he was being asked to decide whether she would live or die. What sort of life could she have, even if the drugs saved her? "Cambodia needs to provide for its people," Wayne told me, and if he refused perhaps they would find another solution, one that would help the people who came after this woman. He liked the way Wat Opot was now, with all his energies focused on the kids, but he was having a tough time saying no and letting this woman die. In the end he could not make this choice alone and decided to consult Vandin, Mr. Sary and the other Khmer staff.

Around the same time, a very sick young man of twenty-four was brought in by his family. Once Wayne accepts someone, that is the end of it: he is responsible for them from then on, often for years. There are no halfway measures. Mr. Sary reminded Wayne that he had made a decision not to accept new adults, and definitely not men. Women who recover join the Wat Opot community to re-create something approaching normal life. They help with cooking and are surrogate mothers to the children. Sometimes they remarry and go back to the world. But male patients are usually solitary and depressed and often turn to drink. In the end, Wayne called the hospital in Takeo and arranged for the young man's care, but while the family was at Wat Opot Wayne never left his office. He knew that once he met the young man he would not

374

be able to say no.

Caring for the dying has always been Wayne's special calling, and I know it troubles him to turn people away. Each time he is presented with an adult patient it is a new agony. Wayne knows that if he accepts one there will be others and then others, and he will once again be running a hospice.

And yet . . . and yet. If Wayne rejects these new patients is there another message? What do the children and the rest of us learn about taking in those we are given to love, even if it is inconvenient or troublesome, as it often is, or futile? What does it mean to love unconditionally, even the ones who seem unlovable? And when you can no longer take care of them all, when it is just too hard, when there are too many children and not enough of you to go round? What then?

MR. SAMADHI

Toward the end of 2006, Wayne had a very difficult patient whom everybody had given up on. He was blind, paranoid, depressed, suicidal and at times physically aggressive. One day he took a swing at Serain, the night nurse, with a metal walking stick. He missed, but he hit a cement post with such force that he bent the stick.

As Wayne tells the story, "I had been up all night with a sick child and was exhausted. I lost my temper, took the stick away from him and threw him down on the bed. I then ordered my staff to take him to the hospital and tell them I would not accept him back unless they could give me medications that could control him. The doctors said they understood, but a few days later the hospital truck drove into the yard and pushed the patient out and drove away. He was covered in shit and looked like he had not had a bath since he left us. I walked out to him and said his name. He responded by saying my name, but I could tell he had lost the will to live. We hosed him off and put him to bed and gave him something to eat. Unknown to him he had only seven days of ARV drugs left, and I had to decide what to do when they were finished.

"Making someone comfortable at the end of his life is one thing, but here was a man who could live for several more years. To stop giving him his medicine would hasten his death not by minutes but by years, and nobody wanted to make that decision for me. I didn't want him dead; I just did not want to be responsible for him anymore, and he evidently sensed that, because his condition deteriorated rapidly, and on the seventh day, as I gave him his last dose of ARV medicine, I realized that he would spare me having to make that decision. He died peacefully later that afternoon with all of us by his bedside.

"I have tried every way to rationalize it in my own mind, but the fact remains that a man willed himself to death, simply to make my life easier. Who am I to deserve that much love?"

30
LEAVING, RETURNING

There's a saying that you cannot wade into the same river twice. Wat Opot is like that. Whenever I talked about returning Wayne would tell me, "Okay, but don't expect it to be the place you remember." New children arrive, timorous and shy, and the pecking order shifts just a little. A mother leaves her children and returns to the village to start a small business, and her older son, suddenly serious, takes on the responsibility of a parent. Wayne makes a dorm into an office, a meeting hall into a bedroom, plants a garden or digs a fishpond, following a master plan in his head that no one else has ever glimpsed. Patients take to their beds or grow strong, or go to the hospital and return as corpses to be cremated. Children are adopted, or move back with their extended families in the village. The sense of mission alters naturally over time, from a hospice for the dying to a community of people living with AIDS, from an orphanage to a family. The emphasis shifts again as the children grow older and begin to ponder how they will live in the world.

Daily life is rarely uneventful. Some days start out quietly, all peaceful and routine, and by noon someone is crying or bleeding or sulking, and then quiet returns with the afternoon heat. Yet there is a measured grace to the days here, a rhythm of meals and medicine, of sweeping and cooking, of the children going to school and returning home, of afternoon naps and after-dinner games. Of the old generator coughing up light for two hours every night and the family gathering to watch Korean soap operas on television. The tucking in of mosquito nets and the freshly showered sweetness of children settling down to bed. Of rain on tin roofs in the monsoon, and the children carrying their mats outside to sleep in the dry season. Of planting and harvesting and ducks quacking; of whispered late-night card games; and of groups gathered around tiny fires, roasting taro in the ashes on hot evenings, or warming their hands on January mornings.

Mark the evening flight to Singapore high overhead; you live in a place where a passing airplane is an event to be noticed. Take the time to savor the shift from rice paddies of green to stubble a dozen shades of dun. Cows and dust and whistling wind and singing kites. Children playing, or dying, or going home.

There were some passages I witnessed, some I only heard about from back home in Maine in snippets of emails or the tales of returning volunteers. I tried each time to imagine the textures of the children's changing lives, yet felt far away, alone, and I knew that no matter how long anyone volunteered at Wat Opot, in some ways they would always be a visitor.

Sometimes I would only find out about a child's leaving after several months, and realize with a start that the person and place I had been picturing woven together had not been so for some time. It has become a process of constantly reminding myself that Wat Opot is not fixed in amber, but is a living, evolving world.

My time away is a sharp discontinuity. A kind of mourning happens, a yearning for the children that never completely goes away, and floods over me when news comes from Wayne that I have missed some milestone. Sometimes just remembering a moment with a child brings with it a longing to embrace with body and heart. Yet something in me impedes the commitment to set aside my life in Maine and go to live at Wat Opot. There are many reasons, including the sheer exhaustion I feel after three or four months in Cambodia, from heat, dust, lack of sleep and, yes, age, and from the constant needs of children, and from second-guessing and doubting myself. When all these things have ganged up on me to such a degree that even a layabout weekend in an air-conditioned hotel room in Phnom Penh cannot restore me, then I realize the well has run dry and it is time to leave — to go away for a while.

This rhythm, this leaving and returning, brings its own deepening. At home I have time to write, reflect and share the stories, time to lecture and raise money. When volunteers from Maine venture to Cambodia and return with their own stories, it integrates my existence by making one half of my world real to the other.

Too, there is a sense of what is still to

come in the other half of my life, things somehow resonating from my experiences at Wat Opot. What happens to me in Cambodia has a way of diffusing into other lives in ways that are unpredictable and often marvelous, through the permeability of the receptive heart. One is a friend who continued his donations even at a time of personal sorrow and financial distress; another friend, though losing her eyesight in one eye, gave precious time to read and comment on my writing; people who were moved to visit and volunteer and form continuing relationships with the children; and for myself, new, sweet intensities of loving.

The comings and goings feel like the tempering of a blade of Damascus steel: heated, hammered, quenched, then forged in a furnace, folded and hammered again. With many layers it is nearly unbreakable; it can bend but it will not shatter. And I feel myself, after each return, each reworking, more pliable, less demanding. And, I pray, more fiercely loving.

It is April now, a blazing dry-season afternoon, and I am leaving again. I lug my suitcases to the pickup. The whole Wat Opot community clusters around the truck to bid me safe journey. And I simply lose it. I weep, understanding at a stroke that all the transient petty dramas, the hurts and misunderstandings, are nothing but an illusion of separateness, and that this moment, this encompassing love, is all that is real.

But for Wayne, who is there always, departures for whatever reason, sad or hopeful, are difficult, like the loss of a child he has loved. Here are five stories of children who left Wat Opot, each under different circumstances, each for a different reason.

MISTER VANTHA: A HUMAN ANNUITY

Every morning before breakfast the children come to the clinic for their medicines. Anything else may change, but not this. AIDS medicines must be taken on an exact schedule, and the twice-daily dosing is the metronome of our lives.

After morning clinic, Wayne takes his breakfast in the little round gazebo that sits on an island, accessible by a narrow log bridge — or, for an agile child, broadjumping from the opposite bank. To the right is the main dining hall, with its dramatic conical roof, and to the left the new three-room schoolhouse, which the children have made beautiful with murals. Behind this a little pond separates the campus from the wat next door. The soil, predominantly clay, makes of the water a whitish slurry. A young monk comes to the pond every morning to fetch water for the garden. He carries two old paint buckets, suspended from a shoulder yoke, back up the mossy steps. Pigs wander by, indifferent to an elderly monk washing himself under his saffron robe; he scoops his bathwater from a concrete cistern. Chickens peck at water splashes in the dust. A raft of ducks pours over the banks and proceeds to feed, quack and engage in frequent and astonishing feats of submerged fornication. After being grasped by the neck and pinned underwater by the mounting males, the female ducks finally shake them off and bob to the surface with squawking, ruffled indignation. There is something altogether mesmerizing about watching this spectacle after one has been living for many months in a celibate community. The ducks leave their eggs here and there along the banks of the pond, where children search for them. A tiny blue kingfisher, iridescent as a hummingbird, hovers and dives, snatching up a dragonfly with a body the crimson of Chinese cinnabar.

From where he sits Wayne can see most everything that goes on: sleepy children leaving for school in their white shirts; the ice man delivering shrinking blocks swathed in burlap in the back of his dripping wagon;

the cook leaving for market to fetch the day's vegetables. Lovely Madame Sophea, the teacher, arrives on her moto, perfectly groomed in an outfit she has tailored herself. She parks her bike and picks her way elegantly along the stony path. Three tiny girls, exactly matched in height and proportion, run to meet her. Miss Raksmai, still too young for school, is herding muddy piglets with a slender branch. Now and then you'll see her, the little boss of Wat Opot, following a few yards behind Wayne, her tummy thrust out, hands clasped behind her back, peering to right and to left, inspecting everything in exact mimicry of Wayne's gait and posture.

Breakfast is usually the same from one day to the next: tea, fried duck eggs, Khmer French bread, packs of instant ramen. We make the noodles with hot water and soy sauce, but the children run around waving bricks of noodles and eating them dry. They are salty and taste like potato chips. Now and then we have sardines canned in tomato sauce. I buy instant oatmeal in Phnom Penh, made in China. To the children oatmeal is a suspicious alien substance, even when I try to explain that it is like their *bobor,* rice porridge. No, this is not rice. Rice is food, but this stuff . . . who can say? I understand completely this need for familiar food. I avoid such Khmer delicacies as duck eggs that are prepared just before the ducklings are about to hatch, so the little ducks are steamed fully formed in their shells, beaks and feet and feathers and all. And the flat baskets of scorpions and great black water bugs laid out for sale on the streets of Phnom Penh. Still, eaten dry, oatmeal has possibilities, and I spend most of my breakfast dispensing pinches of dry oatmeal into little licked palms.

About the time we sit down for breakfast, or for any meal, we see in the distance a determined little boy, Mister Vantha [*Van-TAH*], making his way across the campus. Vantha's progress from any one point to any other point is remarkable. He does not so much walk as wheel through his world with an easy economy of motion. His bare feet are strong and broad, his steps light and sure. Confronted with any obstacle he will scale, swim, climb or tunnel, rather than circumambulate. A tree in his path is an opportunity to forage for a tart green mango, a pile of sand a place to proclaim himself King of the Hill. A fence is a tightrope and a table a diving board. A white humpbacked bull breakfasting on Wayne's bougainvillea invites a David and Goliath face-off, with

Vantha vanquishing the great beast with a volley of gravel and valiant shouts of *"Hoi! Hoi!"*

He is wearing a red striped T-shirt, which disappears somewhere between the clinic and the gazebo, leaving only his green-and-white jersey shorts, which ride long and precariously low on his hips. Sometimes he loses them, too. He does not notice. Vantha marches to a different dinner bell. For he knows when and where there will be food, and materializes unfailingly, as if summoned. Then he will fix you with an expression, not of supplication but of delighted, confident entitlement, as if to say, "I am cute. Feed me." And he is. And you do.

Then he will climb into your lap, or into Wayne's. He is a stocky little boy, with a broad chest, but when you lift him up you are surprised. It is as if he has pushed off from the earth to assist you, and countered the force of gravity, and he is as light as a windblown seed. And when you hold him you feel the unguardedness of his musculature. No armoring, just the generous, supple ease of a being supremely confident, totally at home in his world.

Mister Vantha was born in a nearby village. His mother was a prostitute. When he was born a couple without children offered to buy him. There are no social programs for the aged here, and the elderly count on having children to take care of them, so Vantha was sold to the neighbors. They would raise him, and he would do his duty when the couple grew too old to take care of themselves: a human annuity.

Shortly after he was adopted, Vantha's birth mother was diagnosed HIV positive. The people who bought him, fearing he might be infected, took him to Wayne to be tested. Wayne explained that a young baby who tested positive might just be carrying his mother's antibodies and eventually test negative. They insisted on a test and, sure enough, Vantha was positive. Wayne recommended that the couple take him home and bring him back when he was a year old. But no, they did not want him if there was any chance at all he might be infected. They had paid for a child to take care of them, and they could not afford to raise a little boy who would eat their rice and become a burden, and who might never grow up to repay their investment. They insisted that Wayne keep him, retest him when he was a year old and let them know.

In the end, Vantha tested negative, and Wayne contacted his new parents. They said they would be along for him. When I arrived at Wat Opot, Vantha was five years old. They had never come, had never even called to check on how he was. Wayne said he expected they would let him raise Vantha, feed and educate him, and then claim him when he was old enough to be useful. I thought Wayne was being cynical.

One afternoon, when Vantha was six years old, the people who had bought him arrived at Wat Opot. They told Wayne they were just looking in on him, to see how he was doing. Of course, Vantha did not know them. Wayne asked if they intended to take Vantha home permanently at some point, and they said they did, one of these days. Wayne thought about it for a moment. Vantha was thriving. He was about to start school. He was one of the happiest kids at Wat Opot and everyone loved him. Wayne loved him. He was hoping the people would let Vantha grow up and go to school at Wat Opot with his brothers and sisters, so he decided to force the point. Maybe they would change their minds, or even relinquish their claim.

"It is not fair to take him after he has started school," Wayne insisted. "I do not want him to meet you and then always be worrying about when it will happen. Take him now or leave him." When they said they would take him, Wayne was stunned. He had no legal right to Vantha. Suddenly there was no turning back.

The entire exchange had taken ten minutes. The people gathered Vantha and his few belongings and left. He did not even have a chance to say goodbye to the other children, the only family he had ever known. The few children who were home from school when Vantha left were speechless. Vantha, who hardly ever cries, stared in uncomprehending shock at the world he was about to lose. His new father carried him off in his arms. Vantha's powerful little body was limp, the life force drained out of him. His hand wrapped unconsciously around one of his new father's fingers. He needed something to hold on to . . . anything.

Like seeds in the wind, these children who leave are blown here and there, sometimes to thrive, sometimes to perish. Growing up at Wat Opot with Wayne and a mob of siblings, Vantha might have been educated, given opportunities he will never receive. Now he will grow up in a village, to do the duty of a traditional Khmer boy, working in the fields, taking care of aging parents. Will he wilt, or will he set down roots deep in his own culture, and grow strong?

It was about a year after they took him. Vantha had been ill, and the people who purchased him brought him back to see Wayne. They wanted to know if it would be expensive to cure him — in which case, they did not want to keep him. Wayne admits to having been tempted to tell them it would be complicated and very expensive, but it was not in him to lie, and he said that if they took Vantha to the doctor he would be okay and it would not cost them very much. Wayne had not gone to see the boy in the year since he had left Wat Opot because he didn't want to make it more difficult for Vantha to make the transition to his new life. He told me that Vantha looked confused and unhappy. It broke Wayne's heart to see him, and mine to hear about it.

MISS CHAN TEVY: GOING HOME

The very dramatic Miss Chan Tevy (whom Wayne had dubbed Miss Sarah Bernhardt), the little girl who always demanded shampoo and cookies, and more of whatever you had just given her, came to Wat Opot when she was an infant. Her parents had died of AIDS and she too was failing, although the aunt who had taken her in loved her and did her best to care for her. Her uncle, frightened by the illness, did not want her in his house. Finally, to keep peace at home, her aunt allowed Wayne and Rebecca to take her to Wat Opot, the first child to live there. This was in 2001.

With treatment, Chan Tevy's health improved. Her aunt visited now and then, and when the little girl was old enough she would return to her family for holidays. Perhaps her uncle began to understand that she was not a danger to him. Perhaps she had reached an age when she could be useful around the house. Certainly her aunt had never stopped caring about her. Whatever the reasons, her visits home grew longer and more frequent, and one day it was decided that she would move back to the village to live with her people. Chan Tevy was eight years old.

With support from the Home Care team, she still sees the doctors for her medicine. Sometimes on Rice Day she visits her brothers and sisters at Wat Opot. It is surely a sign of progress that people with AIDS are beginning to be accepted in some of the villages, although Wayne still hears of children isolated out of fear, or of mothers who, too poor to take care of them, abandon their babies in a ditch or in the bush.

BABY LEET: ABANDONED AND RECLAIMED

Some of these abandoned babies come to live at Wat Opot. Wayne writes of a little boy named Leet [*LEE-it*], whose mother was a sex worker. She could not care for the baby and left him with an old woman in the village. She promised to send money for food, as the old woman could scarcely feed herself, but the money never arrived and the baby grew weak. Finally the old woman brought him to Wat Opot, and although he was so ill and malnourished that Wayne feared he would grow up brain damaged if he survived, still Wayne could not allow him to die. Over time Leet recovered, and as the baby of the family he became everyone's darling.

One day a young woman appeared. She told Wayne she was "just checking" on the baby on behalf of the old woman in the village, but Wayne saw at once that she was Leet's mother. Some months later she returned, and this time she wanted to take her little boy with her. Her life was more stable now, she said, and she hoped she could take care of him.

It was a difficult decision for Wayne. Leet was thriving at Wat Opot. Still, she was his mother, and her original abandonment had come about because of poverty and fear, and because she could no longer bear to listen to him crying from hunger. Wayne could see that she loved him and that she would do her best to take care of him, so he agreed, and the entire community turned out to wave goodbye as Leet and his mother rode off on a moto into an uncertain future.

MISS RAKSMAI: ADOPTION

Wayne does not envision Wat Opot as an orphanage, so his focus has never been on finding adoptive parents for the children. To introduce that sense of transience would undermine the feeling of stability, and change the focus of Wat Opot. Some children are more adoptable than others because they are younger or HIV negative — or, for the bald truth, they are just cuter or less emotionally damaged or more socially skilled. Wayne wishes to protect the feelings of the children who would be left behind, lest they feel less precious, more like discards. Already in their brief lives they have endured too much rejection. Why add to their trauma the disappointment of being passed over again and again as their siblings are adopted? Why make adoption the focus of their aspiration, the measure of their worth?

But occasionally a situation arises where there seems to be a match between a child and prospective parents who come recommended by someone Wayne knows personally, a case where he judges that adoption may improve the child's chance for a good life. This is especially true with little girls. A girl growing up in Cambodia without parents still has scant chance of making a good marriage. How would an orphaned child fare if it were known that her parents died of AIDS? Although conditions may be changing, and educated girls may someday have better opportunities, our kids still face many obstacles. So when Wayne heard from a trusted friend that she knew of a couple from Australia who had already adopted a Cambodian boy and were looking for a daughter to complete their family, he thought of Miss Raksmai.

Miss Raksmai was two years old. She was quirky and funny and loved to dance. She had been raised here from infancy, after her mother died of AIDS and her biological father abandoned the family. She was cared for by Sari Yei, a grandmother from the village who had lost a child of her own to AIDS. She is a warm, loving woman with many grandchildren. She took our babies at night to her tiny house in the village, and they were raised as her own.

Miss Raksmai grew up protected and loved and indulged by Sari Yei and by all her brothers and sisters at Wat Opot. She was nurtured, played with, teased and passed from hand to hand to hand dozens of times every day. She was a delightful baby, and with so much attention she grew into a formidable toddler, a climber of window grates and table legs, comfortable with strangers, piglets and large white cows, and happy with all sorts of people. She was strongly independent. She smiled easily, rarely cried and could hold her own with bullies. At Wat Opot, children are safe to wander about by themselves, discovering sand piles and bricks, chasing chickens and climbing mango trees. Once she even jumped in the pond and thought it was hilarious when Mr. Sary, who could not swim, had to dive in after her.

Only once did she cause us worry, and that was the night we almost lost her: a terrible night when she was about a year old. She had been ill with diarrhea for several days and was becoming dehydrated. Wayne tried to give her an IV, but her veins were tiny and elusive. It was late, and there would be no doctors available at Takeo Hospital until morning. Sari Yei was holding her, trying to give her a bottle, but she was not sucking. We were all sitting together in the common area outside the clinic watching soap operas before going to bed. I walked by and looked at Raksmai lying in Sari Yei's lap and stopped short.

Back home in the States I used to collect daguerreotypes and tintypes, the earliest kinds of photographs. In the mid-1800s only professional photographers owned cameras, and when a baby died, mourning parents would sometimes hire a photographer to make one image, likely the only one they would ever have of the child they had lost. I learned to recognize these images — even though the children were often propped up in natural-looking poses — by a characteristic shadowy hollowness about the child's eyes, perhaps caused by the same dehydration that was plaguing Raksmai that night. At least that is what shocked me when I looked at her, lying very still in Sari Yei's lap.

I yelled for Wayne and Rebecca, and they whisked her into the office and began working frantically to rouse her. They examined her eyes with a penlight; her pupils barely responded. Her fontanel, the membrane at the crown of her head, was deeply recessed, confirming that she was seriously dehydrated. Finally, Rebecca sunk her fingernails into the soles of Raksmai's foot, and she stirred a little bit, and Wayne and Rebecca began feeding her fluids with a syringe. At first she sucked weakly, but Rebecca stayed up all night with her, giving her a few drops at a time, and when the hospital opened the next day Rebecca rode with her to Takeo, where the doctors managed to insert an IV. Within a few days Miss Raksmai had recovered.

About a year later Wayne heard from his friend about that young couple from Australia with the Cambodian son. Although Wayne was worried, not having met these prospective parents, he agreed to the adoption. In our conversations, Wayne wondered whether Raksmai would truly be better off leaving all the people who loved her to go to live with these strangers in a more materialistic society. It was not as if she had chosen these people for her parents, he said, not like bringing home the boy you want to marry. She had no choice. It had all been settled before they even met. Reasonable concerns aside, Wayne was a father who had lost many children to death and circum-stance, and I could see that it was terribly painful for him to say goodbye to yet another of his babies.

The Australians arrived, decent folks, living temporarily abroad. Incidents of kidnapping and baby selling had caused the Australian authorities to forbid direct adoption of Cambodian children, but Australian nationals living outside the country were permitted to adopt and then apply for a visa for the child when they moved back home.

As the mother and little boy were solidly bonded, Raksmai seized her opportunity to curl up with her new father. Within a few days they all seemed comfortable with each other, and her new parents were anxious to go on to Phnom Penh, complete their paperwork and leave for home.

The last night before they left, Miss Raksmai sat in the cane chair in my room and played peek-a-boo. She had never played this game before. Had her new parents taught her? Tomorrow she would close her eyes, put her hands in front of her face, and her world would change. And she would go off to Australia with people she had just met. Sari Yei, Wayne and all the children, all she had ever known, would be gone. Did she intuit that? In her new life, would Raksmai still imitate Mr. Wayne, walking around with hands behind her back, her belly sticking out, directing chickens, herding piglets? I wondered what new games she would play.

Did her new parents appreciate the family they were taking her away from? When she was older would they explain to her how loved she had been here, by all her brothers and sisters and the people who cared for her? During the weeks before she left I had been taking many photos of Raksmai with Sari Yei and Wayne and the children, and I assembled them into a tiny album for Raksmai to have when she grew up, so she might see herself with the people who had loved her.

The day she left for Phnom Penh all her brothers and sisters assembled to say goodbye. Pesei told me he hoped Raksmai would not be too sad. Then he showed me a drawing he had made for her the night before, carefully rolled up and tied with a ribbon. But Raksmai hopped into the car before he could even give it to her, hopped into her new father's lap with hardly a glance in our direction. The new family waved goodbye, and suddenly they were gone in a cloud of dry-season dust. Wayne and the children stood around for a moment, a little dejected perhaps that she had not seemed in the least upset over leaving, and then the children drifted back to their games, and Wayne to his office.

Three days later the phone rang. Raksmai's new father, calling frantically from Phnom Penh, explained that there had been a glitch in the paperwork. It seemed that there had always existed a discrepancy between what documents the Cambodian authorities required to release a child as legitimately adoptable and what the Australian immigration people wanted to see in order to issue an entry visa. In a sort of gentlemen's agreement, lawyers would draw up two sets of papers. The fact that the contents did not precisely agree bothered no one. It was just business as usual. But a new official at the Australian consulate had balked at this discrepancy, concerned by past scandals involving the selling of babies. And now Raksmai's new parents could not safely take her from Cambodia, because if they could not ultimately resolve the problem she might never be allowed to enter Australia, and they might all remain in limbo, unable to return home. At the moment there were dozens of other new parents abruptly caught in the same bind. The only solution was to return Raksmai to Wat Opot, leave for their offshore home and hope the lawyers could

400

resolve the problem so they could come back for her as soon as possible. Her grim-faced father dropped her off at Wat Opot. Her new mother could not bear to come. After a week of living as a family, Raksmai was already their little girl.

Miss Raksmai waved goodbye as she watched her father's car drive away in the dust. She seemed bewildered and sad, too young to understand anything except that her new parents were gone. She fitted back into life at Wat Opot pretty well, and the children were happy to see her, but those brand-new clothes and sneakers reminded the other kids that she was the chosen one. It would take six months before the new regulations were clarified, before the differing definitions of adoptability were brought into alignment and the paperwork finally straightened out. During those days and weeks, whenever a car arrived, Raksmai would run up expectantly to see whether her father had come back for her. Finally, one day, his taxi did pull up, and he stepped out looking happy and relieved. Then he scooped her up and whisked her off to a new and uncertain life.

How did the other children feel when Raksmai finally left? Pesei wrote to me:

> This is the story about Mai Mai when she
> left from Wat Opot. We all miss her and it
> is boring too because we use to play with
> her every evening. She use to laugh and
> dance when we had music, but that is
> good for her future. When she left we had
> a party and we were all happy but then we
> cried when we said goodbye to her.

For a year or two her new parents stayed
in touch. They sent pictures at holidays, and
both children seemed to be thriving. But
recently Wayne heard they were divorcing,
and we have not heard any news since then.

FROM FAR AWAY: BABY MAI IN THE DARK NIGHT

It's three o'clock on a January morning in
Maine. I am sitting with a hot-water bottle
on my lap, trying to keep warm, writing an
email to a friend in Japan. We've never met,
and my letter is the sort one writes to a new
friend whom one has found through a series
of apparent errors and accidents, yet whom
one feels certain one is meant to know, and
not for the first time. I sense a subtle
mystery, like a whiff of incense in an old
wooden room. Until now our letters have

402

been a delicate dance of storytelling, cautious revelation and occasional apologies for lapses due to busy lives. Our gestures are nuanced and kind, like feeding a deer in a forest.

A new email arrives, surfacing in my inbox with the sound of a cartoon submarine. It is from Wayne, some gossip about the new volunteers. At the end, a brief postscript reads, "By the way, Baby Mai died on Tuesday morning. She was in hospital for several days but not improving and so they brought her back on Saturday. She died very peacefully in Sida's arms."

Baby Mai was the youngest infant at Wat Opot, only six months old when I saw her last, and recently diagnosed HIV positive. Wayne's note is brief, but I know him, know he's in pain. I have watched him secretly test a few drops of a child's blood for AIDS, blood purloined from an IV needle or a scraped knee, have seen the relief or despair on his face when the answer comes. Tonight, stricken, I add the news to my email, push Send and blurt it electronically to my new friend in Japan.

I know it will be a shock, a slap coming abruptly at the end of the affectionate letter I have been writing. Yet I need to know that someone will share this news in the middle of this frigid night, even someone I have never met on the other side of the world, where the sun is still shining. Then I write just a few words to Wayne — he will know my heart — and finally I begin to cry, and I cry from down deep in the childless, motherless part of my own being.

Alone in Maine, missing Wayne and the children and wishing I could be at the funeral, I remember the day Baby Mai came to Wat Opot. It was in late winter 2007. Her birth mother lived in one of the villages nearby, a pretty young woman with AIDS, who was trying to balance the needs of her aged parents with those of a four-month-old baby. She needed to work to support her family, and her parents were too feeble to babysit, so she made the choice of duty to parents above all and brought her child to Wat Opot. Wayne agreed to keep the little girl until her mother found a way to take care of her. It was a sad parting, the baby bawling, her mother torn, anxious about leaving her crying child with strangers, having no choice.

Wayne entrusted the baby to Sida and her husband, Ty. They are a sweet young couple who live at Wat Opot. Sida is tall and quiet and a little dreamy, with a hint of mischievous sensuality. She and her husband seemed thrilled to have a baby to care for together. For the first few days Baby Mai did not eat much, and she cried often. We all tried to play with her, tried to get her to smile, but she just looked worried and stunned by life without the familiar smell and feel of her own mother.

A week later Baby Mai's mother returned from the village. She had worried all week, imagining her own baby distraught and alone. She told Serain, the night nurse, that she had come to reclaim her daughter, hoping to work out a way for them to be together. But what she found was a smiling little girl, beginning to settle in with her new family. Wayne assured her that she could take Baby Mai home any time her circumstances improved, and meanwhile she was welcome to visit as often as she liked.

Every night Sida, her foster mother, brought her to the clinic at Wat Opot, and she grew fatter and healthier. We all loved her, especially Sida, who looked lighter and happier with every passing day. Over time, Sida and Baby Mai grew to look alike, to mimic each other's expressions. And they were inseparable.

I became fascinated with the pure sensuality of the devotion between them and took dozens of photographs of them together: Sida holding the baby in a ruffled party dress on some special occasion, or nuzzling her in front of a bush exploding with pink bougainvillea. Sida resting in a hammock with Baby Mai asleep between her thighs, as though newly born. At a birthday party, both their faces smeared with icing. The two of them playing, perfectly, ecstatically bonded. And one strange image, where Sida is crouching in the dust clutching the baby with an expression of such haunted agony that I can only imagine that she had been overcome by an intimation of the future.

■ ■ ■ ■

What more is there to say? The baby died. I was not there when it happened, could not go to her funeral or comfort her two mothers or the children, or be comforted, or sit up late that night reflecting with Wayne, as we often did. I heard only echoes from a distance, snippets of emails from volunteers or from Wayne: the baby was not feeling well, was becoming dehydrated; the baby went to the hospital in Takeo for an IV; the baby should be fine and would be home in a few days; there was nothing more they could do; and finally, Baby Mai died peacefully in Sida's arms.

Whether Baby Mai died of complications from AIDS or from one of the many illnesses that babies can suffer from in poor countries, I don't know. At this remove, it hardly seems an important distinction. Could more have been done for her in a hospital with better-trained doctors or more modern facilities? It's possible. I am far away, and the questions trouble me. But I know she could not have been more loved, and that Wayne did all he could to save her with the resources and knowledge available to him. In the end, for all her illness and poverty, Baby Mai lived for one happy year, loved by two mothers and several fathers, and was doted on as the baby of the family by her many brothers and sisters.

There will be a funeral for Baby Mai at Wat Opot, and the monks will inscribe prayers on her shroud and chant over her body before it is cremated. The baby's mother will be devastated. And Sida? I weep again to think of her. The baby was all her joy in this life.

Wayne will mourn in his quiet way. He has cremated three hundred family members already. As is his practice, he will spend a while contemplating the baby's life as he chooses a photograph and tints it with soft pastel colors on the computer. Then he will hang her picture on the wall of the crematorium alongside her brothers and sisters who have died. Afterward, he will walk back to his office looking weary; a few of the children will walk with him, slowly, holding his hands. As Wayne mourned in his way, so I joined him and my family at Wat Opot, by writing this memorial.

The night Baby Mai died, I cried out to my unmet friend in Japan. Mercifully he was at his desk, and across time and space he wrote that the news had made his own heart ache. Nothing more. He did not try to fix anything or put things into perspective, or offer platitudes. It was enough to feel his presence, as we mourned a little girl's death together in the dark of night.

■ ■ ■ ■

PART FOUR:
MYSTERIES

■ ■ ■ ■

31
CALLING THE SOUL

Andrew was staring straight ahead when I walked into the hospice. His eyes were blue mandalas. He slumped lower in the red plastic chair, crossed his arms over his heart and hugged his shoulders. "I just saw a man die." Andrew spoke in a precise monotone. "I never saw anyone die before. I watched his soul leave his body."

Andrew was from Perth, Australia. He had bright red hair and a generous smile. The children called him Andaroo, like kangaroo, only they trilled the *r* and warbled an extra long *oooh* at the end. *An-da-rrrroooooooo!* They loved playing with the unfamiliar syllables, and they loved Andrew, who roughhoused with them like a big brother and took them on hikes and let them look at faraway scenes through his telephoto lens.

I met Andrew on a long bus ride. He was newly divorced, traveling to find himself. He worked as an electrician but liked to take pictures and wanted to see whether he could make a go of it as a traveling photojournalist. None of his friends back home could understand why he would want to leave their comfortable middle-class world to risk dysentery in poor countries with ragged children. He told me he felt he had been divorced twice, once from his wife and then from his friends. He had been traveling alone for months and was becoming weary of his self-involvement. He seemed honest and open, a seeker, or maybe just lonely for family. I invited him to stop by Wat Opot. A week later Andrew hiked in from the main road with his duffel bag over his shoulder and his camera around his neck, all dust and freckles and a big grin, totally open to whatever experience the world might offer him.

He had been here for about a month, and now the world had offered him death.

Vannak was thirty-five, only five years older than Andrew, when he died of AIDS. He had been a patient for just a couple of months. His family had brought him in with a miserable skin infection, a fungus spreading all over his body. Andrew spent long hours sitting by Vannak's bed. They could not speak each other's language, but An-

THE WELCOMING MURAL AT WAT OPOT

The face is the loving mother who looks after the children despite her sickness or death from AIDS. The little white shapes are the souls of all the children, living and dead. Pesei explains that "even though the mother has passed away, Wat Opot still can take care of the baby like the mother giving milk." The cross and the Buddha reflect the partnering of two traditions in the founding of Wat Opot, which is nondenominational. The eye is the all-seeing Protector. The dove is Peace, of course, and the lotus is the purity that rises from the mud. The leaf is life itself. Pesei, who is currently studying at the Royal University of Fine Arts in Phnom Penh, was a teenager when he designed and painted this mural.

drew was there, and when he could do nothing else he would cool Vannak's painful skin with a folded paper fan. Rebecca washed Vannak with sulfur soap, and his lesions began to heal. He fought hard, but his health deteriorated and he passed away with Andrew sitting in the chair next to his bed.

Wayne began preparing Vannak for cremation and sent for his family and the monks. Wayne bent his broad back over Vannak's wasted body, sponging him tenderly with a flowered washcloth. He wiped his forehead and his chest and his palms gently as one would bathe a sick child, rinsing and wringing out the washcloth again and again in a small plastic basin of water. Then he dressed Vannak in fresh clothes, a plaid shirt and khaki pants, and parted and combed his hair and straightened his limbs on the bed. His feet he left bare.

Over the years, Wayne has observed that his male patients often do not do as well as the women. If, as often happens, a man becomes ill before his wife, the family will exhaust their savings on medical care and then be forced to sell their home or rice fields as well. By the time his wife becomes ill there is no money left to pay for her treatment.

Even if a man is not married, if he is too ill to work he may beg or borrow money from friends or family, loans he can never repay. In the end, desperate, he may steal. The family is angry with the man for bringing this disease home, and terrified of this plague whose means of transmission they do not understand. There may also be pressure from the village to force him to leave. So his family may refuse to care for him as his health deteriorates. Even if he receives antiretroviral drugs and his health improves his family may refuse to take him back. He may turn to alcohol if he has not already been drinking. In the end, rejected by family and community, he will feel isolated. He has no life to go back to. He simply gives up.

Mr. Kamra was another young man who lived at Wat Opot. Like Vannak he had an excruciating skin condition. Rebecca tried the sulfur soap on him, and he felt so much better, was so encouraged about his life, that he returned to his village and told his family he was ready to move back in with them. They told him it did not matter that he felt better, he still had AIDS and they did not want him. They threw him out of their house and down the stairs. Then they threw the chair he had been sitting on after him and slammed the door. The chair clattered to the bottom of the stairs and smashed to pieces. When the family came out they found that he had hanged himself from the tree in their dooryard.

Women, by contrast, often have different social skills than men, and are used to supporting each other in the village. At Wat Opot they cook together, share child care, do each other's hair, go to the market, weave silk, dress up for weddings and sit together in the evening chatting under the stars. They may not always get along, and there may be dramas, but women create around themselves a sense of normalcy, of people living together in community. Most important, their children need them, and this gives them something to live for. Even when a mother is very ill with AIDS and possibly TB, even when she feels overwhelmed and hopeless, she may not give up until she can see her children safely settled in at Wat Opot with food and medicine, friends to play with and other mothers to care for them. If she is very ill and the road back is just too hard, she may begin wasting away for no apparent reason. After she dies Wayne may find a neat cache of pills hidden under her mattress, the medicines she stopped taking some time before. He will never tell her children about the pills.

The monks arrived and wrote the funeral inscriptions on a white cloth that they draped over Vannak's face. Wayne had laid Vannak's body on the bed in his fresh clothes, covered by a thin sheet. They spread a towel with blue flowers over his face and upper body and tucked in the edges. The bundle was slender, almost too tiny to have been a man. We were all kneeling on the white-and-green linoleum floor of the hospice, crouching in the narrow spaces between the iron bed frames. Wayne knelt with his hands in prayer. Four monks in saffron robes sat on chairs next to Vannak's bed, chanting prayers. It was a scene Wayne had participated in hundreds of times, a member of our family dead of AIDS. But this time something felt different.

Sama sam poot . . . The monks began to chant the invocation.

Wayne heard a voice inside his head whispering, *Take a photo.*

Namo Tassa . . .

Hail the Fortunate One . . .

Take a photo.

Bhagavato . . .

Freed from suffering . . .
Take . . . a . . . photo.
Arahato . . .
Fully enlightened . . .
Take . . . a . . . photo . . . NOW!

At first he ignored the voice; to stand up and climb over the praying family would be disrespectful and create a disturbance at a sacred moment. But the feeling would not go away. Finally, to quiet the insistent voice inside his head, Wayne struggled up from where he was kneeling, walked to his office, retrieved his small digital camera and took a single photograph from the back of the room. Then he knelt and laid the camera beside him and continued to pray.

After the cremation, Wayne got busy with the children and medicines and the evening's chores. It was not until the next morning that he remembered to look at the photograph. There, hovering over Vannak's face, was a perfect, translucent ball of light. Wayne loaded the image into his computer and examined it close up. The orb was lovely, opalescent, with clearly defined edges. You could just make out details of the room through it, the flowered towel, the white iron bedpost. The orb looked to be four or five inches in diameter. It was delicately poised above Vannak's third eye.

Wayne had never seen such a thing. Andrew was puzzled, but his technical background told him it might only be a reflection. Wayne emailed the image to a number of friends who were photographers or computer experts. He also sent it to a minister he knew who had been his spiritual adviser. Then Andrew and Wayne photographed the room at the same hour, in the same light, from the same spot, but there was nothing unusual about the pictures. Wayne searched the Internet and discovered 3.8 million sites about orbs. He spent a long night reading. People spoke of orbs as specks of dust or aliens or wandering spirits. He looked at scores of photos of orbs, but he found none as precisely placed as the pretty pearl of light floating above Vannak's forehead.

Over the next few days, answers from his technical friends started coming in. They fell into two categories. One group said it absolutely had to be some sort of light reflection or dust in the air or on the lens, and explained how that might have happened. The other group sent technical explanations of why it could not possibly be either of those, but said they had no idea what else it might be. The minister sent Wayne a stern warning "not to go ascribing any spiritual significance to this thing."

We asked the children what they thought. Dara looked at Wayne and then at me with the sort of look only a twelve-year-old can give a clueless adult, and said simply, *"pralung,"* the Khmer word for soul.

Over the next weeks, Wayne and Andrew began taking more photographs at night, and suddenly there were orbs everywhere. After dinner, before the generator went on, or after evening clinic, I'd see cameras flashing like fireflies in the dark, and hear the children's excited exclamations as their shadows clustered about the glowing LCD screens. Then they would run off in all directions, laughing and calling in the darkness.

Sometimes there were no orbs to be seen, but in a second photo taken a moment later, hundreds would mysteriously appear. Some seemed to be only dust stirred up by the children's feet, or insects swarming in the flash. Others were simply odd. A few reappeared night after night in significant places, such as inside the family room in the crematorium, as if keeping company with the living and the dead. One single orb was a frequent visitor outside the children's sleeping porch late at night, after the youngest ones had gone to bed. The children

loved this treasure hunt and would pore over the images on the computer, pointing and arguing the fine points like a convention of tiny taxonomists. They got excited over the occasional anomaly, like a candy-apple-red sphere, or one that appeared to have been caught in the process of hatching into a white flame.

About this time, on a weekend trip to Phnom Penh, I discovered a book called *Calling the Souls: A Cambodian Ritual Text,* published by Reyum in 2005. The author, anthropologist and Cambodia scholar Ashley Thompson, translated an epic poem still recited today as part of a traditional healing ceremony. She described the Khmer concept of the soul, the *pralung,* as a fragile confederation of nineteen separate elements, prone to fracturing at times of physical or emotional stress, or during vulnerable periods of passage, such as puberty, marriage, the ordination of a monk, old age or even a momentary shock such as tripping on the stairs. Parts of the soul can break away and are believed to wander off, lured by demons and spirits into dark and dangerous lands, veiled by illusion. Times of malaise or vague unexplained illness might call for a ceremony where a healer leads villagers into the forest to retrieve fragments of the wandering *pralung.* The verses are moving and tender, reassuring the beloved soul that it will be welcomed home with good food and a soft pillow, that no one is angry, and warning of frightful animals and innumerable cruel spirits that lurk just beyond the safe community and loving home.

If the idea of a fragmenting soul strikes many Westerners as an odd notion, think first of the vestiges in our own language, or of our own rituals designed to ensure the integrity of the spirit. They are so much a part of us, we use them without conscious thought, such as when we bless someone who sneezes to guard against the going out or coming in of spirits. We speak of being beside ourselves with worry, feeling scattered, jumping out of our skin when shocked, going all to pieces, having an out-of-body experience, and we talk about the split personalities of people suffering from schizophrenia and bipolar disorder.

Wayne's office manager told me that her parents had once called an old woman from the village to perform the ritual for her. She was a young woman then, and had been feeling weak and uninterested in life. Afterward she felt much better. I do not know whether any of the Wat Opot children have experienced this ritual, and I do not mean to draw a direct comparison between their searching for the souls of the dead and the calling of the soul as a healing ritual. Yet there seems to me to be a resonance. In a culture where one can go into the forest with a fishing basket to call back wandering bits of soul, it might not seem odd or unusual at all for the children to go abroad at night searching for spirits with a camera.

On one dark night, Wayne and the children

went looking for orbs. They had not seen any for several nights. It was getting late, and they were about to give up. Someone suggested going to Chhang's Place to see if they could call up the spirit of Mister Chhang, a little boy who had died. Wayne told me that he and Chhang had been very close, and that when the child died in his arms, Wayne saw his spirit fly out from his eyes and felt Chhang's soul pass through his own body.

A small open-air dining pavilion was dedicated to the memory of Mister Chhang, and his framed and matted portrait still hangs on the wall. On the front of the building a local artist painted a flowering bougainvillea tree and the words "Chhang's Place." It is very beautiful, with blossoms of several colors on one tree like a real bougainvillea, but the children were not satisfied with the painting. "This is Chhang's Place?" they demanded. "But where Meestah Chhang?" The artist thought for a moment and then painted a beautiful bird with a flowing tail, flying up from the flowers toward heaven. The children were happy to have that image of their friend's spirit painted on his house.

The children ran toward the dining pavilion laughing and calling, "Meestah Chhang!

Meestah Chhang!" Wayne said he would take one final photograph, and then it was off to bed for everyone. He aimed his camera at Chhang's photo, snapped the picture, and the children swarmed around to look at the screen. They gasped and exclaimed. There, just above Mister Chhang's portrait, was an orb, traveling from left to right, with a long tail like a comet. The children were delighted. And Wayne? As with the orb that floated over Vannak's face, he is moved to marvel at the perfection of the moment, and to keep an open mind.

Back home in America, in the cold reality of a Maine winter, I examine the photographs again. It is easy to get lost in theories, yet it seems to me there is a more important question than whether the orbs are dust or bugs or whether a few of them might actually be spirits. What are the children really searching for when they venture abroad at night with cameras, looking for the souls of the dead?

In some ways, the children's search for souls is much the same as their nocturnal hunt for frogs. Instead of running around with little bamboo traps, they carry digital cameras. Watching them, I sense no terrified titillation, no fear of ghosts. Any adult worth his salt remembers clearly that it's a blast to run around in the dark long after his bedtime, whispering and giggling.

But here is the difference: these children have lost, or in most cases been denied, their birthright, to grow up safe and cherished in the family of their birth. AIDS has robbed them of their loving parents, of siblings and close friends. They may have been disowned by their villages, passed along by grand-parents or siblings, uncles and aunts too poor or too frightened or just unwilling to invest scarce resources in taking care of children who may never be anything but a burden. So at night, when they go hunting for the souls of their loved ones, maybe it is just plain comforting for them to believe that the spirits of their brothers and sisters, friends and parents, choose to stay close in the dark night, watching over them and lov-ing them and keeping them safe. Perhaps they are creating their own meaning, in a ritual of reassurance.

In the spring of 2008, as I was preparing to make reservations for a return trip to Wat Opot, I was diagnosed with cancer, a mirror of my mother's illness. I had found a lump in my breast in April, and in the next few weeks there were mammograms and a biopsy, both inconclusive. I lay in the bathtub one day, worrying about the second biopsy. My own mother had died of cancer, and I had spent her last year taking care of her. I knew what a slow death from cancer looks like. Soaking now in hot water I looked down on my own body. I felt small and frightened and alone.

When I told Wayne he wrote, "You join a new family now of people often avoided because of the uncomfortable feeling that others get when they think it could happen to them."

Wayne told the children I was not coming back that winter. They were curious; they didn't even know what cancer was. In their world people rarely live long enough to develop diseases like that. I sent a photo of me without hair. At first the children did not recognize me. Then they laughed and told Wayne I looked very enlightened, probably because monks and nuns in Cambodia shave their heads. Pesei wondered whether we had good doctors where I live. Wayne told me that after they found out the children dedicated their weekly meditation to me.

In the days that followed I often pictured

what it would be like to return once more to Wat Opot, to Wayne and the children. I came to hope that the crucible of my illness would help me remake myself into someone more understanding, more compassionate, more loving. I prayed I would no longer avoid the very ill or dying out of fear of making a mistake or saying the wrong thing. During many long nights I dreamed that through this illness I would finally be able to cross the chasm that divided me from the children, and that we might go on, all of us together, somewhere beyond hope and fear.

■ ■ ■ ■ ■

PART FIVE:
DEPARTURES

■ ■ ■ ■ ■

32
How It Was

Chemotherapy, radiation, the works. Poisoned dreams in a perpetual twilight. Tedious waking hours tinged by nausea. It would be three years before I could return to Wat Opot.

How sweet it would be to arrive all dusty from the tuk-tuk ride and see those kids! Alone in my room in Maine, I savored every moment of my imaginary journey: how I would ride past village markets, past women selling coconuts and soda bottles filled with gasoline, past beaded curtains of red sausages dangling from frames by the side of the road. Motos with whole families on them. Wicker baskets crowded with live piglets, their pink flesh bulging in hexagonal tesserae. Clusters of ducks and chickens strung upside down from poles like living epaulets. Skinny moto drivers with their baseball caps pulled down to shade their eyes from the battering sun.

I conjured minivan taxis so crammed with packages and bodies that you could see no light through the windows, and crowded buckboards carrying workers to the fields and factories, and big smelly buses and the giant SUVs of the NGOs and UNICEF, all honking and passing each other, and passing the passers in the insane life-and-death bumper-car boogie that is traffic in Cambodia, and I wanted to go back.

Finally I pictured my tuk-tuk turning from that paved chaos and riding the last half mile down the dirt road through Ants-in-a-Line Village, and dogs barking and shying away, and children waving, and chickens rising up, each stirring its own tiny dust devil.

Abruptly the dream snapped shut. Something in me decided that homecoming could never be as I imagined, not at all like my idyllic vision of reunion. Surely I had been away too long, and the children's memory of me had faded by now. Many of the children I knew had gone: Miss Raksmai and Baby Cheab had both been adopted to Australia; and Miss Chan Tevy, whose uncle had finally allowed her to come home, would not come running to demand double helpings of cookies and shampoo. Miss Malis lived in the village now with her grand-mother, and Samphos and Sophea, two little brothers whose father was finally well enough to take care of them, were also living at home now. Miss Yanni had not been getting along with her stepmother and had gone to live with relatives. Most of the weavers had moved on, and lovely Lan Tip, with her broad sweet face, and other children whose names I never did learn. Mister Bott, builder of wondrous singing kites, had gone to live with his father, and Dara and Rajana wanted to be monks and were living at the wat. Sovann and his brothers were at the university in Phnom Penh. And of course Mister Vantha, who was still living with the people who had bought him from his mother. And Baby Mai, whose death left a hole in our hearts.

No, I was sure it could be nothing like I had imagined.

I flew to Bangkok and on to Phnom Penh. The Golden Gate Hotel was as I left it, with the same tuk-tuk drivers lounging outside, eager for fares. "Opot! Opot!" They greeted me as if I had never been away. I went to Lucky Supermarket to buy treats for the kids, wavered between oatmeal cookies and less healthy forms of sugar, bought both and piled into my tuk-tuk for the trip to Wat Opot.

It was almost dinnertime when we reached the narrow driveway. We turned into the parking area and the low sun was in my eyes. We stirred up a cloud of dust when we stopped and it glittered in the late-afternoon light. For a moment we were all alone, and when the driver turned off the little two-stroke engine the rattle of the last two hours settled with the slow golden dust.

But the children had heard the sound of the engine and ran to see who had come, and soon there was a crowd. Some I knew at once. Ouen and Kosal and Mister Heng I saw first, still skinny but much taller, and Sampeah smiling with his front teeth grown in. "Is that you, Bopha? Srey Pich?" They had grown up so much that I had to look again to recognize the little girls they had been. Here came Pesei on his bicycle, handsome as a silent-film star with his new pencil mustache. Little Kiri, whose mother still chopped her hair ragged with a razor blade. She looked like a very small Joan of Arc ready for the stake. Rithy was first to scramble up into the tuk-tuk. He climbed into my lap and squeezed me with one of his long melting hugs, and then the tuk-tuk was all little arms and excited faces and hugs and reaching hands and little bare feet, and the driver just standing there grinning at the spectacle. Over to one side two new boys who didn't know me stood there staring, wondering what all the fuss was about.

The kids unloaded the tuk-tuk. A couple of bigger boys carried my luggage and the little ones stumbled on with the bags from Lucky Supermarket so they could be first to peek and see what treats I had brought, and the other children crowded round and grabbed my hands as we walked toward the office to find Mr. Wayne.

33
RETURN TO WAT OPOT

Wayne and I sat in the big gazebo in the middle of campus. It was new since my last visit and serves as a patio, study hall, reception area for visitors and shady breezeway. Miss Punlok and Srey Pich napped, curled up together on the generous cushion of a papasan chair. Sokun, a new little boy, wriggled in and out of Wayne's lap, never sitting still for more than a moment.

Wayne looked relaxed and at ease. We sat for hours, enjoying our friendship and talking about the changes at Wat Opot. One of the volunteers, a young woman from Taiwan, had brought a group of businessmen for a visit from the Taiwanese Lion's Club in Phnom Penh. They had been so impressed that they had raised money and descended on Wat Opot with an architect and builders and earth movers. Soon there was a new dormitory for the children. There were two wings with separate sleeping quarters and bathrooms for boys and girls, and in the center an office for Wayne and a generous common space. The dorm rooms were broad and airy, with high ceilings and a long raised wooden platform on each side. During the day the children used the platforms to play and study, and at night they rolled out their sleeping mats and hung their mosquito nets, and the platform became one huge bed.

Before the new dorm was built the children slept in the old hospice, on porches, anywhere they could roll out a mat. Some of the older boys had hung hammocks in the dining room. Now they slept together, Cambodian family style, several children under each mosquito net. Once, long ago, Wayne had purchased little bedside tables to alternate with the bamboo beds in the old dorm. He arranged the room carefully so that there were drawers for each child's belongings. It all looked very neat and

Wayne was feeling pleased with himself, but by the time he came back that evening the children had dragged all the tables to the other side of the room, pushed the beds back together and were sleeping in their usual puppy piles.

The new dorm stood in the northwestern corner of the campus, safely away from the road. Years ago, when Wayne and Vandin first opened the clinic, the farmer next door had offered one of his fields for sale. He wanted fifty dollars. It was a lot of money back then and Wayne had not wanted to divert funds from patient care to buy a piece of land he might never need. They had five acres already, and with only a clinic and crematorium there was still plenty of room to grow.

When I came back in 2007 there were more buildings, and even more were needed. The land was for sale again, only this time the price had risen to three hundred dollars, nearly a year's wage for a worker in the provinces. Life in Cambodia was improving, and land near Phnom Penh was becoming expensive. The city was beginning to sprawl southward, and it was only a matter of time before the sprawl reached us. Wat Opot needed a new dorm, and the neighbor could see that his land was the only possible direction for the campus to grow. I saw this too, and urged Wayne to buy the land before the price went up yet again. Wayne thought about it, but money was still tight.

We discussed it several times over the next few months, but there was always something more pressing. Wayne complained that the neighbor was being greedy. "I just don't like feeling like I'm over a barrel."

"Damn it, Wayne!" I said finally, in frustration. And then I added, embarrassed at swearing because Wayne tries to avoid it, "In my humble opinion, sir, if you do not buy that land now you will just wind up paying more for it in the end." And to prove I meant it I handed him three hundred dollars.

The new dorm stood partly on that field. I noticed also that the farmer had put some of his windfall into improving his own house and livestock. It seemed a good outcome all around.

Another major change at Wat Opot was twenty-four-hour electricity, wired in from a central generator in town, and there were plans for even cheaper power once the lines were connected to a Vietnamese power plant. Wayne and I had sometimes wondered what Wat Opot would be like if our severely rationed two hours a day of electricity gave way to a taken-for-granted power on demand. Both of us figured that, all in all, it would be a mixed blessing. There would be more light pollution and noise, but power would be cheaper and a lot less bother. Wayne would not have to fetch expensive petrol every day for the grumbly old generator, or depend on an equally stubborn assistant who, being the only one who could prod the behemoth into life, safeguarded his job by refusing to teach anyone else to do it. With full-time power the older kids would not have to do their homework by candlelight, and Wayne could complete more tasks on his computer. But now there were more kids sprawled in front of the TV, soap operas in the afternoon, music videos in the evening. And late at night a single blazing floodlight was enough to blot out the Milky Way. Unlike Wayne and me, the children didn't seem to notice or care. But being from Maine, where our sequined velvet night skies have degraded dramatically, I felt sad.

I missed the twilight hour after dinner when the whole community used to gather in front of the clinic to play and wait for the generator to cough itself to life. Now, many of the children went off to the dorm and played indoors or watched television. And there seemed to be fewer of those wonderful games the children used to play after lights out, like hunting for orbs or catching frogs with flashlights and bamboo traps, or roasting taro in little pit fires, or just wilding on a full-moon night. And the stone bench tucked in among the bougainvillea, where you could sit in the moonlight with a child and talk about the concerns of his heart, seemed less sheltered now.

After Baby Mai died, her foster mother, Sida, seemed inconsolable. She had been a joyous mother and she longed for a child of her own. It was risky; she and her husband are both HIV positive; but they followed the doctor's instructions carefully. Sida is already on medication, and when the baby was born he was immediately given a dose of antiretrovirals. The combination cuts the chance of mother-to-child transmission from around 30 percent to only 2 percent. It worked, and now there is a healthy new baby at Wat Opot with the wonderful name of Savan Tanta, which, I am told, means "More Precious Than Gold." He has fat cheeks and dimples and his mother's playful black eyes. The kids missed Miss Raksmai and, of course, Baby Mai. I asked Wayne whether he worried about Sida and her husband becoming ill and not being able to look after the baby, but he seemed optimistic. And in the worst case Savan Tanta could still be raised by his large and loving family. At Wat Opot everyone loves babies.

After dinner my first night back, Wayne and I walked to the crematorium for the evening service. At first it was just the two of us. Wayne lit a white candle and offered three sticks of incense, and we meditated together in the smoke and dim candlelight under the photographs of family members who had died of AIDS. How many times in the past three years had I ached to be in just this place, doing this simple peaceful observance?

There was a commotion. It was Sokun. He banged the door open and came skidding into the *pa cha* and plopped down in Wayne's lap and began improvising a tuneless version of the Buddhist invocation at the top of his lungs, punching out each syllable, even the ones he didn't know. Wayne and I shrugged and joined in, and the three of us followed that up with the customary song, "Thank you, thank you, Jesus." Sokun was there for the company, and the noise; he could not sit still for meditation but ran outside and skittered around the *pa cha* several times, still bellowing, "Tank you! Tank you! *Saa-ma! Sam poot! Sa-tout!* Jeeee-sus!"

At six years old, Sokun would probably be called hyperactive in the States and put on drugs. Wayne does not know the details of his background, but he seems to be an expert at rooting out fresh trouble and then finding his way to the middle of it. But he also wants to be helpful, to be noticed and praised like any of us. So we try to give him little jobs, which he usually does well for a while. Wayne says he is coming around, and is much better than when he arrived, when Wayne would sometimes have to hold him to keep him from flailing around and hurting someone.

I asked Wayne why there were no other kids at the evening service, and he said that although they still came sometimes, there were fewer regulars than before. It never was compulsory, so he just let it happen as it would.

Wat Opot has matured. It is calmer; the older kids are busy with schoolwork, with art and play. They are more independent, more like teenagers anywhere. The youngest

447

still flock to us by day, and they are the ones who come to the *pa cha* at night, singing loudly, offering their resounding *"Satout!"* at the end. They are still living close to the trauma of losing their families. And they are little kids, and like walking together in the dark to the *pa cha,* clumping along wearing Wayne's huge black Crocs as we circle the crematorium three times after the service. They love holding hands or riding on Wayne's shoulders as we walk slowly back to the clinic for evening meds.

This new calmness, could it be that most of the kids are just further from the essential trauma? When I first came, many had been recently orphaned and there was death all around them — adults and other children sick and dying of AIDS and being cremated. These kids sorted the bones, wondering if they would be next to die, but most of them survived and now, as younger kids arrive, even though they may have recently lost their parents, they enter into a more settled environment. There is no hospice and almost nobody dies. Some of the boys are at the university in Phnom Penh, and with them as examples it is not so outrageous for the others to imagine that they too might go to college one day. Their trauma is no less profound, but the culture they enter here is far more calm, and to my eye they adjust more quickly and settle down into life here. At Wat Opot the focus is on school and art and community, and on the future.

It truly is a change of generations. Mister Phirun, who at fifteen is our oldest boy living with AIDS, straddles the past and present. He has not forgotten the horror days before antiretroviral medication, when he struggled for his own life and watched his friends dying all around him. His body is still scarred from the skin lesions that afflicted him before he went on ARVs. It has taken years for him to begin to believe he may grow up, and to see the point in going to school or thinking about the future.

Maybe this is why many of the children do not come to the *pa cha* for evening services very often now, or search for spirit orbs in the dark. Life has become more normal for them, and the dead are not as present.

Early one evening I took a photograph. The village kids were arriving for their English lessons. They came by foot and by bicycle, a stream of kids from as far away as Phnom Chisor. A crowd of children was playing by the school under the mural of the laughing dinosaur kangaroo that was painted by our kids and the village kids, working together. Wayne looked over from the gazebo, where we were all having our dinner, and smiled. "That's a photo that could never have been taken before," he said. "Village kids playing with AIDS kids, and not being afraid."

Wayne spoke to me about the future. "It's 2009 and I'm sixty-four years old and I feel like I've still got one more project in me, something more I can give in this lifetime. It's not like I want to go sit on the top of a mountain, or find a guru. Anyway, enlightenment is nothing without good works. What's the use of being enlightened if you're not doing something for the world?"

34
THE CRIES OF CHILDREN

Mothers, and some fathers as well, have told me that even in a crowded place they can recognize the cry of their own child. Having not had babies of my own, it took me a little time, but with so many children at Wat Opot there was frequently somebody crying, and after a time I began to be able to guess who was crying and why. I knew when Mister Kosal had constructed one of his elegant towers of playing cards and one of the bigger boys had run by and knocked it over just to savor Kosal's howl of frustration. I recognized Miss Punlok's shrieks of terror whenever anyone looked at her in the long weeks when she was sitting at the foot of her mother's deathbed. I heard Miss Punthea cry out when Mister Leak poked her in the eye and knew hers to be a cry of genuine physical pain. And I could tell when little Rith was caterwauling just to get his older brother to fight his battles so he could be sure he had not forsaken him.

There were other cries, and on this night I learned the cry of abandonment, the sound a small child makes when everything and everyone she ever knew has suddenly been taken away and she is facing her first night among strangers. It is the sort of cry that would make a parent offer his soul to God or to the Devil if only he could take on that child's pain himself, the kind of cry some of us make when we fall into our deepest despair.

A new child arrived today. She is about three years old and only yesterday her mother died of AIDS. There were three siblings, and immediately after the funeral her uncle had them all tested. The older children, a boy and girl, were negative, but when the youngest tested HIV positive her uncle did not take her to his house or even bother to collect her clothes. He just drove her straight to Wat Opot and left her. We do not even know her name yet. Today is Friday and her name is in the paperwork somewhere in the office, and Wayne's secretary has gone home for the weekend.

Wayne asks Madame Neath, one of the "mothers," to look after her. She is a pretty woman in spite of the deep scars that tuberculosis has carved into her face and neck, and she is kind and good with children.

Earlier this evening the little girl was sitting on Neath's hip, clinging to her and looking stunned. But tonight as she bedded down under the mosquito net she began to cry. Neath was moving from bed to bed, settling her brood for the night, and this nameless child just sat there keening, in that same state of fixated shock I remembered with Miss Punlok when her mother was dying. It was — is — a soul-shredding cry, and my only comfort comes from watching Miss Punlok growing up with lots of friends and a wicked sense of humor.

Punlok was there tonight with some of the others. They were doing massage, a complex routine involving finger cracking and step-over toe holds right out of TV wrestling. It's a common family activity, with the young ones massaging the older kids, and switching off, and everybody having a cozy time of it. And I think, maybe in time life will be easier for this new little one too as she starts to find her place. I think it is ultimately the children who heal each other. But for now she is inconsolable, and I need to learn her name.

Some children do not cry. Kids who have lived so long with disappointment and abandonment that they pull themselves away from the world into a kind of shadow, where they accept reality with stoic resignation. Like Miss Srey Mom.

I sat with the kids tonight after dinner, watching TV, and Srey Mom curled up with me and went to sleep. She is taller and prettier than when I saw her three years ago, and she seems to have grown into her face and forehead, which always seemed large for her body. But she is still the hurt little girl I knew, and still needy, though she will shut down at the hint of a slight.

When she does interact with other children she seems to take on more adult roles. Wayne says she is a natural leader. She learned a lot about business from Madame Ketmoni, her first mother at Wat Opot, and

I watch her buying up the evening treats from some of the younger kids and reselling them later at a profit. She also seems to be the local bookie, holding the bets while the kids play at cards and marbles. At these times she looks uncannily like the shrewd Ketmoni.

She lay on my lap tonight, took my hand and placed it on her heart, just as she did when she was younger. She has a cough. She had a second round of TB treatment last year, and with her incessant ear infections I wonder whether she is so often in pain that she doesn't even bother to tell us anymore.

She felt feverish, but Wayne had locked himself in his office, squinting at his computer, trying to finish the annual accounting while nursing a bad cold, and I hated to disturb him. Perhaps I should have called him anyway, but Srey Mom was ready for bed and I figured she might do better just going to sleep. Standing in the twilight of the dormitory, surrounded by the breathing of sleeping children, I watched Srey Mom make up her bed with that same tragic self-sufficiency that I remembered from the night she first arrived. I stepped forward and helped her string up the mosquito net, defining and enclosing her own small space on the sleeping platform. Unlike the other children, Srey Mom sleeps alone. She rolled out her mat. She took two pillows and placed them at right angles. Then she piled up a nest of no less than six folded blankets, these more for comfort than for warmth. Then she lay down and pulled a single blanket up over her shoulders and closed her eyes. Needing to do something, I pulled the blanket up and tucked her in, but she had already turned inward, and was gone.

Once, Papa Steve saw Srey Mom sitting by the crematorium. Srey Mom was examining her arms, he told me, touching the scars left by the rashes and sores that have afflicted her over the years. Srey Mom stared at them in disbelief, and Steve told me he could almost hear the little girl thinking, "Whose arms are these? Could they really be mine?"

Wayne tells me he has to watch Srey Mom carefully. A few times he has caught her palming her ARVs, or spitting them out when she leaves the clinic. The children know how crucial it is to take their medicine consistently so they won't become resistant. Srey Mom is already on second-line drugs. Is she giving up?

Srey Mom receives a phone call from her

sisters. There is a family event, and they want her to come home for a visit. Someone has arrived to pick her up. She gathers her clothes quickly and asks Wayne for her medicine. He asks how long she will be away and she just shrugs, but then she smiles a nervous, excited smile I have not seen on her face before. Maybe this time her sisters have finally decided to let her live with them. Perhaps sharing her fantasy, Wayne gives her an entire month's ration of pills. Srey Mom says goodbye; her face is happy and open. In a moment of hope, her walls come down.

35
RICE IN YOUR EAR

Yesterday two villagers came to see Wayne at the clinic, a boy of about twelve named Samphy and his older sister. They stood to one side, patient and shy, waiting for Wayne to finish his breakfast. Samphy had put on his dress shirt to come to the clinic, green with gold elephants woven through the fabric. Our Ouen has the same shirt, which he reserves for weddings and other special occasions.

Samphy's sister explained that he had rice stuck in his ear. For an hour Wayne tried every trick he knew to dislodge it. First, he used peroxide to bubble the rice out, and then he tried a water flush. He peered through an otoscope and explored gently with long tweezers, and tried to snag it on a fluffed-up Q-tip, without success. The boy's sister stood by, holding the flashlight and looking serious. It appeared that Samphy or his family must have tried to dig out the rice, as his ear canal was already scratched and bleeding. The boy winced and was becoming fidgety, and the blood in the canal obscured Wayne's view. Finally he sent Samphy home with some antibiotics and told him to come back in three days for another try.

How, I wondered, does a bright and sober twelve-year-old boy get rice in his ear? I remembered an old folk song warning kids not to put beans in their nose. Nah. He seemed too smart for that. It was a mystery to me.

It was late December, a few days before the New Year, and the singing kites were flying to celebrate the harvest. Months earlier, the Wat Opot children had planted a field of rice on the eastern end of campus, out near the crematorium. It is good for the land to be cultivated. Wayne had hired a local man to plow the field. All day the great hump-backed bulls struggled back and forth, turning up heavy clods of clay.

It took a whole day for our children to plant the rice, and now it would take two days for the harvest. In the end their small paddy yielded ten fifty-kilo bags of rice, enough to feed everyone at Wat Opot for about two weeks. Wayne can buy rice in the market for about fifteen dollars a bag, and this rice the children grow will cost him twenty, but it is their culture and tradition, and he does not want them to lose touch with that. The older boys will do the threshing, and in the end there will be a special meal of new rice, and everyone will share a sense of accomplishment and thanksgiving.

I watched the children in the field, working in the rice and water and mud, wading through the golden landscape as Brueghel might have painted it, with Phnom Chisor rising misty in the background. Everyone worked together. The bigger boys cut the rice. They twirled the sheaves like pinwheels in the air, and knotted them into bundles with straw. Even the smallest children helped carry in the harvest, stepping high like egrets through the shallow water, climbing the banks and passing sheaves to others to lay out in the sun to dry. Each carried a bundle of rice on one shoulder. The heavy grains slapped against their cheeks and necks as they labored through the mud.

As they carried the bundles of rice on their shoulders to the threshing floors, they tilted their heads away at the perfect angle for a few grains of rice to shake loose and fall.

And that is how a little boy gets rice in his ear.

36
FUND-RAISING

A yoga teacher came to visit one day to lead a class, and to choose some of our kids for a teacher training program. Yoga and meditation are beneficial for children with AIDS, and yoga instructors in Phnom Penh can earn a living doing meaningful work in a healthy environment. Our kids take naturally to yoga. They are agile and light and most of them are physically fearless, never having had parents to warn them about climbing trees or balancing atop barbed wire fences.

Accompanying the teacher, who was Khmer, was a lady from Australia who asked me for a tour of the campus. I walked her through the main attractions: the fishponds, the clinic, the new dormitory and school, the crematorium, the flowers and rice field, and I told her the story of Wat Opot. She was quiet, until finally she said, "Well, you certainly don't need *my* help. I was thinking of leaving a donation, but you are too successful. I want to give money to the truly needy."

I thought of our dwindling bank balance, and cringed.

By now we had come to the gazebo, and were cooling ourselves in the papasan chairs. Wayne happened by and joined us. Our visitor began telling Wayne about a place she had visited in Phnom Penh, an orphanage way more in need of her donation than Wat Opot.

"How did you find it?" Wayne asked.

"I saw a brochure at the hotel, and my tuk-tuk driver said it is a good place. The driver knew all about it. It is run by an old monk who is building a dorm and school for the orphans."

"An elderly monk, with no teeth?" asked Wayne.

"Yes, that's the one," she said, excited. "All he needs is five hundred dollars and he can finish the whole thing. When I go back to Australia I want to raise the money with my church committee and send it to him. We can make it our special project."

Wayne leaned back in his chair, closed his eyes and sighed. Finally he sat up and began to tell the visitor about a time, many years before, when he met the same toothless old monk. Actually he was not a monk, and the school and dorm, they were almost done back then too. All it would take was five hundred dollars to finish the job. Wayne was touched, and he dug deep into his own pocket and gave the monk the money. But the buildings remained unfinished. Later, Wayne learned that the children he had been shown were kids from the community, not even orphans, but hired to deceive visitors.

Unfortunately, this sort of fraud is all too

common, with hotel desk clerks and tuk-tuk drivers getting a commission for herding tourists to "orphanages." In some cases there are indeed orphans in residence, but they are kept out of school and trained to put on a show for guests with little songs and dances. Sometimes children whose families cannot afford to feed or educate them will go to live at an orphanage. This is true even for a few of the children at Wat Opot, and points to the need for aid to poor families to help them keep their children at home. There are some good organizations working in Cambodia, but others exist mostly to funnel money to the owners. Still others, with good intentions, simply do not work efficiently. Some are frauds, pure and simple. It's a mixed bag, and recently the Cambodian government has begun evaluating and licensing orphanages and other NGOs.

For some people, running an orphanage is a career move. Find a generous congregation back in the States to support you. Begin by building a nice house for yourself and your family. Buy a Toyota Land Cruiser. Find a few orphans — not hard to do — and build them a small house, and — *voilà!* — a comfortable living.

One young man whom Wayne knows

asked him to be on the board of directors of a new orphanage he was hoping to open. "Why do you want to do this work?" Wayne asked him. "I grew up in an orphanage," the young man told him. "I learned the job from the director. I want to get married. It is the only business I know." Wayne said he did not want to be on the board. As a rule Wayne objects to these business ventures because although a few children may benefit, a disproportionate amount of the money collected goes to support the lifestyle of the director, and the well-being of the children is not the primary focus.

Wayne paused, examined the calluses on his hands, embarrassed to go on. Mister Sokun ran into the gazebo and climbed onto Wayne's lap. "When someone does not donate to Wat Opot because we seem too well-off," Wayne explained, "I feel like we are being penalized for having a place that runs well and actually does something for the children. People fall for the desperate places, but many of these places have been operating for years and have a stake in remaining that way. That 'kindly old monk' was once charged with fraud, but he bribed his way out and now he is up to his old tricks."

Our visitor was pensive, and admitted that

she had felt a little uneasy about the old monk's operation. A few weeks after she left we received a generous donation from her church in Australia.

In 2012 the operating expenses for Wat Opot averaged around $7,000 a month, with the majority of money going to education, food and staff wages. The budget for March that year included the following categories:

Education	$1,767
Kitchen and food	$1,694
Staff wages	$1,357
Transportation	$43
Office	$59
Supplies	$150
Buildings and furnishings	$399
Medical and dental	$151
Grounds and gardens	$61
Children	$489
Community service	$62
Electric	$255
Arts-and-crafts supplies	$261
PayPal and other bank fees	$102
TOTAL EXPENDITURES	$6,850

In March 2012, this money supported fifty-nine resident children and six in university in Phnom Penh, plus approximately twenty-five adult residents. Now that Wat Opot has passed the government licensing inspection, Wayne says he expects the authorities will begin sending many more children to live here, some of them from NGOs that have been closed because of substandard care. The figures include the cost of feeding and housing volunteers (who pay a nominal fee for room and board and often donate additional money or raise funds when they get home). Figuring an average of a hundred people, this comes to $60 to $70 per person per month. Most medical care is supplied by outside agencies at no cost to Wat Opot.

Staff wages include local people who work at Wat Opot: Wayne's secretary, an assistant, a cook and her helpers who prepare three meals a day, and a stipend for Vandin San, Wayne's codirector. Wayne himself does not receive a salary.

Transportation includes gas and maintenance for an aging van (also donated), and shuttling the children and other patients to see the doctor in Takeo, about an hour away. There are also a couple of motos used for food shopping in the market, and bicycles for older kids to ride to high school. With gas growing ever more expensive, Wayne recently purchased a tuk-tuk.

The cost of utilities has improved since round-the-clock power became available. Formerly Wat Opot relied on a gas-fired generator. Wayne was able to sell the old generator for nearly what it had cost him many years before.

Child care includes wages for the "mothers." Then there are schoolbooks, uniforms, village school fees, and wages for teachers at Wat Opot's own school; these all cost more as the children grow older, as do the "gratuities" paid to public school teachers to assure that kids graduate. As more children go on to university, the cost of lodging, food, tuition and books will also rise.

While Wat Opot's primary expenses remain relatively steady from month to month, income does not. Donations from individuals constitute more than two-thirds of what comes in, and can vary widely. Most individual donations come from volunteers and their families, friends and communities, visitors, or friends of Wayne's. The rest comes primarily from small grants received from assorted organizations. Cash flow is always unpredictable, which makes managing Wat Opot's finances a challenge. Sometimes, when money is tight, Wayne will put out an email appeal to friends and past volunteers who have been generous with their support even during economic downturns in their own countries. Every three months Wayne posts a financial report on the Wat Opot website.

From time to time Wayne is visited by fund-raisers who encourage him to set up a sponsorship program, where people send money to benefit a specific child and in turn receive their child's photo and the occasional letter and progress report. He has always refused, especially when they insisted, "These children are so beautiful, you could get each of them sponsored a dozen times!"

Some years ago a group of Maine volunteers established the Wat Opot Children's Fund, an official 501(c)(3) fund-raising organization, to enable U.S.-based supporters to make tax-deductible donations.

However the money comes, the intention is always the same: feeding these young bodies to keep them strong, and nurturing their young minds and spirits to keep them flexible, generous and compassionate. Sometimes it is necessary for a donor to be flexible as well, to understand that needs may change, that Wayne may need to make an abrupt about-face as situations reveal themselves. But in the end the money is scrupulously managed and well spent.

37
"SOMETIMES I HOPE IT NOT RAIN"

"I will fly in an airplane," Ouen was saying. "I am afraid. Maybe it will fall out of the sky."

"It's very safe," I assured him. "I flew to Cambodia three times, all the way from *Amérique.* You will fly high up over the earth and the ocean, and you can look out the window and see little houses and pagodas and fields, and the people look so tiny. Then you fly right up through the white clouds and the sky is bright blue. It's beautiful!"

He seemed to relax a little. "Can you open your window?"

I am sitting on the stone bench near the volunteers' dorm. The air is comfortable and warm and a three-day moon smiles down through a froth of stars. A flowering bougainvillea screens out the single watery bulb that lights a sign welcoming visitors to Wat Opot. Here in the shadows the bench feels sheltered and private.

Mister Ouen, the boy I accompanied to the eye clinic on my first visit, five years earlier, is telling me about his plans for the future. Ouen is fifteen years old now. He has dyed a blond streak in the top of his hair and has a new prosthesis for his eye. It's a bit large still, giving him a slightly pop-eyed appearance, but the doctors tell him he will soon grow into it. And he's growing fast; his limbs are long and he has a little acne and the light fuzz of his first mustache.

Wayne tells me Ouen has not been going to school. His weak eyesight makes it difficult for him to study.

"I will go to Malaysia," Ouen says. "I will work in a paper factory."

A growing number of Cambodians travel each year to Malaysia as domestics and factory workers. It is said that employers in Malaysia like to hire Cambodian workers because they are patient and tractable, and because Cambodians are Buddhists, and unlike Muslims, they do not have to stop work to pray five times a day.

"My big brother is there now. He wrote a letter. It is hard work, but he make *loy j'rarn,* money a lot of. Better than in Cambodia. He says if I come we can save *loy.* Stay two, maybe three years. We can start a business when we come home. Maybe buy a tuk-tuk."

My guts congeal at the thought of Ouen driving anything in Cambodian traffic. Once, only once, I allowed him to carry me to the market on the back of a moto. But the idea of the brothers pooling their earnings to start their own business makes sense. Without much education their prospects are limited to rice farming, construction or menial labor.

Boys like Ouen who get a late start in school often do not do well. They are embarrassed to be sitting with the little kids, and they're bored, and the cycle of defeat only gets worse when they begin cutting classes and cannot keep up. Often as not, they just stop going to school entirely.

For a time Ouen took classes at a Chinese language institute. It was formal and strict, and after a few months he stopped going. Then there was music. He studied with a master in Takeo. But after selling Wayne an expensive instrument the master turned Ouen over to his son, an indifferent teacher, and Ouen lost interest.

"My uncle will help me go to Malaysia."

The man whom Ouen calls "my uncle" or "my teacher" lives in Takeo. Though not a relative, he has been a family friend for

470

many years. Ouen and his mother lived in the man's house when she was ill, and it was he who brought them to Wat Opot when she was dying. Now he is arranging for passports and travel documents as he did for Ouen's brother. He is also helping Vuth, another Wat Opot boy, to go with him. They are only fourteen and fifteen years old, and the man had to swear they were both eighteen to apply for papers. Vuth, who has no family, is listed as Ouen's brother so that both boys can claim to have a relative working in Malaysia. Ouen admits to me that he has not told his uncle about his poor eyesight.

In spite of the irregularities Wayne is allowing them to go. He says they are both good kids and that this trip will allow them to get work experience and see something of the world. With Ouen's older brother already in Malaysia, Wayne is less concerned that the boys will get into any serious trouble.

Still, Ouen worries about leaving Wat Opot. He has lived here since he was seven years old, when he lost both of his parents to AIDS. Since then Wayne has been Ouen's father, and Wat Opot his family.

We sit on the bench for a while, watching

the stars, not saying anything. Then Ouen begins to tell me about his father. He has never spoken to me about his family before.

"My father traveled for his work. He went to Thailand sometimes. Then he got sick and we took care of him. He was dying of AIDS, but we didn't know. Then the doctor told him he had AIDS, and my mother was sick too. Then my father felt very sad. He told me he went to a party in Thailand and got drunk and caught AIDS and gave it to my mother. He said he was a very bad man. He told me he was sorry he brought AIDS home to his family.

"When I was a little boy before my father was sick, we used to sleep together, my whole family. When it rained we all stayed in bed and played in the morning. I was very happy. Now when it rains I remember my family . . . and I cry."

He is quiet for a moment, and then he adds, "Sometimes I hope it not rain."

Ouen continues, "One morning I woke up and my father was sleeping next to me. I tried to wake him up to play with me, but he was dead. When Wayne told us you were sick in *Amérique,* I used to ask him every day if you were okay. Wayne asked me how come I asked so often. I told him it was because of the time you went to the eye clinic in Takeo with me."

We reminisce about our trip to the clinic, and I tell Ouen how proud I had been because of the way he took care of me that day, how he treated me like his *yei*. He says he had been worried about going alone and it made him feel good that I went with him. His words move me deeply. With all the plans we make about what we will do as volunteers, it is what we offer each other as human beings that endures; it is the simple and mutual acts of kindness that remain.

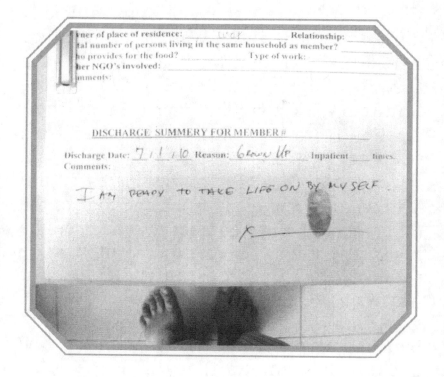

■ ■ ■ ■

The day came when Ouen and Vuth were to leave Wat Opot. Impatient for their new adventure to begin, they had decided to move to Takeo and live with Ouen's uncle while they waited for the arrangements to be finalized for their journey to Malaysia.

We all stood around Wayne's office, trying not to look worried. Wayne and I were there and a few of the children who happened to be home from school. Ouen and Vuth grinned nervously and teased each other. First there were papers to sign, officially mustering them out of Wat Opot. Each boy signed his name and made a thumbprint in red ink. Under the heading "Discharge Summary," Wayne had written as their reason for leaving "Grown Up" and "I am ready to take life on by myself."

I doubted that. Ouen was in tears, and Vuth shifted nervously from one foot to the other, avoiding eye contact. Wayne gave the boys fifty dollars apiece, plus a little more to cover their expenses until they left for Malaysia. We took a few photos, and Wayne gave each of them a bar of soap, a toothbrush and some toothpaste, and a few packets of shampoo. They had one small suitcase between them, a cardboard carrying case that had once held a laptop computer; in it they put the toiletries with their few personal belongings. Then they shook Wayne's hand and prepared to leave.

Pesei was there, standing quietly in the background. In two years it will be his turn to go, and he will have his younger sister to think about as well. Pesei has worked hard in school and his English is good, and he is a wonderful artist. His life will likely be much different from Ouen's and Vuth's, but he looked on, clearly moved by what he saw. Our eyes met for a moment, and I think we each understood what the other was thinking, but we didn't talk about it. Sok was there also, an older boy who refuses to go to school, and whom Wayne allows to stay because, really, he has nowhere else to go. After lunch Wayne overheard Sok encouraging his little brother not to be like Ouen and Vuth, but to remain in school.

Wayne walked the two boys to a waiting moto and said goodbye. It seemed a lonely leave-taking, marked by but a brief ceremony — a red thumbprint on a paper, some money and a few bars of soap. Some of the other children were present, but they seemed stunned and could not say goodbye. The whole proceeding felt to me like a scene from a movie of men being released from prison. One minute everything is provided, but then they walk through a gate; the next moment they are on their own, boarding a bus on a lonely road. I longed for a gathering of the clan, for some recognition that these young men were loved, that they had been and always would be part of this community, this family, some celebration of their maturity and a boost for their confidence as they departed. And some reassurance for the children who remain behind.

That night after we close the office, I follow Wayne as he walks with Mister Baing toward his sleeping porch. Baing is fourteen years old and doesn't go to school. He is illiterate in his own language, but he is smart. He spends a lot of time with the volunteers and speaks English better than most of the other kids. He has apprenticed himself to the bricklayers and carpenters around Wat Opot and works hard, and he is learning a trade.

Baing is clearly worried. He repeatedly asks Wayne whether Ouen can come back if things don't work out for him in Malaysia. Wayne says, "No. Ouen did not go to school, so he has to go out into the world and work." Baing asks whether Ouen could come back if he goes to school. Clearly it is not only Ouen he is worried about. "No," Wayne answers. "Ouen is a man now.

He will be fine." And Baing protests, "But . . . he cry!"

In the end, Ouen and Vuth never did get to Malaysia. They knocked around Takeo for a few months, their departure repeatedly delayed by conflicts between the Cambodian and Malaysian governments over exploitation of foreign workers.

When I visited in 2012, Ouen was living in Phnom Penh. He had gone from one tedious job to another, getting restless, rarely lasting for more than a few days. He constantly asked Wayne for money, inventing a series of family deaths and memorial ceremonies. Wayne paid bribes for jobs and fees for uniforms, but nothing much came of it. Finally Wayne told Ouen that he was on his own. When I left, Ouen had gotten himself hired by a taxi company, washing the cabs. He had no place to live, and was sleeping at the car wash office.

Sink or swim. Sometimes it turns out that a young person must be hurled into independence before he faces the reality that parents — biological or surrogate — cannot support him for the rest of his life. After he had been living completely on his own for some time, Ouen thanked Wayne for making him understand that he needs to be responsible for his own life.

Ouen's poor eyesight makes everything more difficult for him, but Wayne says it is harder for children from impoverished backgrounds to find and then hold in focus a vision of what their life could be. For their part, children like Pesei, whose families were more structured and self-sufficient, are driven to reclaim all that was lost to them.

As more children reach high school age, Wayne has begun a series of one-on-one meetings and counseling sessions where the children discuss their education and career plans. Wayne asks them to come up with several careers they might be interested in, and then offers them realistic guidance on how to reach their goals. Wayne has also invited students from universities in Phnom Penh — many of them rural kids themselves — to visit Wat Opot and speak with our children about scholarship opportunities and to encourage them to make plans to attend college.

At the other end of the spectrum from Pesei is Mister Sampeah, the boy who came to Wat Opot hiding in the back of his mother's ambulance. His mother had been viciously beaten and died without regaining consciousness and, understandably, Sampeah refused Wayne's offer to try to find his village and reunite him with his family. As Sampeah grew older he began skipping school a lot. Maybe he was scared — scared of going out into a world that has only bad memories for him. Sampeah knew that some of the boys had been asked to leave Wat Opot because they refused to go to school, so he studied just enough to keep up appearances.

One day, Wayne was talking with some of the kids who had played hooky from school. He singled out Mister Sampeah as an object lesson. "Sampeah doesn't go to school," he said. "Maybe he will have to go home."

Mister Baing looked very serious. "Sampeah not have home."

Recently, Wayne found a foster family for Sampeah, and he tells me he is doing well now, living in the village.

Some of the older kids are aware that the little ones need advice and encouragement, and they talk about giving back to Wat Opot by setting an example for the others. As more Wat Opot children graduate from high school and university, Wayne is planning a wall of graduation photos to remind the younger kids of what is possible. But he can see that in the coming years one of his biggest challenges will be to convince all the children, HIV positive and negative alike, to

479

avail themselves of the opportunities that Wat Opot has to offer, and to set high goals and not to be afraid to work for them.

38
GEEWA: IN HIS OWN WORDS

"Geewa [*CHEE-wah*]. It's the name my family calls me. It means 'Monkey.' I was born in a monkey year."

"Not *s'waa*?" I asked. That was the only Khmer word I knew for monkey.

"No. It's different. Like maybe 'Little Monkey,' a funny name old people like to call you. And Pesei, it's not my real name either. They call me that at Wat Opot because it's the name my mother called me. My mother liked that name. Pesei is a girl's name, a soft name, because I am quiet."

"What is your real name, then?"

"Rathanak. It means diamonds, gold, everything you have that can make you rich. In school they call me Rathanak, my given name."

Before Pesei's father got sick there *had* been wealth. The family had a trucking company and a car and land. But his father caught AIDS and brought it home to his wife.

"My father was sick, and my mother borrowed gold on our land."

The fact that his mother borrowed the money in gold will prevent Pesei from reclaiming his family's rice fields. Ten years ago, when his mother took out the loan, gold prices were low. To reclaim his patrimony Pesei must pay the lender back the same weight of gold, and the price has risen dramatically. These days the gold is worth much more than the land.

His mother spent all she could borrow to take care of his father's medical bills.

"After my father died, they took everything. So my mother went to Phnom Penh

481

to work. Me and my sister Jorani stayed with my father's mother in a little house. My *yei* did not want my father to marry our mother. My mother's family was very poor and she did not have an education, and her skin was very dark. But she was beautiful and smart and had lots of friends.

"My mother had HIV, but it didn't show yet. She went to Phnom Penh and did makeup and hair style for movies. She worked very hard, visited us every three months. No one knew she was sick. They had no ARVs yet, so she took the old medicines. One day when she was working, someone saw the pills and asked. She was afraid they would know she had HIV, so she stopped the job. She came back home to visit. She was very thin.

"Then she went back to Phnom Penh and worked cutting grass to feed cows. But it was very hard work. After, she was getting very sick, so she stopped working, came to the hospital in Takeo. She lied to the doctor, told him no one was at home to take care of her, nothing to eat, so the doctor took her to Wat Opot.

"So she stayed at Wat Opot and Jorani and I stayed home. Some people told me maybe she died. I kept crying, but I still went to school and I missed her. Finally she came to see us. I said, 'Where you stay? People say you die!' She said, 'Opot, but you cannot come because it HIV place.' I had no clothes. Only my *kramah* and short pants. After we ate she took a truck back to Opot, and I jumped on the back of the truck, and we went to Highway Two to get the bus. She saw me and she cried. It was very far so I could not go back. She said I can come to Opot, but only for a short time, but I came and met Wayne and some of the kids here. Then I stayed and took care of my mother."

"What was it like when you first came to Wat Opot?" I ask Pesei.

"It felt strange. Everything was different. Smelled different. Even the rice was different. The rice was the wrong size. People all looked very strange, sick, all smelled of medicine, disinfectant. But after, I got used to it.

"My mother needed money, so she sometimes went to Phnom Penh to ask her friends. Friends gave her money, but they were scared of HIV so did not let her come inside their house. I slept outside on the street with her. We did that six or seven times. That made me strong. I can live anywhere, sleep anywhere, because I wanted to go everywhere with my mother."

He was ten years old.

"We stopped going to Phnom Penh because she was so thin they would not pick her up, because they were afraid she would die on the bus. Sometimes we waited two, three hours for a bus to stop. My mother had a good voice. On the way to Phnom Penh she used to sing on the bus. Then people liked her, gave her money.

"One day at Wat Opot she fell down from the bamboo bed under the tamarind tree. She broke her hip, made skin problem [bedsores]. I took her to the hospital, took showers with her, cleaned her. After three months we went back to Wat Opot, but it hurt. She always screamed and cried.

"After she died, I decide to stay here at Wat Opot. My *yei* came and wanted me and Jorani to go back to live with her in the village. But I decided to stay because Wayne said we could go to school.

"At first it felt very strange, but people liked me because I am polite, I am a good kid. And I always make friends with volunteers."

Abruptly, Pesei began to tell a story he had never told me before. Unlike the Khmer, Chinese do not cremate their dead, but bury them in tombs carefully oriented according to the laws of feng shui. After some years the bones are dug up, cleaned and reburied.

"My father was half Chinese, half Khmer, so after he died they buried him. About four or five years later, we had to get the bones out and have a ceremony and put them in a good place. I am the son, so I had to do it. I climbed down into the grave. Jorani was there, crying. I was crying. My family were all crying and holding hands like a chain and I reached up, held on to my family with one hand, cleaned the bones with my other hand. I had to take everything off the bones, old clothes and skin and everything. I felt very scared, but I am the only one who could do it. I cleaned all the bones: head, arm, finger, everything. I took the bones out and put them in a nice box, and we buried it with my grandfather's bones. After I did that, I can do anything."

Pesei is twenty years old now. He is about to leave Wat Opot to study at the Royal University of Fine Arts in Phnom Penh. The Schmitz-Hille Foundation, which sponsors the art program at Wat Opot, has given Pesai and Sambath, another talented twelfth-grade boy, full scholarships, but they must still pass their final exams to graduate. These tests are notoriously difficult, the more so for students from village schools. Most students find it necessary to take extra classes after school to get a passing grade. Sambath, who wants to be an architect, is an excellent student, but he failed the exam last year. Some of the better students inform me that on occasion an especially good exam paper is swapped with that of a wealthy student, one who skips class a lot. This can be crushing to the diligent pupil, for a good grade on the exam not only allows the student to graduate, but also may help him qualify for a scholarship. Now, to go to university, Sambath must wait a year to take the exam again. Meanwhile he has been attending special exam-prep classes in Phnom Penh, where he can live with his older brother.

Pesei has decided to join Sambath to prepare for his exam, but living in Phnom Penh is expensive. Wayne tells Pesei that with so many other kids in school he cannot afford to support him there until he is enrolled in university. Pesei worries about it for a few days, and then remembers an uncle in Phnom Penh. He has not seen him in many years, but surprisingly the uncle and his wife invite Pesei to live with them while he prepares for the exam.

Pesei and I are just leaving for Phnom

Penh in a tuk-tuk when his uncle's car arrives unannounced and whisks him away to a party at his grandmother's house. His extended family has gathered there, people he has not seen since before his parents died. They have a feast and his family wish him well in his new life.

"Everybody was happy to see me. They called me Geewa, Monkey," a name he had not heard for a long time.

Pesei had been living in Phnom Penh only a few weeks when he spoke to a cousin who was making a trip to see their maternal grandmother. He asked to go with her.

"I went to see my mother's family because my mother wanted to go before she died, but she was too sick. I have only one cousin from there. She took care of me when I was little and my parents arranged a marriage for her. It was very far away. We had to take a bus, then a moto, then cross the river, then another bus, another moto. My cousin is the only one who knows the way back home. I wanted to go for a long time because my grandmother is very old, but I didn't have the money, didn't know the way. They are very poor and live very far away, near the Vietnam border.

"After I came there, I met all my family,

and told my grandmother that my mother was crying before she died. She wanted to come here. My grandmother asked me to pray and light incense and ask my mother's spirit to come. I called Jorani and asked her to go to the crematorium at Wat Opot and pray and tell my mother.

"Everyone was excited to see me in Prey Veng, where I was born. They had not seen my face since I was seven years old. They said, I am my father; I look exactly like him, but I have my grandmother's feet.

"And they called me Geewa."

I remembered the night Miss Jorani came to the crematorium to pray to her mother's spirit because it was the only time I ever saw her at the evening memorial service. I asked Jorani why she had never come before, and about her childhood at Wat Opot.

"I was four years old when my father died from AIDS. Pesei was six years old. I didn't go to school yet when he died. When I was very young, my mother made me to plant rice, to cut rice. I was eight years old or seven years old.

"When my mother was sick she left home. She rode on the moto on the back and I couldn't go with her, and I cried. Then she came to visit and brought me here to Wat

Opot. I was nine years old. There were three dorms and one kitchen and no buildings or landfill or palm trees. Only one place they planted a garden, near the kitchen. The flowers were very beautiful.

"At night I rode my bicycle around the crematorium. My mother told me, 'Don't go near that place! It full of ghosts to burn!' I wasn't afraid. I really liked that place. But when I knew about the ghosts I don't go back again.

"Other children were here before me. They brought me shoes and clothes. They were very kind. They came to speak with me. Kalliyan, Sida, Sovann, Punthea, Rajana, Srey Pich, Sun Tevy, all were here. Mister Chhang and the others, they all died.

"I helped Pesei take care of my mother. Clean her sores, take baths with her. She always cried, 'I going to die! I cannot stay with you anymore. You have to take care of yourself.' She told me I have to study hard, stay at Wat Opot and have a better life, not go with our grandmother.

"I had one piece of my father's bone. He was Chinese and Khmer, so we could not cremate him. Pesei cleaned the bones. My mother gave me one piece and Pesei one piece, but we both lost them."

I asked Jorani whether her mother had been angry at her father for infecting her with HIV.

"She was not angry at my father. She took care of my father. She was very kind. When my father died, she very very cry. She tried to takc care of my father, sold everything she had, her car, her other house in Phnom Penh, gold. Now I have nothing, but I have Wat Opot.

"She told me, 'Don't trust the man. Take care of yourself, study hard.' She always cried when she gave me advice. When I saw she cried, I always cried too.

"Pesei came here maybe half a year before me. When he brought me to Wat Opot he taught me to say, 'Good morning, Wayne,' but I was really shy. I could not say that. I was very afraid of Wayne. He wore a black shirt and black pants. He was a big man."

Miss Jorani tells me about the volunteers and about the other children at Wat Opot.

"Volunteers come because they like the children and it's a very nice place. The children have a good heart. They pity the children and like to play with them. They tell the world about the children, that they lost their parents, but they can still play with a happy smile.

"Sampeah doesn't have a grandmother, doesn't have anything, but he's still happy. He doesn't have any family. I very pity Sampeah. One day if I have money, I'll bring Sampeah to a town, play some games. He lost everything. He never goes home, doesn't have any family come to visit. I share with him if my *yei* brings me some potato, and with the other girls.

"Srey Mom is my best friend, and the little girls. Punlok only had one underwear when she came. Red underwear. Nothing else, no shoes, only red underwear, and her hair was very curly."

Miss Jorani is thinking about going into medicine. She sees getting an education as one way she can be an example to the younger children.

"Pesei tells me I have to work hard. When I get sad or angry, he says, 'Do you want to go back to the rice fields? If not you have to study hard. Be strong!' He never hits me, but he worries because my mother never went to school.

"I don't want to marry anybody before I finish my education. That way, if the man

491

leaves, I can take care of myself.

"I always think about my parents before I go to bed, but I never dream about them. I keep their picture next to my bed. I always hope my mother will come back, but I never see my mother again.

"I need to work hard to take back what I had before."

Pesei has been teaching English at Wat Opot. He is curious about words and shades of meaning, and he thinks in stories and parables. Like Jorani he looks for ways his own story can inspire the younger children.

A few years ago he painted a picture of a glowing ball flying on wings of light. He showed it emerging from a dark cloud into the sunshine. At the time he told me he had made a choice to turn away from his dark memories and live a good life.

"When I teach the children, I tell them stories. 'You have a choice. Do you want to go back?' That's the way I teach. I also believe in the Spirit. Something always protects me. If you do good things, the good Spirit will stay with you and always protect you.

"The kids are different from me. Some of them, they don't listen anymore. I want to help them by showing them my painting of

the ball and wings. The ball is like the world.
And you have the wings. If you do not fly,
you will never see the world is beautiful.
People helping you at Wat Opot are the
wings. So use the wings to fly up and see
you are beautiful. Use your wings to fly
from darkness to light."

"At Wat Opot they call me Pesei. At school
they call me Rathanak. But my family, they
call me Geewa, and in Phnom Penh, my
new friends also call me Geewa. Back to my
family. Back to Geewa."

39
KANGHO'S BROTHER DOES NOT BELIEVE IN YOGA

Kangho is a tall, handsome boy with a winning personality. Like Pesei he makes friends
easily and is a favorite of volunteers. He has
a great sense of humor and flirts outra-
geously, but harmlessly. At heart he is serious and responsible. The youngest son of a
colonel in the military who died of AIDS
before antiretroviral drugs were available,
Kangho is too young to remember his father
clearly, but his oldest brother, Sovann, has
become father to the family.

After their mother died, Sovann took care of their father. He learned from watching Wayne how to give his father an IV, and stayed with him after he moved back home to the village to die. His father was a respected and dignified man who valued status and education. When he was dying he charged Sovann to take care of his sister and three younger brothers and to make sure they all receive an education.

When his father died Sovann drove his father's car to Wat Opot and informed Wayne that he was going to live there, and that Wayne was going to put him through school. He was about fourteen at the time. This was in 2003, and there were only half a dozen kids living at Wat Opot. Sovann did not ask Wayne; he simply walked in, as upright and dignified as his father had been, and announced that this would happen, and Wayne agreed. After that, as each of his siblings came of age, Sovann would an- nounce that it was time for that one to leave their grandmother's house in the village and come to live at Wat Opot so they could learn English and go to high school, and then Wayne could pay to send them to college.

Sovann went to medical school, but after the first year he found he could not afford to pay the bribes necessary to advance to second year and he transferred to nursing school instead. He has graduated and has begun working in Phnom Penh. During a recent flu outbreak, Sovann returned to Wat Opot to help Wayne take care of the children.

To date, one younger brother has entered law school, and another has a scholarship to study architecture. Kangho is about to graduate from high school, and the youngest, a sister, has recently moved to Wat Opot and may go into nursing.

Even though he is in school in Phnom Penh, Sovann remains a stern taskmaster to his siblings. He calls Kangho at midnight and he will berate him if he is not studying. When other children are asleep or watching television, I will see lights at the school and find Kangho pacing back and forth, drilling his little sister in English in an empty classroom. Kangho worries that when he leaves Wat Opot his sister will not apply herself, and that she will spend time with the boys from the village. He knows how easily a girl can ruin her reputation.

When a kundalini yoga teacher from Phnom Penh came to teach classes at Wat Opot, Kangho became interested in yoga and was invited to take a teacher training course. The yoga studio was in need of male teachers, and Kangho could earn some money while going to the university. Now, every Sunday, Kangho teaches yoga to the children at Wat Opot. Sovann does not approve. He does not regard yoga as a suitable profession for a member of his family. He does not see spirituality as something Kangho needs, only education. For his part, Kangho is intrigued by yoga, and feels its subtle, balancing effect, yet he seems to be pulled between a longing for social standing and material success, and the benefit he intuits from his practice of yoga. One night he informs Wayne that when he is a rich man he will have bodyguards, a sign of wealth and status. Other times, he seems to understand that flaunting wealth creates the need for protection from the envy of the world.

Wayne tells Kangho a story from his days as a barefoot doctor in Honduras. The area where he lived had a lot of gangs. They robbed stores and delivery trucks, and many people were beaten and killed. Once a month Wayne would go to the city to get money for supplies. He would return with a thousand dollars. Everybody knew he went for money, but he was never robbed. Years later, Wayne visited some of the boys he took care of in the village. Wayne had taken them in and helped them through school, and they have remained friends. One of the boys said that after Wayne left he had asked a gang member why they never robbed Wayne. "Are you kidding?" the young hoodlum replied. "With those two huge bodyguards who were always with him? Not a chance!" Wayne tells Kangho that he never had any bodyguards.

Wayne respects Sovann, respects his efforts to reclaim the life his family had before their father died. If he succeeds, Sovann will have accomplished the impossible, something out of reach for most adults. He will have put four orphaned siblings through college.

Sovann still has friends from the old days, when his father was important and respected. Even though he grew up at Wat Opot he keeps his connections in the village. His siblings feel comfortable associating with the upper class, but only up to a point. Kangho is frequently invited for dinner at the home of the village chief. The chief has a pretty daughter, and one day I teased Kangho about whether the chief was trying to make a match. After all, Kangho is a fine young man with a lot of ambition. Kangho laughed it off and then, abashed, he told me that no, he would not be a suitable match for the chief's daughter. He was serious. "I have no money, no land, no parents."

40
Turning Points

Wayne does not often tell visitors about Toon Hang, and when he first mentioned him to me I sensed that I should not press him for details. The death of any child is tragic, but it was clear that this little boy had been special to Wayne, and that there were unsettling mysteries surrounding his death. Late one night, as we sat watching fireflies dart over the pond, Wayne finally told me the story, and it spilled out as full of emotion as if it had happened yesterday.

Hang was only four years old when his mother died of AIDS. They lived near Wat Opot, and Prak Vutha used to bring Hang regularly to the clinic for medicine and rice. But this week they had failed to appear, so Wayne walked through the dusty rice fields for a home visit.

He found Prak Vutha lying on an open-weave bamboo bed under a tree outside her hut. Little Hang came running down a path through the dry grass to greet Wayne. His mother, hearing him shout Wayne's name, tried to rise in welcome, but she was unsteady and weak. Walking toward her and meeting her eyes, Wayne held his palms together before his face in the respectful *sampeah* greeting and urged Prak Vutha not to get up. He offered to start her usual IV, but she told him it would not be necessary. Wayne was worried about her, and as he examined Hang, he noticed the little boy glancing over at his mother again and again. To check Hang's ears and look down his throat, and to feel his neck to see whether his glands were swollen, Wayne kept having to turn the boy's tiny face back toward him with his large gentle hand.

"I prepared to leave, and I went back to the bed of Vutha and raised my hands in farewell, but to my surprise she took hold of my hands and held them tightly, and with tears in her eyes, she whispered, 'Please take good care of my son.' On the walk back to the pickup I wanted to cry, but like the rice fields around me, my eyes were too dry to produce tears."

Prak Vutha died a few days later and Hang came to live at Wat Opot. It wasn't long before he became Wayne's buddy, his caboose.

Sitting on Wayne's lap at meals, playing

on the clinic floor while he took care of patients, curling up next to him under the mosquito net when he slept, Hang was inquisitive, creative, funny and wholly good-natured. He rapidly picked up English, and by the time school started he was excited to be able to go. He was the first HIV-positive child to start public school in our village, and in no time he became the teacher's pet. Until that time the teachers had not let any kids with HIV attend classes, but Hang was so lovable they could not refuse him, and his going opened the public schools to the rest of the Wat Opot children.

Hang's mother died in September of 2001, long before antiretroviral medicines were available in Cambodia. It was a terrible time; all Wayne could do was comfort the sick in the villages, and wash their bodies and cremate them when they died.

When testing finally became available, Wayne began checking everyone who came to the clinic. To his horror, most of the people he tested were HIV positive. "It was relentless bad news, a nightmare," Wayne told me. "I felt as if I had stepped into Hell. It seemed as if everyone in Cambodia was HIV positive; adults, children, young women who had been virgins when they married, and young husbands who married them not knowing they themselves were HIV positive."

By 2003, Wayne was losing two or three patients a week. Sometimes several were cremated in a single day. According to the Cambodian National AIDS Authority, the country's first cases of HIV were reported in 1991, and by 1995 more than a third of the country's sex workers and nearly 10 percent of its military had been infected. By 2002, Cambodia had the highest prevalence of HIV infection in Asia.

Then in 2003, Médecins Sans Frontières arrived, bringing with them a single line of antiretroviral drugs.

"But the doctor in charge had not received training in pediatrics yet, and he wanted to wait before starting children like Hang on the medications," Wayne told me. "I was assured, however, that Hang would be the first one to get them once he received the training.

"It was just before New Year's of 2004 that I took Hang to the hospital in Takeo for his appointment. The doctor informed me that he would be leaving in the afternoon for Thailand to receive instructions for using ARV medicines for children. Hang had a bit of fever and had started to have some diarrhea the previous night, and so the doctor wanted to keep him in the children's hospital in Phnom Penh so that he could start the medications immediately upon his return. I was reluctant, but the doctor was just as concerned as I was about Hang and so I let him convince me that it was the best thing to do.

"I called each night for an update and was assured he was doing fine."

But Hang never had a chance to begin taking ARVs.

"On the morning of the fifth of January, the day the doctor was supposed to return and start the medications for treatment, I called to see what time we could pick him up from the hospital, only to be told that he had died during the night. I was stunned and in tears. I told them we would be right in to pick up the body, but was informed that they had already sent his body to the crematorium and all that was left were his ashes.

"I still wait for Hang to come home from the hospital. I imagine him jumping out of the car and running into my arms, arms that have held so many other children since then, children whom I also had to let go of as I placed them into the crematorium furnace. The difference is that with Hang I couldn't hold on to him for that one last time, I couldn't look into his face and see that he was at peace, and I couldn't release him from my heart with the first puff of smoke rising out of the crematorium chimney.

"The doctor came out to pay his respects the following day and, as he was lighting a candle and incense, he offered to open an investigation into Hang's death. Something didn't seem right about how things were handled, and I could tell he felt deeply responsible. We told him there was no point in having an investigation because it would only create hard feelings and it wouldn't bring Hang back to us anyway.

"They say that time heals all wounds, and I suppose that is true . . . but time seems to have stood still since the passing of Toon Hang, and even the mention of his name brings back all of the memories."

It was February 2010 when I returned to Maine, during one of the warmest late winters on record. At home in my hundred-year-old house I was grateful for the sunny days and lack of snow, even as the little voice in my head kept insisting, "Global warming." As spring approached, an oil rig in the Gulf of Mexico exploded, beginning a saga of environmental desecration that has more recently been eclipsed by the nuclear catastrophe in Fukushima.

In May the *New York Times* ran a front-page article on the state of world efforts to control and treat HIV/AIDS ("At Front Lines, Global War on AIDS Is Falling Apart," May 9, 2010). They reported that because of the global recession, major donor nations and charitable foundations were cutting back on programs to provide anti-retroviral drugs. As a result, doctors and nurses in the developing world were being forced to turn away growing numbers of new patients, as well as existing patients who had become resistant to the cheaper lines of ARVs. Particularly disturbing was their report that in families where one person infected with HIV was receiving care, but another was turned away, patients were known to share their drugs with their loved one, rendering each patient's dose ineffective and possibly resulting in the development of drug-resistant strains of HIV. These powerful mutant strains could in turn be passed to others and spread ever outward through the global village.

Donor nations and charities, beset by "donor fatigue," were beginning to concentrate their resources on diseases that could be cured cheaply by one-time treatment, or prevented by distributing affordable items like mosquito nets or water filters. The new buzzwords were "cost-effective" and "more bang for the buck." While I was in Cambodia, I was told that a grant proposal had a better chance of approval if it was couched in terms like "community development," or "mother-and-child health," and although nations and charities all continued to make large donations to HIV/AIDS programs worldwide, these were not enough to keep up with the rising numbers of new cases.

In the grimmest terms, the *Times* article predicted that "for most of Africa and scattered other countries like Haiti, Guyana and Cambodia, it seems inevitable that the 1990s will return: walking skeletons in the villages, stacks of bodies in morgues, mountains of newly turned earth in cemeteries." I shuddered, remembering Wayne's stories of his early days at Wat Opot, when the village was too poor to have a crematorium, and dogs roamed about eating the remains of victims who had been only partially cremated in shallow pits in the earth.

In Cambodia, oil and gas exploration were poised to bring more money into the economy. Land prices were booming and new commercial developments, upscale housing and tourist resorts were drastically changing the landscape. Almost every day the Cambodian press ran stories about people evicted from their homes and land to make way for new development. Mysterious fires broke out in the city. The land around Boeung Kak, the lake area in the middle of the capital, which some call the lung of Phnom Penh, was being cleared and filled to make room for upscale development, and people living around the lake were fighting eviction. Villagers in the provinces complained of illegal lumbering and mining operations that forced them off their land and polluted the environment, and foreign powers were investing in hydroelectric dams and power lines that could light cities and run factories, but that would change the ecology of rivers where their ancestors had fished for generations.

Médecins Sans Frontières had initiated the HIV/AIDS program that served not only our children but also thousands of people affected by AIDS in Cambodia. After their initial five-year commitment was over, the Khmer government took over the program and the administration of international funding. Although Wat Opot children are still receiving medication and care, they are not seeing the doctor as frequently.

In these hard times, funding for the Home Care teams has dried up, forcing Vandin to lay off half his outreach staff. Many of these people are themselves living with HIV. Although Wayne says that fewer people in villages need Home Care services now, the cutbacks leave no one in place to follow up when a patient misses a doctor's appointment, or to check that they are taking their pills on schedule, or to find ways to counter discrimination against people living with HIV/AIDS. And people whose health has stabilized on ARVs still need social services and help finding work.

In fall of 2009, MSF reported in its newsletter, *ALERT,* that its physicians in Africa were seeing more patients who were resistant to second-line antiretroviral medications. Resistance can evolve naturally over time as the virus mutates, or it can result from an interruption in treatment, as when a child has been living with elderly relatives who cannot get them to the doctor regularly, or do not give them their pills on time every day. Wars and civil disturbances also rupture the life-sustaining routines that are the basis of ARV treatment. Outdated drugs — or, worse, counterfeit pills — compound the disaster. The article spoke of the overwhelming despair of both doctor and patient when the many infected with ARV-resistant strains of AIDS must be turned away like refugees without a country to return to. In Cambodia, I had heard of the plight of AIDS patients who lost their homes to urban renewal and were forcibly resettled to the outskirts of the city from which it became too expensive for them to travel to work, let alone to reach a doctor. This can be a disaster, when even the briefest interruption in care can result in drug resistance.

Today, only two lines of ARVs are manufactured cheaply enough to be commonly available in Cambodia. More advanced and much more expensive medications are available in the West, and allow many AIDS patients here to survive for decades. With more choices, doctors can better tailor treatment to individual patients and strive for fewer side effects. MSF reports that negotiations are under way with major pharmaceutical companies to create patent pools, through which drug manufacturers in the developing world would collectively pay royalties for licenses from the companies that hold the patents for more advanced lines of ARVs. If adopted, patent pools would allow these drugs to be produced at low cost. They could then be provided to those who need them throughout the developing world. Although the picture may ultimately improve, many drug companies have so far resisted loosening their hold on lucrative patents.

Several of the children I have written about in this book are currently on second-line ARVs, and the Khmer doctors promise that if any become resistant they will do their best to procure further lines. But in the current climate this will be on a case-by-case basis and is likely to be difficult and very expensive. Without patent pools, as more patients become resistant to second-line ARVs the cost will surely become prohibitive, and people who have been doing well for a decade will sicken and die.

As I read the reports from the Western and Cambodian press, and from MSF, I found myself becoming depressed and pessimistic. It began to seem to me that we might ultimately look back at the first decade of the twenty-first century and see it as a calm between storms, a halcyon age when there were both the means and the dedication to take on the epidemic. The misjudgment, greed, fraud and lack of oversight that brought down the world economy in 2008, and the massive public indebtedness brought about by war without end, have unleashed an epidemic of neglect that is murdering the poorest of the poor. This is not a natural disaster, but an unnatural perversion of the human heart. A mentally healthy society takes care of its neighbors' children, and a spiritually healthy society provides for the needs of its children's children, down all the generations of humanity. We must learn to care for people we will never meet, and, as Wayne insists, "There must be acts!"

Think of Toon Hang, who would be in high school today if only he had been treated a few days earlier. Will any of our children at Wat Opot be denied the medications that let them run and play and grow up to go to school? After all the effort, all the scrimping and struggling to create a community from nothing, after long sleepless nights nursing them when they fell ill, after all Wayne's tireless devotion and love, is it possible that we will allow these children to slip away from us?

Wayne seems a bit bemused to find himself father to a passel of teenagers. It is an outcome he could not have hoped for in the early days of Wat Opot. Many of the kids are doing well, going to school, developing outside interests and friendships with people in the village. In 2013, Wayne reported that three of the children had graduated from university, two with law degrees. One boy was in his final year of civil engineering and two others were in the second year of art studies, with a third studying architecture. One was in school for midwifery and yet another in an international school of design. Sovann, Kangho's older brother, has gone on to work on his master's degree in nursing. A few have become Buddhist monks. Five have married and are raising families, and some are now in trade schools or working in Phnom Penh. Our oldest HIV-positive boy is in high school, hoping to become a teacher. Others will soon follow.

Wayne is confronted by the problem of how to counsel young adults after they leave Wat Opot. And, like many parents today, he is also faced with the phenomenon of grown children moving back home. He is beginning to reconsider the meaning of Wat Opot as a community — whether it is a place where children grow up, only to leave for the world, or whether it might offer some of them a place to settle and raise families and continue to live their lives together. Mao, an older boy who left Wat Opot to work a construction job in Phnom Penh, has returned to marry a village girl. Mao and his wife and baby live at Wat Opot now. Mao works with the animals and manages the fishponds. Perhaps it is a good outcome for everyone. Mao came to Wat Opot from another orphanage and has no family. His wife, whose mother died when she was young, was raised by her grandmother Sari Yei in the village. Sari Yei, who has nurtured many of our infants as well, is raising other grandchildren in a very small house nearby and has no room for another young family. Living at Wat Opot, Mao and his wife can offer support to Sari Yei, and they can be part of both extended families.

Perhaps Wat Opot will evolve over time into an intentional community of children and adults, some who came because they were orphaned and sick, and some, like Mao and his family, who remain by choice to live in community and raise their own children. Wayne asks, rhetorically, I think, whether that makes the ones who stay dependent on Wat Opot. I suspect this is a Western concern more than a Cambodian one. In contrast to the American preoccupation with rugged individualism, I have never gotten the sense that anyone in Cambodia puts a premium on moving away from their family. Having many family members to pitch in, and elders to look after the grand-children, and children to look after their parents when they get old, seems the most natural thing in the world and a good way to spread the responsibilities over many generations. It is only in cultures that make a fetish of independence that you find cities of high-rise studio apartments, and single-serving isolation, as if we were planning for loneliness. We expect every family unit to stand on its own, and, unless we live for a while in a place like Cambodia, most of us have no idea how atomized our own families have become.

Wat Opot is constantly changing. For now, Wayne says he wants the community to continue to find its way, to evolve, "to become more and more itself."

Wayne and I used to talk about whether there could be another Wat Opot, whether another leader could duplicate the plan. Wayne wonders now whether this is even an important question. Things are what they are, rooted in time and place, in circum-stance and personality. Even if founded on the same principles, a Wat Opot without Wayne would be different, and whoever is the leader would set the tone according to his fundamental humanity. A day is made up of a series of moments, and each moment is a year in miniature. It is the sum of interactions, of choices, of attitudes and examples, whether compassionate or otherwise, that sets the tone of existence.

41
SWEEPING THE TEMPLE

Casual visitors to Wat Opot will marvel at the well-groomed campus and buildings with fishponds and ducks and gardens and murals on the wall, all built by a man whose pockets are almost invariably empty. If they pay a little more attention, they will begin to think about the significance of the fact that our children live together, regardless of whether or not they are infected by HIV. They might put this fact into the historical context of how people with HIV/AIDS have been treated around the world. Then perhaps they will begin to fathom the changes in attitude that have occurred in the villages around Wat Opot, changes that have led to the opening of the gates between our children and the world around them, a world a little less afraid now of people with AIDS. Some visitors might be sufficiently im-

pressed that they will return home determined to end discrimination in their own villages and schools and orphanages. Such an opening of the eyes is wonderful and hopeful.

Still, the opening of the heart may remain more elusive. It may take more time for some of us to comprehend just what we have experienced here, for the goodness of this place to seep into our psyches, so we do not fall back on our old habits of thought and judgment.

For those of us who come from societies steeped in statistics, who see cost-efficiency and replicable results as the main event, it may be necessary to linger for a time in this community to perceive its light, which, like many mysteries, may only be made visible by contemplating shadows cast on a wall. For it takes awhile to see past the form to the spirit, and it is in the small day-to-day events that the lessons lie. By watching Wayne with the children, and the children with each other, you may, over time, begin to grasp the true depth of compassion of this place, so that even a small event might become, for the visitor with an open heart, a hologram of the whole and worth contemplating.

The children have been my teachers. The grandmother of Jorani and Pesei came for a visit one day, and Pesei asked me to take a photo of the three of them.

Another little girl wanted to join them.

"Why do you want to be in the picture?" I asked her. "She's not *your yei.*"

The girl stepped away, abashed.

Pesei put his arm around her shoulder, drew her back into the frame and said, "But *she* is our family too."

Another example is an incident that happened during my first winter at Wat Opot.

Makara is an older boy whose mother lives in the village. She is HIV positive. He came to Wat Opot so that his little sister could receive medical care and both of them could attend school. Makara and some boys from the village school stole a fancy bike and it fell to him to fence it at a bike shop near the main market. The bicycle, as karma would have it, belonged to the son of the shop owner, and Makara found himself in a lot of trouble. Theft in a close-knit community is a serious betrayal, and Wayne might have thrown him out, but that would have left his little sister here alone and Makara would likely have stopped going to school. On the other hand, the incident reflected badly on Wat Opot in the eyes of the villagers, and letting him off would set a bad example to the other children.

Wayne called a meeting and left it to a jury of Makara's peers, the other boys his age, to decide whether he should be expelled. In a quiet voice Makara promised to do better, and not to bring shame on his family. The boys listened gravely, eyes discreetly averted, weighing Wat Opot's reputation in the village against the repercussions of expulsion on their friend's future. Each boy knew that he himself might easily have been the one on trial. Finally, they agreed to give Makara a last chance. But that was not the end of it. Each boy on the jury promised that he would watch over Makara and steer him straight if they saw him getting into trouble again. By assuming responsibility, each boy accepted the roles of father and older brother. From being a jury, they became even more a family.

Watching this scene — a group of boys under a tree at twilight considering what was best for their friend and for their community, sitting in judgment with no malice but soberly aware of the ramifications of their decision — I was touched. Still, coming from the world of breaking news reports and paparazzi, I observed with no little personal disdain my own impulse to monitor the boys' expressions and reactions. How addicted I have become to these glimpses of what we think of as authentic: the naked moment, captured in a snapshot or newspaper photo, laid out for our dissection. As I watched these modest children, with their innate sense of courtesy, I felt nosy and intrusive. I wondered whether the new thought that had come into my head, of perhaps one day writing a small book about their lives, had squeezed me back through some invisible membrane separating Wat Opot from the world, whether the mere thought had changed me from a participant to an opportunist.

Yet in that moment I realized that here was something well worth observing, that it might indeed be transient and was in any case so remote from most Western people's experience as to be as far from imagining as life in another galaxy. Stranger, even, because we have more images from film and television, and might have more of a concept of an alien culture than of the scene of simple decency unfolding before me that evening.

Before one of his rare visits to his family in the States, Wayne gathered the community together to say goodbye and to reassure everyone that he would be coming back. They were sitting in the temple after their weekly cleanup of the grounds and the dharma lesson with the head monk of the wat. Around them were painted scenes of the life of the Buddha, and the lovely gold-papered statues smiled down at them with compassion.

"Do you know why we come here every week?" Wayne asked the children. "Why we pick up the trash and sweep the temple and listen to the teachings of the Buddha and chant the lessons?"

A small voice called out, "Because you like us to?"

Everyone laughed, and Wayne answered his own question by telling the children once again the tale of how he and Vandin went looking for a place to build their clinic. How they went to many villages and wats and at each place people said they would like to help, but always there was some reason why they could not. Underneath every excuse was the same fear — fear of living near people with AIDS. Of all the places they looked, only Wat Opot, a dilapidated temple in a very poor village, gave them a small piece of land, a few parched haunted acres that was all they had to offer.

"We clean the wat every week to say thank you to the monks for our home," he told them. "And we go to the temple to remind ourselves that we do not want to be like the people who rejected us."

I was reminded of one Christmas party when Wayne had asked the children whose birthday we were celebrating and the kids sang out, "Yours!" I imagined Wayne and Vandin, wandering about a shattered country, searching for a little land for a clinic to care for the poorest of the poor, and finally being taken in by a group of destitute monks who had nothing to offer but an

abandoned field where ghosts roamed. To have watched this fragile seed flower into a thriving place where people who were near death found life and hope again and shared community — how like a miracle play that seems to me! And I am struck by how the repetition of this simple tale has all the power of a foundation myth, one that sets a standard of spiritual understanding for a people and teaches them how to live.

A visiting scholar once asked Wayne whether he could have accomplished all he has without having a spiritual background. He replied that he did not think so.

"What aspects of spiritual practice do you

want to pass on to the children?" the man asked.

"I want them to learn to look into themselves, through meditation and contemplation, and to make an open and honest evaluation of their lives, without putting it into words like 'God' or 'Jesus.' "

At the end of one of Wayne's visits to the States, I called from Maine to say goodbye. He seemed upbeat, looking forward to going home and getting to work on some of the projects he had been thinking about while he was away, particularly the one-on-one counseling sessions with the children. We talked about some of the issues that had been getting me down: cutbacks in help for AIDS patients, my fear that some of our children might become resistant to available medicines yet have no access to other lines of ARVs, my worry that we might be backsliding to the days when kids like Toon Hang died from lack of treatment — the whole vortex of anxiety I had been feeling since I returned to America and started reading the newspapers again.

"How do you function in the middle of all that's happening?" I asked him. "Doesn't the impossibility of it all get to you?"

"Maybe I'm stupid," he began, "but I try

not to look at the news very much. And I try not to get too involved in what's going on in Phnom Penh. I just take care of what's in front of me, things I know I can do something about."

I guess that's it then, I thought. Just start where you are, and do what you can, and don't let yourself be paralyzed by the nay-sayers.

And that was all we said on the subject. Because then Wayne started talking enthusiastically about some new project he had begun planning while he was at his mother's house.

Wayne always told me he tries not to worry, and as if to prove his point, news of two new grants was waiting for him when he got back to Cambodia. New government regulations concerning orphanages required a security fence, and the same Taiwanese businessmen who had donated the new dormitory had offered money for a wall around the entire campus. At last the marauding cows could be kept out of the gardens, and Wayne could get serious about growing crops to feed Wat Opot. There might even be enough surplus to sell in the local market. It was another step toward making Wat Opot self-supporting.

KHANA, the Khmer partner NGO of the International HIV/AIDS Alliance, had offered some money for extra education, and Wayne decided to send six of the older girls to beauty school to study hair styling and makeup. Even in small villages, Khmer weddings are lavish stylized affairs, and it seemed like a great way for the girls to be able to begin saving for university. I imagined them painting elaborate wedding makeup on all the little kids for practice and laughed out loud. I longed to be there. It would be a pure, joyous hullabaloo!

The beauty classes might accomplish another function as well. They would get the kids out into the community, and continue to integrate children with AIDS into village life. When I was last there, people from the village had begun dropping by in the mornings to buy fish from our fishponds and have a cup of coffee at a little snack shop Wayne had started at Chhang's Place. I remembered the first year I was at Wat Opot, when a villager had asked me whether he could get sick if he bought a fish from someone with AIDS. In those days, local people were afraid even to come through the gate, and I reflected on how far Wat Opot has come.

Even as a new brick wall is being built,

the invisible walls between Wat Opot and the surrounding community are coming down, and more and more, our children are beginning to live in the world.

42
IN A ROCKET MADE OF ICE

At the end of the rainy season small dragonflies hatch and fly up from the rice fields. The children capture them. They pinch their wings together and tie threads to their bodies, like fishermen tying flies. The threads are thin fibers teased from the raveled edges of rice bags. The children hold the threads between their thumbs and forefingers and run in circles as the dragonflies trail above them like tiny kites. Or they release them, tossing them in the air to fly free. Then the slender filaments float in their wakes, and undulate like the messages towed by biplanes that buzzed over the beach when I was a child.

Here boys buzz about, pretending to be airplanes. A shiny green mango leaf torn and twisted onto a twig becomes a propeller, and the little boys skip back and forth, leaping into the air. They are so joyous and light I imagine them rising up like dragonflies, heedless of gravity, heedless of all that holds them.

It was evening. I was sitting alone on the low wall that surrounds the crematorium. I had lost track of hours. The moon was almost full and about halfway up, so maybe it was not very late. I was feeling stunned. I needed a quiet moment just to breathe and gather my emotions for the impossibility of saying goodbye to a hundred people I loved.

So many times I have come and gone from this place that sometimes events become confused in my mind. Four times I have visited Wat Opot and then left, and I hope I will return again and again. But this story happened on the last night of my second visit, sometime in May of 2008. The very next day I would leave Wat Opot and fly to America. I had been steeping myself in this place all week, breathing it in, imprinting my memory with its smells and sounds, loving the weight and the embraces of the children on my lap and the touch of their hands in my hands as we walked.

After a while Sovann wandered by. He was only seventeen then, about to graduate from high school. In those days I didn't often get to talk with him. He shared a house with the older boys at the far end of the compound, and usually he was busy studying, still hoping at that time to become a doctor.

Wayne had told me about how Sovann had promised his dying father that all the children would get an education, and even at seventeen Sovann was feeling the weight of his responsibility. He had already brought two of his younger brothers to live at Wat Opot, and in future years he would bring his youngest brother, Kangho, and his sister too. He knew Wayne would help him put them all through school.

That night, sitting alone with me on the low wall of the *pa cha,* Sovann admitted that even though he studied hard he would have to give the teacher money to graduate from high school. He confessed even to hoping someone might sell him a medical degree. "If I buy a doctor's degree maybe I can make money sooner, take care my family. Maybe come back here, help Mr. Wayne."

We sat holding hands, watching the moon, sharing the gentle evening in the easy, affectionate manner of people who speak different languages but manage to communicate eloquently with few words.

After a few minutes he said, "My teacher say people fly to the moon in a rocket ship. Is it really true?"

I told him it was, and that men had even walked on the moon. "How does your teacher know about people going to the moon?" I asked.

"He say he read it in the science book yesterday. And today my teacher tell me the sun is bigger than the moon. I don't understand. How can that be? They look same-same."

I assured him the sun was much larger than the moon.

Then I told him about the solar system, and the stars, and I diagrammed the different kinds of eclipses with a twig in the dust. He still could not grasp how the little moon could darken the big sun.

"Well," I said, "do you see that tree way over there? Hold up your hand. Now do you see how your hand covers the tree? Is your hand really bigger than the tree?"

He got it and smiled.

"So do people ever fly to the sun?"

"No, the sun is very, very hot," I explained. "It is so hot, if they get close they would burn up."

He considered this for a minute. Suddenly his face brightened.

"Maybe they could fly to the sun in a rocket made of ice!"

■ ■ ■ ■

We sat together, Sovann and I, both very quiet under the full moon. Somewhere there was music. Maybe it was the song of a night bird, or a funeral chant, or maybe it was a flute, a simple melody played on a hollow reed: one line, and then a single, pure note, resolving into silence.

GRATITUDE

In a Rocket Made of Ice grew from an article I wrote for *Kyoto Journal* in 2008. I had never written for publication, and the night before I was to submit my manuscript I met, by chance, a professor of writing named Dianne Benedict. Dianne told me she loved working with new writers and offered to come by the next day to put some finishing touches on my piece. In a single marathon session, Dianne blew the breath of life into a factual, arm's-length account of Wat Opot. She taught me to write in the first person, to be less shy about my own experience, to more warmly engage the reader. For her extraordinary gesture and her encouragement for a novice writer and complete stranger I offer my deep gratitude.

All along the way, as I wrote and rewrote, edited and reedited, other wonderful people would appear in my life to offer their help and support. Though it never ceased to amaze me, I came to see that it was not to me so much, but to the work itself that people responded, a manifestation of the compassionate bodhisattva in all of us. For I have come to feel strongly that we are each of us in service, and give according to the fundamental good in our natures, and that my own contribution is merely as a story-teller, a scribe. I write this at a point in my life when cancer has returned and threatens to cut my own time short, and when I struggle against drug-induced fatigue to craft a decent English sentence, but with the full confidence, learned from Wayne, that if I need to lay this project down someone else will pick it up and see it through. For some, their help would flow from friendship and love, or from sympathy for my commitment over the past seven years. But fundamentally we are all in service to the children. The stories of their courage and compassion, and yes, their tragedies too, deserve to be told.

As I told the stories and wrote the chapters, I pestered my friends relentlessly, and from their questions and insights came a richness of perspective. Thank you: Alison Woodman, Harry Hurlbert, Benjamin Thelwell, David Rosen, Paul DeVore, Jennifer DeVore, Cheryl Corson, Laurence Craig-

Green, Ralph Shapiro, Ellen Goldman, Luke Powell, Marjorie Speed Powell, Ingrid Sunzenauer, Susan Frost, Deborah Ceranic, Jeff Kaley, Jim McQuaid, Nick Humez, Jo Diggs, John Compton, Miriam Senft, Marilyn Handel, Martin Love, Matthew Zuschlag, Ed and Patricia Lueddeke, Lawton Vogel, Scott Wolland, Nate Berger, Chris Vincenty. There are others, and their omission will haunt me.

To all the people of Bar Harbor and Mount Desert Island, Maine, who came to readings and talks and who donated generously to children in a far-off land, and to those who felt called to travel to Cambodia to volunteer. To the children of Mount Desert Elementary School, who asked the most perceptive questions. To Barbara Baron Gifford and her sewing circle, who made it their summer project to craft a doll for each Wat Opot child. Thank you for helping me to unite the antipodes of my world into one embrace.

Grateful bows to Laura Bonyon Neal and the True Nature Zen Sangha, for welcoming me to abide with them.

To Belinda Yalin, dear friend, who suffered the little children by listening to endless tellings of the stories, thanks, thanks, and ever thanks.

Special appreciation to Renee Fox and Judith Swazey, whose relentless encouragement has kept me grounded while simultaneously helping me over some especially high hurdles.

My dear friend Luke Powell has spent his career photographing the peoples of Afghanistan and the Middle East. His gentle images reveal the dignity and humanity often lost in the headlines and badgering news cycles of our age. It was Luke's work in the mountains and minefields of Afghanistan that inspired me to search for service. He taught me, I hope, to avoid the traps of journalistic sensationalism while still allowing people to reveal their stories with a dignity that allows us to see them as very like ourselves, rather than using their hardships as an excuse to distance them as the Other, fantasize our own superiority and rush in to "fix" what we cannot comprehend is not broken.

A huge shout-out to Bennett "Buck" Stevens for intercepting a prayer made to the Universe for service and introducing me to Wayne and Wat Opot, for calling me on my nonsense and for skillfully deflecting all excuses, even when I was really scared. Without Buck, I would never have gone to

Cambodia and none of this could have happened.

My gratitude to Andy Gray for allowing me to quote from hours of recorded interviews of Wayne. Andy's probing questions, so different from my own, gave me a much more rounded understanding of Wayne's spiritual journey.

Years ago I took a workshop with Jay O'Callahan, master storyteller and national treasure, and over the years I have returned to Marshfield, Massachusetts, where Jay does much of his teaching. Jay believes that we are all very good at telling ourselves what we do wrong, but rarely do we have any notion of our strengths. I cannot thank Jay enough for his joyous, gentle and heart-centered teaching.

To all the volunteers I met at Wat Opot over the years, each with their own insight, especially to Shelly Hill, Andrew Jamieson, Deb Leavitt, Bonnie Woolley, Ron King, Miwa Ikemiya and Caroline Broissand. To Melinda Lies, who found her home at Wat Opot too late to be included in this story, but who, with Wayne, is writing much of the next chapter. And to the memory of our beloved friend Steve Jessup, "Papa Steve the Giant Tasmanian," who showed us all that love is not a language learned from a phrase book.

I thank as well the many doctors and healers, traditional and otherwise, without whose tender mercies I surely would not have survived to finish this project: Philip L. Brooks, John Swalec, Charlie Hendricks, Ormand Lee Haynes, Michelle Kinbrook, Joyce MacIntosh, Melanie Clauson, Rachel Sharp, Stephen Curtin and Christine Cuneo. And to Lynne Assaf, David Walker and Lawton Vogel for helping me to hold fast to my humanity through all the dramas.

To Wayne Dale Matthysse and all the people of Wat Opot, young and old: every word of this book is written in gratitude to you. Loving my extended family of tumbling children has been one of the greatest joys of my life.

To the people of Ants-in-a-Line Village and the surrounding communities, thank you for graciously welcoming me into your world. To Arun Chea Meier, for afternoon tea in her lovely pavilion under the mango trees, for her insights into village life and for allowing me a glimpse of the value of meditation in coming to peace with the terrible history of the war years. To the staff of the Golden Gate Hotel Annex for their warm hospitality whenever I returned to

Phnom Penh, and to the tuk-tuk drivers on Street 278, who carried me safely home to Wat Opot.

To Beth Kanji Goldring for her love and resolute grounding, and for always telling me the truth, whether or not it was what I had in mind. And to Mary Dunbar for her gentle optimism.

To Pico Iyer for his gracious encouragement at a moment when all seemed lost. And to Anne Fadiman and Dr. Paul Farmer for generously taking the time to read and support this work.

To Robin Desser, my editor at Alfred A. Knopf, who allowed this book to touch her heart, and whose gentle guidance created an aura of safety as she urged me to reach yet a little deeper to prepare the text for this edition.

I would like to thank the editors of *Kyoto Journal* for their unfailing courtesy and encouragement to a beginning writer. To John Einarsen, *KJ*'s amazing founding editor, for diving into this project with his whole heart and keeping me focused on The Work, for traveling to Cambodia to "sniff the air" and get to know Wayne and the children and understand what is so extraordinary about Wat Opot and for his unfailing optimism, dedication and tenacity. To Ken

Rodgers for his ever-wise and sober suggestions.

And finally, and above all, to Stewart Wachs, who, as associate editor of *Kyoto Journal,* recognized and nurtured the writer in my soul, and who, as my first editor and at incalculable personal cost, parented this book from its inception. Dear friend, without you this book would not exist.

PHOTO CREDITS

Unless otherwise noted, all photographs are by the author.

ABOUT THE AUTHOR

Gail Gutradt has volunteered at the Wat Opot Children's Community in Cambodia since 2005. Her stories, articles and poems have appeared in the Japan-based *Kyoto Journal,* as well as in the *Utne Reader* and *Ashé Journal.* Her first *Kyoto Journal* article, "The Things We've Gone Through Together," was nominated for a Pushcart Prize. She lives in Bar Harbor, Maine.